CARL MAXEY

CARL

a fighting life

MAXEY

JIM KERSHNER

A V ETHEL WILLIS WHITE BOOK

UNIVERSITY OF WASHINGTON PRESS

SEATTLE AND LONDON

THIS BOOK IS PUBLISHED WITH THE ASSISTANCE OF A GRANT FROM THE
V ETHEL WILLIS WHITE ENDOWED FUND, ESTABLISHED THROUGH THE GENEROSITY
OF DEEHAN WYMAN, VIRGINIA WYMAN, AND THE WYMAN YOUTH TRUST.

University of Washington Press, PO Box 50096, Seattle, WA 98145
www.washington.edu/uwpress

Library of Congress Cataloging-in-Publication Data
Kershner, Jim, 1953–
Carl Maxey : a fighting life / Jim Kershner. — 1st ed.
p. cm. — (A V Ethel Willis White Books)
Includes bibliographical references and index.
ISBN 978-0-295-98846-7 (hardback : alk. paper)
1. Maxey, Carl, 1924–1997. 2. African American lawyers—Washington (State)—
Spokane—Biography. 3. Civil rights workers—Washington (State)—Spokane—
Biography. 4. Boxers (Sports)—Washington (State)—Spokane—Biography. I. Title.
KF373.M377K47 2008   340.092—dc22   [B]   2008008657

The paper used in this publication is acid-free and 90 percent recycled from at least
50 percent post-consumer waste. It meets the minimum requirements of American
National Standard for Information Sciences—Permanence of Paper for Printed
Library Materials, ANSI z39.48–1984. ∞

CONTENTS

PREFACE AND ACKNOWLEDGMENTS

In April of 1997, I interviewed Carl Maxey for a historical newspaper article about segregation in Spokane. He answered my questions about restaurants, hotels, and swimming pools, but for some reason he was particularly insistent on telling me about his own upbringing. I remember thinking, "Well, I can't really use most of this. But if Carl Maxey wants to tell me his life story, I should probably shut up and listen."

This was probably the last interview of Maxey's life. He died three months later. I kept the interview tape, but I didn't give much thought to it until a year later, when I delivered a version of my "Segregation in Spokane" story at the Pacific Northwest Historical Conference in Boise, Idaho. At the end of my presentation, I mentioned that Maxey had died suddenly. A woman in the audience asked if anyone was writing a biography of Maxey. When I said no, she replied, "Well, why don't *you*?" I could think of dozens of arguments against, but all were eventually trumped by one argument in favor: Maxey's life was a remarkable story that deserved to be told.

About eight years later, I delivered the finished book to my editor at the University of Washington Press. Her name was Julidta Tarver, and she was the woman who had raised her hand and said, "Well, why don't *you*?" I am indebted to her for not only planting the seed for this project, but also for allowing me to carry it to fruition. I would also like to thank Julie Van Pelt for her outstanding editing and Mary Ribesky for shepherding this book through to completion.

This biography would not have been possible without the cooperation and assistance of the Maxey family. Ninon Schults, Lou Maxey, Bevan Maxey, and Bill Maxey granted me many hours of interviews. Through them, I was able to see the full picture of the private Carl Maxey. I am also indebted to the late Milton Burns, who helped bring Maxey's dramatic early years to life.

I also wish to thank the archivists at the Northwest Museum of Arts and Culture (MAC) in Spokane, especially Rose Krause, Jane Davey, and Laura Arksey. I also appreciate the help given by Stephanie Plowman and staff at the Gonzaga University Archives and by John Clute at the Gonzaga University School of Law. The archivists at the Seattle office at the National Archives and Records Administration helped me to fill out the Seattle Seven story.

As a staff writer for the *Spokane Spokesman-Review*, I had the distinct advantage of access to the invaluable *Spokesman-Review* reference library, which has clipping files covering Maxey, his many cases, as well as many important background topics. I would like to thank the reference library staff, Sara Lindgren, Angie Flint, and Jeanette McDonald Olson, for their help and patience. My heartfelt thanks as well to photo editor Larry Reisnouer, who generously helped gather images from the *Spokesman-Review*'s photo archives.

Adam Lynn of the *Tacoma News Tribune* helped track down old newspaper clippings from the Seattle Seven trial. Rick Bonino of the *Spokesman-Review* provided valuable first-hand insight into the Ruth Coe trial. And I cannot forget the role played by Betty Brown, my barber/counselor at the Lincoln Barber Shop, who, when I complained that I didn't have time to finish the book, looked at me and said, "Well, what are you waiting for?" The next day, I requested a three-month sabbatical. *Spokesman-Review* editor Steven A. Smith generously granted me the time to make this book a reality.

Most importantly, I would like to thank my wife Carol and children Mike and Kate, who encouraged me from the beginning and gently prodded me when I faltered. Finally, I would like to thank all of the people who gave me interviews for this project (listed in full in the Note on Sources). Many of them knew Carl Maxey intimately; through them, I hope that you will come to know Maxey too.

JIM KERSHNER, July 2008

CARL MAXEY

AN ORPHAN'S FIRE

Carl Maxey once said he wanted to be judged in life the same way he had been judged by referees in the boxing ring: honestly, without prejudice, and based strictly on blows landed. He landed enough blows, both legal and political, for the *New York Times* to run a tribute to his life headlined "Type-A Gandhi" shortly after his death in 1997 at age seventy-three. The *Times* called him one of the best-known lawyers in the country: a black attorney who had smashed color barriers in a creamy white town and made national headlines with lurid murder cases and outrageous war-protest trials. Yet Maxey also wanted—urgently needed—for people to understand where he began. He once said he wanted his hometown of Spokane, Washington, to realize that he was "a guy who started from scratch. Black scratch." This was his way of saying: He didn't start from square one. He started from square zero.

A more luckless childhood is hard to imagine, at least outside of a Charles Dickens novel. His very birth was inauspicious enough. He had a mother who wouldn't or couldn't keep him, and a father who was nowhere to be found. His birth certificate lists his birth date as June 23, 1924, and his birthplace as Tacoma, Washington. Yet the mother and father listed on the certificate, Carolyn and Carl Maxey of Spokane, were not his birth parents at all. They were the black couple from Spokane who took him in sometime after his birth. The birth record was evidently revised after the Maxeys formalized the adoption in 1927.

By his own admission, Maxey never knew who his birth parents were, and in later life he never even wanted to find out. He usually said only that he had been "born illegitimately." Only a set of official adoption papers reveals the name of his true mother, Elizabeth Cooper. The 1920 U.S. census shows an Elizabeth Cooper living as a boarder in Tacoma—a widowed black chambermaid. As for his father, there is no mention, although we might guess that his last name was Alfred, because the child's birth name was Emmett Alfred. Many years later, Maxey's first wife, Ninon King (later Ninon Schults), would joke with Carl by calling him Emmett, and laughingly would speculate that he was the scion of some rich family. He laughed along with her but he knew the more likely truth. He was the child of a poor black woman in Tacoma who had no means to support him and no way to keep him.

The adoption put an official end to the name of Emmett Alfred, and from that time forward the little boy was named Carl Maxey, after his new father. In those days, under those circumstances, he was probably lucky to be adopted at all. In the adoption papers, the court had pronounced itself "satisfied of the ability of the petitioners to bring up and educate said child properly." But those words proved to be hopelessly optimistic. As an adult, Maxey remembered little about his time with Carl and Carolyn Maxey—he said he had no memory of his father and only a thin memory of his mother. The elder Maxey was listed on the birth certificate as a railroad employee, but he later worked as a janitor at a pool hall and tavern in downtown Spokane. One day in the future, the little boy would help open up employment opportunities for black men in the Northwest, but in those days, these kinds of jobs were as much as a black man could hope for.

The young parents, both thirty, lived near downtown in what passed for a black neighborhood in an almost entirely white city. Spokane had only about 700 black residents in a city of more than 100,000 people. Because of this, and because of its place in the upper left-hand corner of the U.S. map, Spokane in the 1920s had somewhat schizophrenic attitudes about race. On one hand, black residents did not have to sit in the backs of buses or trolley cars. Washington had passed a law barring the segregation of public accommodations in 1890 and had strengthened the law in 1909 and 1910. This was not the Jim Crow South. At times, though, the Northwest teetered on the brink of de facto segregation. Up until a few years before Maxey's birth, black residents in Spokane were told they couldn't sit on the main floors of some theaters; they were restricted to the balconies. When the Pantages Theater in Spokane ordered a black patron named S. S. Moore into the balcony in 1919, he filed suit. Moore won two hundred dollars in damages and a unanimous decision from the all-white jury. "All of us were for damages from the start," a juror was quoted as saying in the *Spokane Daily Chronicle*. "All of us declared that even if a man were black, he had the right to sit where he wanted to."

Nor did Spokane have segregated schools, possibly because of an enlightened Northwestern attitude, but just as likely because there were too few black students to make it practical. Yet segregation of the most egregious kind existed in other aspects of life in Spokane, as it did in many other northern cities, more by custom and social pressure than by law. In 1900, a prominent Spokane citizen named Emmett Holmes tried to take his family to dinner at a restaurant at Natatorium Park, Spokane's premier amusement park. The restaurant refused to serve them. Holmes sued the owners of the park for five thousand dollars and lost after the restaurant claimed it had simply been "overcrowded." In a further insult, the *Spokane Spokesman-Review* reported that jurors "appeared to treat the entire matter like a joke and were overheard bandying back and forth jokes and remarks suggested by the restaurant bill of fare." So Carl was born into a world where black residents carried around a list in their heads of restaurants where they were welcome and a larger list of those where they were not. When it came to jobs, housing, clubs, and hotels—as well as restaurants—black people had to know their place.

With a black population too small to be a political or economic force, that "place" was narrowly defined. In employment, for instance, blacks were restricted to janitorial jobs, laboring jobs, and domestic service in homes, clubs, and hotels. Census records show that, out of a total of 320 black residents with jobs, 211 were in "domestic and personal service." The rest were mostly laborers or railroad workers. Professional jobs were off-limits, except for clergymen (2) and musicians (11). In 1930, Spokane had yet to have a single black doctor or dentist. Spokane didn't even have a black teacher, although some bright black students had gone so far as to get teaching degrees from nearby colleges before being rejected by the school board. Spokane certainly did not have a black lawyer. Even Seattle, with a black population four times larger, had only two black lawyers.

In fact, the black employment situation in Spokane was sorry and getting sorrier. By the 1920s, the region's mining boom had tapered off and the city's affluent white families weren't hiring as many domestics. Perhaps this helps explain why the Maxey family began to run into trouble around 1927 or 1928. At some point in Carl's first few years, something split this little family apart irrevocably. Carl never knew what it was, and no one else remembers either. Maybe the elder Carl Maxey lost his job and couldn't find another. Maybe he was tired of a wife and child and just wanted to ramble. For whatever reason, his father disappeared from the Spokane City Directory, and apparently from the picture, in 1928, leaving his wife with a four-year-old boy and no visible means of support.

The neighbors did what they could to pitch in. Frances Scott, who as a child lived near the Maxeys on Third Avenue in Spokane, said that she remembers her mother, Louise Nichols, looking after little Carl on a number of occasions. Mrs. Maxey was incapable of taking care of the boy by herself, possibly because she was already having heart troubles. She was also having money troubles as the Great Depression arrived. This was a time when people all over the city, even in the middle-class neighborhoods, were converting their backyards to chicken coops, just to keep a supply of eggs. The poorer neighborhoods were already stretched too thin. "As much help as other people were able to provide, even that wasn't enough," said Scott, who was three years older than Carl.

So in January 1930, when Carl was five years old, he was taken to the Spokane Children's Home as a "charge of the county." Why Carolyn Maxey felt she had to take this drastic step, Carl himself never knew and never wanted to know. Once, when he was grown and married, his wife Ninon, a caseworker, offered to look up Carolyn Maxey's welfare case report in an archive. Maybe it would shed some light on his early life? "But he didn't want me to," said Ninon. "He said he didn't want to know. Usually he was pretty humorous about everything, but he said it in a way that I knew he seriously didn't want to. It was my impression that he would find it rather painful."

So from age five until twelve, Carl's home was the huge brick Spokane Children's Home. Most of the 106 children there were orphans—others, like Carl, were charges of the county, whose parents couldn't or wouldn't take care of them. Charge or orphan, it didn't matter—the place was a nightmare for any child. Though it looked like a turn-of-the-century university building, complete with massive redbrick walls, long dormitory halls, and ivy twining up the drainpipes, it was more like a prison to many of the children, and not a humane one. Carl's six and a half years there shaped the course of his life in ways that he couldn't possibly anticipate.

One of the few things he remembered clearly of his early years at the home was that, one day, somebody drove up in a car and took him away—not to a new home and a new loving family, as most of the children no doubt dreamed of, but to his mother's funeral. Carolyn Maxey died on May 8, 1933, alone in a downtown apartment. The cause of death was heart failure, and beyond that the death certificate is heartbreakingly spare. The entries for spouse, marital status, occupation, parents, and even date of birth are all filled in by the same abbreviation: "Unobt" (unobtainable). Even her age is merely guessed at: "About 45" is typed in and then crossed out and "54" written in. Neither number was even close to correct. If the information on Carl's birth certificate is accurate, Carolyn Maxey would have been only thirty-nine.

The only entry filled in with any confidence is "Color or Race: Black." The doctor who signed the certificate said he had attended her exactly once, six days before her death. She was buried in Fairmount Cemetery in Spokane, in the corner set aside for "public assistance" cases. No stone marks her gravesite. A visitor searching for it finds nothing but a large, featureless lawn, with no markers to provide even the slightest evidence that hundreds of the city's indigents lie beneath. It looks like a lonely soccer field, yet it was Spokane's potter's field in 1933. As the eight-year-old Carl was led away from that potter's field in May 1933, he had become, for all practical purposes, an orphan. His adoptive father was nowhere to be found.

His own memories of the home he doled out sparingly. He remembered sweeping down off the hill to go to school at a nearby public elementary, tearing through the neighborhood stealing apples off of trees. He remembered a dark and dank closet in the basement where kids were sent for disciplinary reasons. It was called, at least among the kids, the Dungeon. He told his second wife, Lou Maxey, that he remembered that black spots often decorated their breakfast oatmeal. Those black spots, he later learned, were rat droppings. Other than that, he spoke of the home only as a place to be endured.

But at least one other child at the home, Milton Burns, retained vivid, and horrific, memories of those years. Burns was at the Spokane Children's Home for most of the same years as Maxey. He became Maxey's best friend and actually more than a best friend. In a sense, Burns, a charge of the county, was one of Maxey's charges too. "My first recollection of Carl was that he was always protecting me," said Burns, two years younger than Carl. "He was a bigger kid, and he identified me as another minority and I think that was basically it with him. Carl thought I was black and I never said anything different to him."

The people at the home thought that Burns was black, too, the only other black child in the home. He may have looked black, but his mother was Native American and his father was—who knew what? Hawaiian? Burns never found out because his mother was a prostitute, haunting the Skid Roads of both Seattle and Spokane. She had no idea who the boy's father was. So this was another thing the two boys had in common—illegitimacy, no small burden to bear in that era.

This relationship with Burns was the earliest manifestation of an enduring theme in Maxey's life: a compulsion to protect the underdog. Carl recognized immediately that young Burns needed help to endure both the physical and psychological hardships of the home. Some of these were the garden-variety hardships common to most orphanages of the era, the kind that people were reading about every day in the popular comic strip "Little Orphan Annie." The children worked hard, doing all of the manual labor for the compound and tending the big vegetable patch out front. Inside, the kids were required to polish the hardwood floors every day by a method called blocking. The children would pull big wooden blocks, weighing about fifty pounds, up and down the halls. The stronger kids, like Maxey, would pull the blocks with ropes; the weaker kids, like Burns, would ride on top for extra weight. Burns also remembered rigorously enforced order and quiet during meals. No talking was permitted at the table except for a politely murmured, "May I?" or "Please pass the salt." The children were kept quiet, obedient, but by all accounts, well fed.

When visitors came, the children would put on a show. The superintendent would make the kids sing and dance, and quite often, for the further amusement of the adults, the superintendent would have the kids strap on boxing gloves and stage boxing exhibitions. This is where Maxey first donned a pair of gloves. As for Burns, all attempts at boxing ended in failure. "Oh yeah, all I could do was stand there and cry," he said, more than sixty years later.

Yet there were good memories too. Burns still remembers the excitement of the holidays, when all of the kids were given gifts. He said those were the times when "you'd get presents, you'd get clothes, and they really treated you pretty special." To the outside world, the home seemed like a good-hearted, well-intentioned institution. "The children are given all they can eat, with fresh milk three times a day," reported the *Spokesman-Review* in 1929. "The health of the children is watched closely, and in some cases where dental or medical care is needed, the child is taken to well-known doctors or specialists." As for order and obedience, the paper reported that "discipline with a smile, but with firmness and justice, is being dealt the orphans and 'semi-orphans.'"

As it turned out, discipline was being "dealt," all right, but not with a smile. The orphanage attracted supervisors, who, in Burns's words, "had their own agendas and who spent their time taking it out on the children." In the dark of night, things were going on at the Spokane Children's Home that the paper didn't know about. Even the well-intentioned board of directors, made up of prominent society women, had no idea what was actually going on after lights out. Yet the kids knew. The kids saw it and heard it every night, as they lay awake in long rows of beds.

"You lived in constant fear," said Burns. "You lived in dormitories and Schueler [Fred Schueler, the assistant superintendent] had a room at the end of our dormitory. I can remember very vividly at night— the door would come open. Of course the dormitory was dark and the light from the office would light him up from behind, and he'd stand there with his arms crossed." Schueler's shadow would stretch down the rows of beds, each bed containing a child who was proba-bly too terrified to be asleep. "You lay there and wondered what you had done wrong during the day," said Burns.

Slowly, Schueler would walk up and down the rows of beds, his footfalls echoing ominously on the well-blocked wooden floor. The children had no idea at whose bed he would stop; but they knew he would stop at someone's. "Whatever his agenda was in picking the particular kid, it had to do with what he perceived you had done wrong," said Burns. "So you laid there in constant fear of what was going to happen to you."

Then, suddenly, Schueler would stop at a bed, yank the blankets back and jerk a boy out of the bed. He'd make the boy hold on to his ankles, and he would beat the boy across the backside. "He beat them with a strap," said Burns. "He always had a leather strap." Burns said he "operated on the basis of fear" for most of his childhood and has blocked out a lot of these memories. But he believed that Carl was one of the children who felt the sting of the strap. "I think Carl had his share of abuse, but he would never talk about it with me," said Burns. "He just didn't like the place and wouldn't talk about it."

According to Burns, Carl had already developed a strategy for dealing with this kind of abuse and humiliation: he pretended it didn't bother him. He discovered this put him in a position of strength. If he never showed fear, they couldn't hurt him. "I remember one time, I was in the garden with him, out in front of the home," said Burns. "Carl was standing there and one of the staff who didn't like Carl came and broke a rake over his head. Carl just stood there and smiled. He wasn't going to let that so-and-so know he was hurt at all. And you break a rake over a kid's head, that's got to hurt." Even worse things were going on in the shadows at the Spokane Children's Home, things that would not be revealed for several more years.

Meanwhile, Superintendent Fred M. Hunter and his assistant, Schueler, continued to impress the board with their efficiency and their "discipline with a smile." The home was practically a mini-food-factory, producing more than 19,000 pounds of vegetables from the garden, more than 4,000 jars of home-canned fruits and vegetables, and more than 1,500 eggs from the home's flock of hens every year. Even Maxey remembered some good times, days when he and other kids were able to sneak away, down to the Spokane River or down to Natatorium Park. Making an escape was difficult and risky, but apparently not impossible. "Literally, you can't control kids in that setting without them being corralled, all around," said Maxey just before his death. "I knew Spokane like the back of my hand. I knew it real thoroughly. I've been thrown out of Nat Park more times than . . . [laughs]."

Even then, Maxey was learning some of the ugly truth about racism. He remembered once that all of the kids from the home were invited out to Camp Cowles, a Boy Scout camp on an idyllic lake in the forested mountain country north of Spokane. "They wouldn't let me in the water at Camp Cowles," said Maxey. "I couldn't swim with the rest of the kids. I remember that, and having to wash dishes for the rest of the kids. And that's why I never joined the Boy Scouts." At the same time, he was beginning to develop some of the traits that would serve him well in later life. Certainly, he began to develop his lifelong urge to protect the weak. "He always told me, 'It was us against them [at the orphanage]. We learned to stick together,'" said Ninon. "And he also learned not to be afraid of the establishment."

To the outside world, life continued to be benevolent and idyllic at the Spokane Children's Home, at least if you were reading the fund-raising brochures. One boasted, "A healthful recreation is provided for these children—with opportunities for baseball and football, fun on a well-equipped playground and a small wading pool." A later poster even included a picture of a smiling Carl, along with several other boys, accompanied by the slogan, "Some of them were babies . . . orphans . . . kids from broken homes . . . some were sick . . . but all of them say . . . THANK YOU for your help."

Then, on August 15, 1935, when Carl was eleven, the facade came crashing down. Three girls, all about fourteen, ran away from the home that day and started toward Coeur d'Alene, Idaho, about thirty-five miles from Spokane. These teenage orphans were walking down the highway, past midnight, ten miles from the home, when they flagged down a sheriff's patrol car for a ride. The officers asked the girls what they were doing out so late. The girls first tried to make up a story, but it wasn't long before they admitted to running away from the Spokane Children's Home. When the officers told them that they would have to go back, the girls begged to be taken anywhere else besides the orphanage. Something seemed to be bothering the girls, something unspoken, reported the officers. Finally, the girls admitted the real reason: Superintendent Hunter was having "improper relations" with young boys at the home.

Alarmed, the officers brought the girls to the county's juvenile hall, where the girls were questioned thoroughly and separately. When morning arrived, the officers contacted the Spokane County prosecutor's office. "Due to the fact that the charges were so serious and the acts so obnoxious, it was decided to make a careful investigation so that there would not be any injustice done by accusing an innocent man," stated the prosecuting attorney's report to the court. "The Juvenile matron was called and she questioned the girls individually and at great length. The girls claimed that it was common talk among the boys and girls at the home that Mr. Hunter was having improper relations, particularly with one boy, and that it had been going on for a considerable length of time." The girls said they would rather be locked up in detention than be taken back to the home, and they gave the names of some boys who had witnessed some of these acts.

The officers brought six boys from the home in for questioning. The boys said they had been climbing down the fire escape by Hunter's room one night and had seen Hunter and a boy, fourteen, in the room doing . . . well, the prosecutor's report does not disclose exactly what the boys described, except to say that they witnessed them having "improper relations." The boys also said that Hunter commonly showed this boy favoritism by taking him into town for shows and giving him extra desserts. One boy went on to say that Hunter had also performed "improper relations" with him.

This was enough to send the officers out to the home. They knocked on Hunter's office door and asked him to come down to the station for questioning. Hunter, age fifty, denied the accusations at first. But as the officers described the charges and the number of accusers, Hunter's facade collapsed. "He soon admitted that he had had these improper relations many times with one boy who was then 14 years of age and who had been an inmate of the Home for many years," said the prosecutor's report. "He admitted that three or four years previously he began having these improper relations with the boy and that it happened many times during that period of time and that the last occasion was about a week or so prior to his arrest. The defendant's wife died about a year or so ago and although these acts occurred prior to that time, according to him they happened more often afterward. The defendant for the past year had the habit of taking the boy to his room where the acts took place. The defendant stated that in looking back over his life, he could blame one man for his course of conduct in regard to the acts he committed and he also stated that he fought very hard to keep from giving in to this weakness. He stated that this was the only bad habit he had, and that his conduct otherwise was temperate and above reproach. The writer is inclined to agree with him." The writer, by the way, was prosecuting attorney Ralph E. Foley, the father of Tom Foley, who would become Speaker of the U.S. House in the 1980s, and a friend of Carl Maxey.

Hunter adamantly denied that any other boy was involved. And, in a classic example of irrelevancy, considering what he had already admitted, Hunter "emphatically denied" that those boys on the fire escape could have seen him and the boy. Yes, it happened many times in that room, said Hunter, but those boys were lying if they said they ever saw it. Hunter agreed to make this confession and to plead guilty to sodomy in order to avoid bringing children from the home to testify against him at a trial. That "would have a further injurious effect on the Home on account of the unfavorable publicity it would bring," according to Foley.

The publicity was bad enough as it was. The *Spokesman-Review* reported that Hunter had been jailed "relative to revolting accusations." Those accusations were left up to the imagination, and even in later stories the word "sodomy" was never printed. The paper substituted the term "morals charges," and the public was allowed to imagine exactly what the superintendent might have been doing to whom.

Then, just when it seemed that the publicity couldn't possibly get worse for the Spokane Children's Home, it did. After the deputies took Hunter in for questioning, several more young boys ran away from the home later that night and somehow ended up in a detective's office at the Spokane police station. They said that the assistant superintendent, Fred Schueler, aged thirty-three, the man who beat the children at night, was guilty of the same things that police had hauled Hunter off for. The next day, police and prosecutors questioned a number of young boys, and late that afternoon, just one day after Hunter's arrest, officers went back out to the home and arrested Schueler.

Like Hunter, he first denied everything, but before long he too crumbled. He said he had "a habit of handling young boys of the Home improperly and had different ones of the boys handle him improperly." He admitted improper relations with one boy, who was fourteen, and with another boy, who was fifteen. He had done this with the fifteen-year-old many times. "The boy worked in the engine room at the home and [the] defendant stated that he would go to the engine room and that he would have improper relations with the boy and the boy would have improper relations with him," said Foley's report.

"He admitted that this took place off and on over this period of time, maybe every two or three weeks, and that the last time it happened was a few days prior to his arrest. The defendant stated that he had had a weakness for these revolting practices for a long time and that he had fought hard to overcome his habits. He denied that there were any improper relations between Hunter and himself and stated that he was totally unaware that Mr. Hunter had been guilty of the same acts, and he felt the latter did not know of his unlawful practices."

With these confessions in hand, justice moved swiftly. Both men pleaded guilty to sodomy, or more specifically, to "carnal knowledge of himself by the mouth of another male person." On August 19, 1935, both men were sentenced to "not more than 10 years" in the state penitentiary. Only four days after those girls flagged down that sheriff's car east of town, both Hunter and Schueler were behind bars at Walla Walla. They both ended up serving five years of their sentences.

This speedy justice was orchestrated to have the least possible negative effect on the Spokane Children's Home, as an August 22 story in the *Spokesman-Review* made clear. Foley told the paper that conditions at the home were "completely remedied and that the court expressed pleasure that the institution was given a clean bill of health." He continued, "I could not believe it until we had the actual facts. I want to advise the court that this situation is completely cleared up. Steps were taken immediately to protect the children. No girls were involved and but a few boys. The unfortunate part was that the information got around in the home."

If it got around, neither Maxey nor Burns, ages eleven and nine at the time, heard about it. Neither of them was mentioned in the prosecutor's reports. Yet Burns said that, decades later, when he found out about the scandal, it brought forth some dim memories of Schueler making him sit on his lap and "playing with me, sexually . . . When you're a kid and you are experiencing something like that, you just kind of block it out. I did a lot of that in my early years." Maxey, near the end of his life, expressed contempt for the two men who, in his words, performed "angry and mean acts against both little boys and little girls in that orphanage." But he said "nobody ever bothered me in that regard." Lou Maxey recalled that "Carl's favorite line has always been, 'Thank God they didn't like black kids.'"

Yet even though Maxey and Burns were not involved in the scandal, they came to believe that they were turned into scapegoats. A little more than a year after the arrests, in October 1936, Maxey and Burns were evicted from the home. The authorities gave no reason. The new superintendent just called them in one day and said they would no longer be living at the Spokane Children's Home. As to where they were supposed to go next, well, that was the county's problem. Burns later believed that their eviction had something to do with the sex scandal, but the connection is not clear. Burns thought it might have been part of a general sweeping-under-the-rug process, the same process that whisked Hunter and Schueler to Walla Walla in four days. "What they were doing was, I can look back now and say, they were trying to cover up for a lot of things," said Burns.

Maxey, in later discussions of the incident, agreed that the scandal must have been the trigger, but he saw an even more ugly underlying motive: racism. He thought that in the racial climate of the time, and in that city, it was only too likely that the "good society ladies" of the board believed that the first order of business in any housecleaning ought to be kicking out the two black kids. And the minutes of the board for October 8, 1936, provide plenty of evidence:

"It was moved by Mrs. Irving, and seconded by Mrs. Paine, that the two colored boys, Carl Maxey and Milton Burnes [sic], be returned to the County, having been in the Home for years. Motion carried.

"It was moved by Mrs. Sutherland, seconded by Mrs. Bartleson, that the Board go on record as voting to have no more colored children in the Home, from this time forward. Motion carried—unanimous."

Decades later, when Burns found a copy of these minutes in the archives, he took a copy to Maxey at his law office. "I showed that memo to Carl and he just couldn't believe it," said Burns. "He went around the office showing it to everybody." To Maxey, it was bald confirmation of what he had already suspected: that he had been kicked out of an orphanage—an orphanage!—because of the color of his skin.

For a kid who had already been virtually twice orphaned, this was a particularly cruel blow. The home was already the refuge of last resort. And he wasn't even welcome there. Two months before he died, he talked about the profound effect this had on his life.

"They threw us out [because we were black]," he said. "It sure as hell says that. We must have been pretty bad. And the incident that precipitated it was sexual misconduct, all involving white people. So if you wonder where some of my fire comes from, it comes from a memory that includes this event."

2

A FATHER IN BLACK ROBES

As Maxey remembered it, he was just plain tossed out on the street. "I ran around until they caught me after a while," he said, some sixty years after being evicted from the orphanage. Under some circumstances, Spokane might have had its attractions to a young boy on the loose: the ballpark at Natatorium Park, where Babe Ruth had recently come through on a barnstorming tour; the Nat Park ballroom, where black patrons were admitted only when the musical star was black (Fats Waller, Louis Armstrong, and Duke Ellington all played there); and the vaudeville houses downtown, where a young Spokane singer named Bing Crosby had recently learned his trade before going on the road to Hollywood.

But in 1936 the reality was far starker. The Great Depression was at its height. The mining industry was half dead and the demand for timber had crashed right along with the housing market. Unemployment in the city hit 25 percent. Tent cities and shantytowns mushroomed in the railroad yards and beneath the big bridges spanning the Spokane River. Packs of unemployed men haunted the rail yards, hiding from the "bulls"—the hired guards—whose purpose in life was to keep the hoboes off the freight trains. And these hoboes weren't all adults. "Hundreds of them are boys and girls, as young as 10 years, who are traveling in bands," wrote *Spokesman-Review* reporter Margaret Bean, who visited the rail yards and hobo jungles in October 1932. "With a through freight, composed of 100 cars, it is impossible for a freight car to keep this swarming army from crowding their train, especially the mobs of children. They are too agile for a train crew. Chase them from one empty car and they are half a mile down the train and scrambling into another."

Refugee farmers from the Dust Bowl wandered the city only to find that eastern Washington was suffering its own record-breaking drought. Large portions of Spokane—like much of the hard-hit Northwest—had a hangdog air. If there was ever a good time for a twelve-year-old black kid to be wandering aimlessly through Spokane, this was not it. "I can't imagine why nobody in the black community didn't take him in," said Lou Maxey. "But, at the time, I guess I can. Nobody had any money."

Some tried their best to help. Mildred Elliott, who was a child at the time, remembered her mother marching up to the door of one of the Catholic children's homes in Spokane and asking them to take Carl in. In fact, "asking" is hardly a strong enough word. She begged them. "They said, 'No, we don't take colored,' and the nun slammed the door in my mother's face," said Elliott. What could a black woman do in the face of that? She turned around and made the long trudge home. She didn't have a nickel for the trolley ride.

In any case, Carl probably didn't remain on the street for very long. Milton Burns, his one and only companion through these times, said that he doesn't remember being out on the street long, if at all. "We went straight to the juvenile home [the Spokane County Juvenile Detention Center]," said Burns. "There was no other place for us to go, because we were county charges." The juvenile detention center was in a built-on annex next to the bizarrely chateau-esque Spokane County Courthouse, which loomed on the city skyline like a misplaced French fairyland castle. Burns remembered the detention center as a home to twenty or thirty kids at most, the majority of whom were juvenile delinquents of varying degrees. Maxey and Burns were two of the youngest and definitely two of the most innocent inmates. "We hadn't committed any crime except that of being kids too young to take care of ourselves," Maxey said.

The two boys stayed in juvie, as they called it, for the entire school year, which was sixth grade for Carl. They walked to Audubon Elementary School for classes, where they were quite a novelty. "I was always a hit at show-and-tell," Carl once said, chuckling. "'The juve- nile delinquent . . .'" Black kids were rare enough in this middle-class part of Spokane, not to mention black kids who made their home at the detention center. Possibly some parents whispered about the juvie kids and their imagined bad influence, but Burns remembered that Carl was well liked and got along with everybody, both students and teachers. Carl had already developed the beginnings of the charm that later disarmed many of his enemies. He also discovered that he had a gift for telling a story and for making a persuasive point in front of his sixth-grade peers. Maybe that was another thing that made him a hit at show-and-tell: his fledgling oratory skills.

Compared to the Spokane Children's Home, juvie was easy to tolerate. Neither Maxey nor Burns had bad memories of it. Burns remembered it as "just another type of institution," but at least one in which no cruelty was served along with the three square meals a day. For both Maxey and Burns, the manner of their leaving was the most memorable thing about juvie. According to Maxey, the county received deliveries of milk from an Indian mission boarding school, the Sacred Heart Mission, run by Jesuit fathers on the Coeur d'Alene Indian Reservation in DeSmet, Idaho, about fifty miles away. Sometimes, the priests themselves would bring the milk. On one of those deliveries, the head of the mission school, Father Cornelius E. Byrne, met the two black children. He saw two boys who needed a home.

"He said he'd take us both in if we wanted to come," said Maxey. "I didn't know anything about Catholicism. But he invited us down, and we took him up on it." Ninon Schults recalled that "it was the port in the storm when there didn't seem to be any." The mission school was an unlikely port for a black child. Almost all of the students there were Indians of the Coeur d'Alene Tribe. A few white children had found their way there, too, but for the first time Maxey and Burns were in a place where the white children stood out more glaringly than the black children.

At first, Carl couldn't believe what he found when he got to the reservation. "There were kids in his class who were in their twenties," said Lou Maxey. "But they were all stunted physically and in such bad shape from chewing snoose [chewing tobacco], and from poor nutrition." The reservation was a poverty-stricken place, with the disease and alcoholism endemic to many reservations of the time. Yet soon Maxey grew to love the people and the school, and he began to consider the mission school his first real home.

The Sacred Heart Mission was a vestige of what had once been the most powerful "civilizing" influence in the Inland Northwest. In 1842, before any white settlers had arrived, a group of Jesuit missionaries established a mission church and school on the St. Joe River, near the southern inlet to Lake Coeur d'Alene. After the wild St. Joe flooded a few too many times, the priests moved the mission to Cataldo, Idaho, northeast of the lake (that mission building still stands and still attracts daily tourists on Interstate 90 east of Coeur d' Alene). The old mission became the cultural center of the Coeur d'Alene Tribe, which had converted overwhelmingly to Catholicism with the coming of the Jesuits. But by the 1870s, prospectors struck silver just upstream from the mission. Now, instead of river water flooding the land around the mission, boomtown civilization rushed in, with its miners, prostitutes, and gamblers. Not only did the silver boom threaten the Coeur d'Alene's territorial holdings, but, according to the priests, it also threatened the morality of the Coeur d'Alene women. Chaste behavior, it seems, was far more difficult when surrounded by hundreds of lonely miners. So in 1878, the Jesuit fathers persuaded the tribal elders to abandon the Coeur d'Alene river valley and move to a less crowded spot in the fertile Palouse, far across the lake and at the opposite corner of their reservation. They built a new mission at DeSmet, complete with boarding school.

Both this new mission and the tribe itself suffered through poverty and disease over the ensuing decades. And, in a process of attrition that afflicted many of America's Indian reservations, the tribe's landholdings were whittled down to about a one-third of their original size. White settlers decided that Lake Coeur d'Alene and the big rivers that entered it were too desirable to be left to Indians. But the Jesuits kept their church and their little school alive. The mission continued to be the center of tribal culture, much as it was when the first Black Robes, the Jesuit missionaries, held forth at Cataldo in the 1850s and 1860s.

However, Father Byrne was a new kind of missionary. Byrne, who eventually devoted over forty years of his life to the Coeur d'Alene and Flathead Indians, did not believe it was his job to "civilize" the Indians. He believed it was his job to save their culture. "Our missionary days are over," he once told a reporter. "The Indian missionaries did what they had to do under past circumstances. A kind of dark ages followed after that when everything was confused. Now, we are in a period of clarification where the Indians are becoming educated to their own needs and are able to act accordingly."

A fellow priest, years later, described Byrne's work as "one man's unremitting fight for a people and their culture." Byrne encouraged the use of Salish, the tribal language, and became fluent in it himself (he was already fluent in Latin and Spanish). He encouraged Native handicrafts and even had a tribal member make traditional beaded buckskin garments for the priests to wear as vestments. He was a tireless fighter for the rights of the Indians, and he was especially adamant about preserving tribal lands. "The land is the one unifying thing that you have left that will hold you together as a people," Byrne once told a convention of the Affiliated Tribes of the Northwest. "With the land, you are a people. Without it you will be individuals whose cultural background will disappear."

He said the same thing before three Senate subcommittees, testifying on behalf of the Indians, although if anything, he said it even more forcefully. His style in those hearings was later admiringly described by a fellow priest as one of "heat and fervor." He was even accused of "defying governmental authority," according to the *Spokane Daily Chronicle*. "The Coeur d'Alenes are proving that the Indian can take his place in American society without losing his identity," Byrne told the *Chronicle* in 1949. "The Indian feels it would be a calamity to lose his traditional heritage through assimilation by the whites. He wants to accept all the things this country has to offer, but he does not want to lose his right to contribute as an Indian."

Byrne's family name alone made him part of Spokane's elite. He was the oldest of six children of Dr. Patrick Sheedy Byrne, mayor of Spokane from 1901 to 1903 and a well-known physician. Dr. Byrne was considered something of a reformer, too, but he had other things in mind for his eldest son. He wanted Cornelius to go to West Point and begin a military career. When Cornelius instead announced that he wanted to become a priest, his father said that if he persisted in such a foolish course, he could pay for his Jesuit schooling himself.

"So I got a job washing windows and worked in the celery fields at the old Kelly Gardens in Spokane," Father Byrne told the *Spokesman-Review*. "My father, in a letter written to me just before his death a few months later, wrote, 'Now that you have made public your determination to be what you are, don't disgrace us by coming back.'" Young Cornelius did no such thing. He spent five years in the novitiate at Los Gatos, California, three years at the Jesuit seminary at Mount St. Michael near Spokane, two years teaching the Basques in Ona, Spain, and two more years in Madrid, learning Spanish and continuing his studies.

In 1927, he came back to Spokane to teach at Gonzaga, both the high school and the university, prompting an adoring profile in the *Spokesman-Review*: "The solemnity of holy orders and the somber shadows of monastery walls, where only cassocked men study and pray, have not dulled the merry twinkle in the eye of Father Byrne," wrote the reporter. "Father Byrne is an Irishman and—well, you know how the songwriters sing of 'the light in Irish eyes'; it never goes out. And he is most genial. In his lean black cassock he looks to be of slight build, but we have an idea that he will end up as a fat priest to match the geniality of his nature." He stayed slim all of his days and was genial when he wasn't confronting bigotry and intolerance.

Meanwhile, education—a rigorous, Jesuit education—became the key to Father Byrne's work at DeSmet. It was also the goal he set for Maxey and Burns when they arrived at his school, just two years into his tenure. Burns remembered the school as a place of strict discipline. Order was enforced to an almost military standard; whenever the students walked, they walked in single file. "We went in line everywhere," remembered Burns. "The Jesuits, so much of their modus operandi is discipline-oriented. They're a highly disciplined order for themselves, and they treated us kids with a lot of the same." Burns remembered that "one of the scholastics was pretty rough on the kids. He would come up behind you and get you to recite the Latin verses and if you missed a word, he'd hit you. He'd hit you in the back. They had this thing: scare the hell out of them, and that's the way they learn. And I learned all right. God, I was smart. I was so damn fearful as a kid, it wasn't even funny."

Carl, surprisingly, thrived in that atmosphere, probably because he sensed real caring behind the discipline—quite different than what he had experienced at the Spokane Children's Home. "Carl was a better-put-together personality than I was in a lot of ways," said Burns. "He handled things much better than I did. He was well liked by the priests and by the other kids. The Indian boys always wanted to knock me around because I was one of the smallest ones. But Carl wouldn't put up with it. And they soon learned that."

Carl was a good student, a good learner, and an insatiable reader. His tastes at that time ran to the popular adventure novels of the day, the Tarzan novels by Edgar Rice Burroughs and C. S. Forester's seafaring tales featuring Captain Horatio Hornblower. But it was on the athletic fields that Carl first discovered that he could cut a blazing figure in the world. Under the encouragement of the priests, he soon was playing every sport and starring in almost all of them. "Carl blossomed in a lot of ways there," said Burns. "It was very evident he was a good athlete. He was fast; he was quick." Lou Maxey recalled that "the old-timers who were there loved to talk about how everything changed when Carl came. They had a baseball team, they had a basketball team, they had a football team, but they never won anything. I don't know what Carl brought to them at the age of twelve or thirteen, but suddenly they started winning football games. Suddenly the other kids developed these talents."

DeSmet is where Carl learned the science of boxing, having acquired only the crudest rudiments of the sport during those sad "exhibitions" at the Spokane Children's Home. Byrne took the boys to their boxing matches in the tough mining and logging towns of the Idaho panhandle—at Civilian Conservation Corps camps, Catholic Youth Organization camps, and Amateur Athletic Union gyms. "The first fight I ever had in a ring that I can remember, I fought a man who was 33," Maxey later told *Spokesman-Review* sports columnist John Blanchette. "And I was 13." Maxey won, but "looked like the loser," he said. "That was a lesson. Fighting is a man's job, not a boy's delight."

He also began to run track and he learned that he had blazing speed. In fact, he was so fast that DeSmet's football team was suddenly steamrolling its opponents. Decades later, when Carl had a full mane of white hair, he waxed nostalgic as he drove past some of those small towns in the Idaho panhandle: Wallace, Mullan, and Priest River. He talked about how the fans in those towns used to shake their fists at him because he scored so many touchdowns during the games.

His athletic prowess was not the only reason fans got ugly. The rough mining towns of the Silver Valley (Wallace, Burke, Wardner, and Kellogg) had a particularly virulent reputation for racism, dating to 1899, when black troops of the Twenty-fourth Infantry, stationed at Fort George Wright in Spokane, were brought in to quell a violent miner's uprising in Wardner. Striking miners commandeered a train, stacked explosives in the middle of Kellogg's main street, and proceeded to blow one of the biggest mine buildings in the world into a heap of jutting timbers. Troops were called in, and thousands of miners were rounded up and put in the Bullpen, a hastily constructed barracks that was virtually a concentration camp—a concentration camp where the inmates were all white and the guards were almost all black.

The black troops were used as guards because military authorities felt that white troops might identify too much with their prisoners. This racially loaded situation was inflamed further when union agitators spread rumors in the Bullpen that black soldiers were sleeping with the miners' wives. There was little, if any, truth to these rumors, but they served to focus all of the miners' rage and frustration on the black troops. Not only were the troops despised as strikebreakers, but they were also feared as devilish polluters of their women. The animosity lingered long after the Bullpen was dismantled. It set the stage for an uncommonly poisonous racial atmosphere in the Idaho panhandle, which some say lingers to this day.

The venom brewed in the Bullpen was still relatively fresh in the 1930s, and it may explain why a fourteen-year-old running back was treated like some kind of criminal when he entered some of those panhandle towns. "When I first went up to Wallace to play a football game, they had to keep me in the sheriff's house overnight, because there was a big sign up that said, 'Nigger, read this sign and run,'" said Maxey. "Really, literally, that was true. For the whole city." After a probably not-so-restful night at the sheriff's house, Maxey was allowed to play the game. "And we beat 'em, too," said Maxey, laughing. "Carl said he would make a touchdown, and just keep running," said Lou.

At DeSmet, Maxey also had his first and only brush with show business. The Spencer Tracy movie *Northwest Passage* was filming near Payette Lake in Idaho, and the producers needed some Indians. So they sent a bus out to various reservations to pick some up. Ninon Schults remembered the story like this: "When they were filing in to get on the bus, the bus driver said, 'Hey, wait a minute, you're not an Indian.' And Carl said, 'Yes, I am. Blackfeet Tribe.' And the guy thought that was hilarious and he let him on the bus." After he arrived on the set, Carl's characteristic brashness got him a cameo in the role of . . . Indian falling off cliff. It was a battle scene, and the director needed someone to fall into the river. Nobody wanted to do *that*. Except Carl. If you watch *Northwest Passage* closely, you can see an "Indian" dive off a cliff into the river. That's Carl Maxey. "He looks like a young Indian man-boy," said Ninon.

Carl didn't have many black role models at DeSmet, or anywhere else for that matter, but somehow he managed to find one far up in the mountains during those years. In the high country outside of DeSmet lived a man named Jake Barker, who was known as the Black Wrangler. He lived alone except for his horses. No one knew much about him except by legend. One day, Father Byrne got word that Barker was sick, so he gave Carl a pair of snowshoes and a vial of medicine and sent him off to Barker's cabin.

Carl trudged his way up the mountains and ridges, powder snow sparkling beneath his snowshoes. Walking in snowshoes is strenuous work and it took much longer than he or Father Byrne had planned. By the time Carl got to the cabin, his feet were frozen. He was in no condition to make the return trip. Barker asked him, presumably with some irritation, "Why'd they send *you*?" Carl had no answer for that. Jake got up, put Carl on the back of his horse, and rode him safely back to the mission. On the way, Carl told Jake that he thought he had heard a baby crying on the way up. "That was no baby," Barker said. "That was a cougar following you."

"And that Jake Barker has always been a hero to Carl," said Lou Maxey. "He didn't know anything about his background—Carl thought he may have been from the 9th or 10th Cavalry—but he could shoot, he could ride and he was a cowboy. And then one day, he was just gone." To the end of his life, Carl carried scars on his heels from the frostbite he got that day.

His three years at DeSmet left other imprints on Carl, of a much more positive kind. Father Byrne's interest in justice for the Coeur d'Alene Tribe was part of a larger, distinctly Jesuit interest in social justice and equality. For Father Byrne, justice was an attainable goal, and he was never shy about projecting these principles onto an unwilling public. For instance, when he first arrived at DeSmet in 1934, he learned that some of the local citizens objected to Indians attending the local movie house. He also heard that at least one white citizen was boycotting a restaurant because an Indian worked there. "Young Father Byrne immediately began a thorough investigation," said the *Spokesman-Review*. "He then enlisted the aid of a weekly newspaper in the area and through its columns challenged readers on the question of the rights of Indians as citizens of the United States. He added the potent reminder that the Indians, whose bank accounts were then substantial, might boycott businesses in the area. Prejudices quietly subsided."

Father Byrne fought on behalf of the Coeur d'Alenes, but he also spoke out publicly whenever he perceived racism against blacks. After a *Spokesman-Review* columnist ran an account of Spokane's shameful treatment of the all-black cast of the touring musical *Carmen Jones*—they were denied service in most of the restaurants and hotels in town—Byrne weighed in with a blistering letter to the editor about "conditions of intolerance in Spokane that almost challenge belief." He closed his letter with this thundering cry: "Its stench rises to the high heavens!"

So when Father Byrne first saw those two kids at juvie, he might have seen more than just two boys who needed a home. He might have seen two boys who had never received a fair shake and deserved one. He undoubtedly saw two boys with enormous potential. "Father Byrne right away recognized that Carl had something," said Ninon Schults. "He was free of the Indian culture; he didn't have to balance two cultures. He had to only make his way in one. And Father Byrne encouraged him to do everything, to be a good student, to be a sports person. He gave Carl a real chance."

"Father Byrne did that for a lot of people," said Burns. "But he had a special interest in Carl. Me, he had under his nose most of the time, and he put up with me, I guess. He saw special qualities in Carl right from the word go. I think what he really saw was Carl's wanting to achieve, his motivation to achieve and to do for other people. Father was very good at that sort of thing. He expected more out of me, but I don't know whether he was disappointed or not. All I know is that if I had the kind of drive Carl had, I would have done a lot better than I did."

Neither of them turned out too badly. Burns went on to a successful career in the field of corrections, working in adult parole and probation and later being named the assistant superintendent of the state prison in Purdy, Washington. Maxey went on to forge an incendiary career as a civil rights lawyer, politician, and all-around establishment gadfly. "It's kind of ironic that the two kids who were booted out of the children's home because we were minorities, achieved more than anyone could have anticipated," said Burns. "And I really attribute that to Father Byrne. He just affected both of our lives."

Years later, during Maxey's huge and emotional memorial service, Ninon remembered sitting there thinking that one man was not getting quite the credit that he was due. "All of these people talked and were saying all of these wonderful things and all of these interesting things, but not enough was said about Father Byrne," she said. "They *couldn't* have said enough good things about Father Byrne." If it was any consolation, plenty of good things had been said before about Father Byrne. In 1952, the Coeur d'Alenes bestowed upon him the name "Hest Spoo-os," which means "kind heart." In 1962, the tribe named him an honorary member, and during the ceremony they presented him with a small token of gratitude: a brand new car, which they drove right out of a teepee to the delight of the crowd. By 1972, when the tribe honored him again, the Spokane newspapers were referring to him as the "Apostle of the Coeur d'Alenes."

And Maxey himself paid tribute to Father Byrne many times over the years. Maxey told everybody who would listen that Byrne was the most influential person in his life, bar none. Maxey kept in touch with Byrne for more than four decades, exchanging visits, letters, and viewpoints. In 1983, when Maxey weighed in with a scathing guest column to the *Spokesman-Review* about discrimination in the judicial system, Maxey quoted his old mentor, who had just written to him on this subject: "My dear friend, Father Cornelius Byrne, a 90–year-old Jesuit priest at DeSmet, Idaho, who took me in as an orphan child, said it best in a letter to me about that very editorial: '[The Judiciary is placed] where it should be, as foundation sine qua non of our Bill of Rights—for all, regardless of race or culture or religion.'" Obviously, Maxey was still learning from his teacher.

Father Byrne was more than just a teacher. He was the kind of strong, compassionate man that an orphan boy probably prayed for. "I haven't known any fathers in my life," said Maxey in a 1981 interview. "And I suppose the closest thing I had to one was that Jesuit priest." Maxey later met some other people he considered father figures—at college, at law school, and during his working career. But without Father Byrne, he could never have accomplished what he did. Not only did Father Byrne spur Maxey to blossom while at DeSmet, but Byrne was also responsible for the next crucial phase of Maxey's life. Byrne finagled a full scholarship for Maxey to Gonzaga High School, the Jesuit prep school in Spokane.

So if his early years in the orphanage were square zero—more like a desperate holding action than a true beginning—by the time he was fifteen Maxey was finally up to square one and ready to blow back into Spokane as a scholar-athlete with a full ride at the best school in town.

3

THE COUNT AND THE CLUB

O ne more thing about Father Byrne: He was connected. He made many friends and connections during his years at Gonzaga in the '20s, so when he told his Gonzaga friends that he had a young man, soon to be a sophomore, who was bright, driven, and who also just happened to be a fine all-sport athlete, they listened. "At DeSmet, Carl's athletic ability had become quite obvious, and the Byrne family was pretty well ensconced at Gonzaga, so they recruited Carl," said Ninon Schults. "It wouldn't be legal now, but they actually gave him an athletic scholarship to high school," said Lou Maxey.

Carl entered Gonzaga High School in 1939 with a scholarship for football, basketball, and track. He was a tall, skinny fifteen-year-old, built for speed. Not only did Gonzaga help with his tuition, but the school authorities arranged for him to board with an elderly black widow named Celestia Mash, who lived in a small frame house at W. 917 Shannon, in a middle-class neighborhood a mile or so away from the high school and college. "It was a white neighborhood, but she had been there so long that other people had moved in around her, so nobody was fussing about that," said Ninon.

As part of his scholarship, Carl had to work. At first, one of his jobs was to stop in at the Episcopal Church along the way to school and light the fire in the furnace every morning. Soon afterward, with the help of his Gonzaga patrons, he ended up getting a job at the City Club (still in existence today as the Spokane Club), which was the city's "power" club. "All the major persons were in the Spokane Club— every mayor, every doctor, every lawyer," Maxey once said. The city's power elite would lunch there in almost Gilded Age splendor, waited on by a deferential crew of black servants in white jackets and white gloves. A black man had no chance of joining this club, at least not until thirty years later. But many dreamed of working there, since it was *the* most important employer of blacks in the city. One black Spokane resident, who grew up during those years, went so far as to say that nearly every black man who came to town applied at the City Club at one time or another. Maxey eventually worked his way up to the relatively high-status job of waiter and bartender, despite being a minor.

Maxey had a standard joke when he talked about his pay in those days: "twenty-five cents an hour and all you could steal." It wasn't entirely a joke. One of the perks of working at the club, especially important to a growing teenage boy, was finagling some of that high-toned food out of the black cooks. Carl was enjoying the same dishes that Spokane's mining heirs, business barons, and railroad big shots were shoveling down every day. "He would give the cook some liquor, and he would get to eat right off the menu," said Lou Maxey.

Carl loved many of the people he worked with, a group he later called "reflective of the old black community in Spokane, people of integrity." The headwaiter, Ross Houston, become another of his father figures. As for his other feelings about the City Club . . . those feelings were what later observers would call a "Maxey mix"—a complicated mix of conflicting emotions. "I have a lot of good memories of the City Club, contrary to what a lot of people might think," Maxey told the *Spokane Daily Chronicle* in 1981. "Even though we were humiliated in pay and by the snapping of the finger and the command, 'Boy!' I also had a lot of respect for the members . . . The stories they told were fascinating. You could see they were the sources of power, that they had an effect on lives. I got along well with 'em. I listened well. The white man taught me many things."

Maxey said he was intrigued to finally meet the men who were in control of people's lives, including his own. He was not cowed, or awed, or filled with insecurity. Instead, he was filled with a desire to someday "get on an equal footing" with them. He soon found that these were men who could help him get where he wanted to go—not that he was entirely certain where that might be. "I don't mean to suggest that they pulled me aside," said Maxey. "You didn't do that at the City Club in those days." Yet he made some contacts, some of which paid off years later. Maxey asked for career assistance from some of those clubmen, and sometimes they even gave it to him. "I could feel affection for the guys at the Club," he told the *Chronicle*, again in 1981. "Yet I know what they thought about me. [Now] I fight 'em all the time, but I don't hate 'em. As the guy said, some of my best friends are white." Maxey soon worked his way up to assistant manager in one of the lounges, where one his jobs was to serve booze to the big shots. Even fifty years later, he could reel off the drinks favored by some of Spokane's founding fathers. Carl always remembered that J. P. Graves, Spokane's richest real-estate tycoon, was partial to old-fashioneds.

As a black employee at the City Club, Carl had to constantly remember that a fine line existed between being friendly and being *too friendly*. He had to know his place, as the saying went, and that rankled young Carl. Sometimes, he rebelled against it. Ninon Schults remembered Carl talking fondly about one incident that must have scandalized most of the prim socialites at the club, not to mention most of the fathers of the prim socialites. Carl was working a club dance as a waiter, doing his job, minding his own business, and probably enjoying the chance to hear the big band jazz he loved. A young white woman, daughter of a prominent Spokane couple, walked up to Maxey and asked him to dance. It was an alarming violation of protocol, of custom, of taboo. So Carl said, sure, I'll dance with you.

"And boy, that shocked everybody to pieces," said Ninon. "But that was the kind of girl she was. She didn't care what anybody thought. She was on top of the social heap, and when she asked him to dance, he did." So there they were, the rich white girl and the tall, slim, athletic black waiter, waltzing around the floor of the City Club. The whole place was apparently buzzing. Carl loved this sly bit of social subversion, and he was probably a bit flattered too. Ninon remembered that he always admired and respected that girl for what she did that night.

He also said that his "social awareness" began to take hold while working at the City Club. Lou Maxey remembered a story about one ugly altercation in the club: "There was some stag party, and there was someone from the air base, I mean a bigwig, and he did something to a woman," said Lou. The man had either insulted the woman or otherwise violated her honor. "I think she might have been a black lady, but frankly, that doesn't even matter," said Lou. "Whatever he was doing, it was even out of line for these jerks. And Carl told him to stop, or else. So Carl decked him."

To Lou, this story was an early example of what would become a continuing pattern in Maxey's life. He would see someone being treated badly, and he would be unable to stand aside and watch. He had to jump into the middle of it, even at his own peril. "That was Carl," she said. "He had developed that much of a sense of how the world was supposed to be, even at a really young age. A sense of justice, a sense of protecting those who couldn't protect themselves. Pretty amazing, I think. Because this stuff could have made an asshole out of most people. But with Carl, it didn't." Lou remembered that the punching incident terminated his employment, while Ninon thought the beginning of the end might have been the dancing incident. In any case, his employment ended after high school, and he never worked there again.

Nor did he ever join the club, although there came a time when he could have. In the 1970s, the Spokane Club (so-called by that time) finally opened up membership to blacks. But they did so only when threatened with court action by a one-time waiter at the club, who was crusading to open up all of the social clubs in the state. Maxey, no matter how much he might have dreamed of being on an "equal footing" with the clubmen, never felt truly accepted in that kind of company. Instead, he was more comfortable creating what amounted to his own miniclub, holding court nearly every lunchtime in the restaurant of the Ridpath Hotel, one of the city's big downtown hotels. This busy, loud, everybody-invited coffee shop better suited his more democratic style.

Maxey's years at the City Club not only gave him some much needed cash, but the experience forced him to develop a work ethic that, in later years, became his pride. "I would work there from five at night until one in the morning," he said, "and then get up and go to high school."

Gonzaga High School was an all-boys school, in those years tacked onto the much larger Gonzaga University. The high school was actually housed in the first floor of the big university building. The campus, dominated by St. Aloysius Catholic Church, called St. Al's by all the boys, was on the bank of the Spokane River, within easy walk of downtown Spokane. Gonzaga was the only boys' Catholic prep school in Spokane—the girls had two other Catholic schools to choose from, Marycliff and Holy Names, which the boys called Homely Dames through time-honored custom.

The power elite in Spokane was largely Protestant—mostly Episcopalian and Presbyterian—led by the Cowles family, which owned both local newspapers and unfailingly championed conservative Republican editorial policies. However, Spokane was a more Catholic community than many places in the West, possibly because of the missionary history of the region, but more likely because of the pull of Gonzaga University itself, which was established in 1887, just after the city got its start. Like most Catholic schools of the era, it was by no means reserved for the upper crust. It served Spokane's entire Catholic establishment, from the sons of mayors, like Father Byrne, all the way down to the sons of Irish miners and Italian shopkeepers. Maxey was certainly not the only student there who wasn't paying full freight.

Nor was he the only black student. Kenny Carpenter was a grade ahead of Carl. He became one of Carl's best friends, and his example proved that a black student could not only endure at Gonzaga High School, but could thrive. Carpenter was a class officer, member of the debate team, and made the honor roll for three straight years. He was also captain of the track team and played basketball, tennis, golf, and football as well. In the 1941 annual, his classmates jokingly predicted he would become the commissioner of the WPA (Works Progress

Administration), one of President Roosevelt's controversial Depression-fighting agencies and one that was providing wages for one million black families, as well as for millions of white families.

The Gonzaga students circa 1940 had lived through the trauma of the Depression and couldn't help but be alert to the possibly momentous decade on the horizon. In the yearbook's class prophecies, the students predicted that one of their classmates, "Dr. Thomas B. Gibbons, noted surgeon," would receive the Nobel Prize for operating on the brain of Adolf Hitler. "The patient failed to survive," the yearbook noted sardonically.

American popular culture had become worldwide in reach during the preceding three decades. Like most young Americans of the time, Carl's fellow Gonzaga students were particularly immersed in the world of Hollywood and radio. The 1941 yearbook listed a few of their class favorites, chosen by vote:

Favorite radio star, Bob Hope.

Favorite radio orchestra, Glenn Miller's.

Favorite singer, Bing Crosby (an old Gonzaga boy).

Favorite actor, Spencer Tracy.

Favorite actress, Bette Davis.

Favorite movie, *Gone With the Wind*.

Least favorite movie, *Tobacco Road*.

As befits a group of boys receiving a classical education, they also picked Shakespeare as their favorite classical author and Strauss's "Blue Danube Waltz" as their favorite classical song. As for sports, they were partial to Notre Dame in football, Joe DiMaggio in baseball, and Don Budge in tennis. The list was all-white, except in one category. In boxing they chose Joe Louis, a particular hero of Carl's. Louis, nicknamed the Brown Bomber, had recently defeated Max Schmeling to become the heavyweight champ of the world. Boxing was one of the few arenas of American life in which a young black man could win respect.

This conventional Catholic schoolboy culture must have been an adjustment for Maxey, and he did not exactly blaze his way through the school, especially at first. Even in athletics, it took him some time to prove himself. He played football for his entire three years, but did not make the varsity squad on a regular basis until his senior year, where he was a fast, darting halfback. This was one of the glamour positions of the era, but he shared the position with a bigger star, Nick Scarpelli, who was one of his best friends throughout high school. Maxey scored several touchdowns that year and helped the team win the city league championship. Carl was also instrumental in the final sixty-five-yard drive that led the team to a victory in the Catholic state championship game. But that was only after Scarpelli, the star right halfback, went down with an injury.

Maxey was more of a star in basketball, which he played his junior and senior years. He was a starter, along with his friend Scarpelli, both of those years. The team, however, was a disappointment, being knocked out in the first round of the playoffs. But in track, Maxey's favorite sport, he became a true star. He was fast enough to be a threat in both the 100–yard dash and the 440–yard race, and lithe enough to excel in the high jump. He qualified for the state track meet in his junior year and also in his senior year. At the state meet, he almost won the state 440 title. He finished second.

During that same state track meet in Pullman, Maxey experienced one of his high points as an athlete. His 880–yard relay team won the state championship. His friend Scarpelli ran the first leg, and Maxey ran the anchor. "He had a pretty good lead, but the fellow who beat him in the 440 was running the other anchor," said Scarpelli. "We were all standing there screaming, and Carl outlasted him and maintained his lead. That was a big day for us."

"That record wasn't broken for years," said Lou Maxey. "And I remember when it was, Carl was so pissed off. And more recently, some woman ran a faster time than he did in something, and he was really irritated about that." Scarpelli remembered Carl as "very competitive . . . And he got even more so later on." Yet for Carl the hunger for competition was only part of it. Athletics played a deeper role in the soul of this young boy, who was still intensely aware that he had no mother, no father, no family, and nobody to rely on but himself. In an interview many years later, he said that athletics "filled vacuums of unhappiness and loneliness."

Scarpelli remembered that Maxey was well liked at Gonzaga, but did not belong to any of the cliques that make up any high school. He said that Carl tended to run around with the people on his athletic teams. The trio of Scarpelli, Maxey, and Kenny Carpenter was especially tight. Another good friend was named John Bogle, and he used to share lunch with Maxey, who didn't usually bring one of his own. "Mrs. Bogle was a very nice lady and when she found that her son was sharing his lunch, she made enough for two so that Carl could have a good lunch too," said Ninon Schults. "I thought that was nice."

In his senior yearbook, Carl's nickname is listed as "Count," presumably Count Carl. His favorite saying, according to the yearbook, was the '40s hipster expression, "That's coin, ole man." In the "Favorites Among the Grads" section, in which the class voted on such categories as "Most Likely to Succeed," Carl was voted the class "Beau Brummel." He was a snappy dresser—at least as snappy as someone could be on City Club wages. He remained a flamboyant dresser all of his life. "He used to spend all of his money on clothes in those days," said Lou Maxey, which may explain why he rarely had much money for lunch. "That was when zoot suits were just coming into fashion, with the pegged trousers," said Scarpelli. "So we both bought corduroys that were pegged at the bottom. We thought we looked pretty sharp."

Academically, Carl was a good student, but not a great one—which isn't surprising for a student who was out most nights until 1:00 A.M. waiting tables at the City Club. He made the Gonzaga honor roll his junior year, but not as a sophomore or as a senior. His skills as a speaker, which brought him so far later in life, had not yet developed. He did not join the Debate Club or the Public Speaking Club. Except for the G Club, composed of athletic lettermen, he did not join any of the other clubby groups at Gonzaga High School, such as the Knights of the Leash, an honor society, or the Sodality Society, a Jesuit-oriented devotional and charitable society.

And he most certainly didn't join the Knights of the Altar, an altar-boy group. In fact, Maxey didn't even consider himself a Catholic, even though he had been attending Jesuit schools for six years and had to attend mass regularly, right along with the rest of the boys. "Everybody always assumed he was Catholic, because of Gonzaga, but if you asked him he would say, *no*," said Lou Maxey. He later became involved with the Unitarian Church, which fit his liberal philosophy better.

Whatever qualms he had about Catholicism as a religion, he seemed to have none at all about a Jesuit education. In 1984, the Gonzaga University alumni bulletin interviewed the man who by that time was considered one of its most distinguished graduates. He described himself as a "strong advocate of what Jesuit education is all about. I am profoundly indebted to the discipline of Jesuit education, although I do not ascribe to the religious persuasion. Jesuits march to a different drummer, as did Martin Luther King, Jr." Maxey considered a Jesuit education a good fit for a young black man of conscience and commitment. Gonzaga High School was also a good place for a young black man to get a taste of what life might be like in college—which had probably seemed a ludicrous dream to him just a few years prior. Maxey said there was "tremendous exposure to the university" environment at the high school, since the high school was actually in the college building.

Maxey also had fond memories of some of the characters who taught at the school. One of his most vivid recollections was of a particular Jesuit brother, Brother Peter Buskins, SJ, who was in charge of the athletic department's property room. He was quite a picture, in his black cassock and big stogie clamped between his teeth. "He was just a great guy, and all the boys loved to talk to him," said Scarpelli. "He would always tell us these stories about his religious life, and various things that had happened to him."

The school seemed relatively free of racial prejudice. Scarpelli remembered that Maxey was "treated very well." But this was 1942, and many stereotypes remained unquestioned. That's the only explanation for what his classmates prophesied for him in the 1942 yearbook. Carl Maxey was not destined to be a Nobel-winning surgeon, or commissioner of the WPA. Written as if it were a detective tale set ten years in the future, the "Class Prophecy" read, "Carl Maxey, the chauffeur, states he heard noises in the garage but was engrossed in a game of Harlem Billiards and failed to remember it."

The story was intended as humor, and other classmates took some ribbing too. Nick Scarpelli was destined to be a butcher, "serving time for hacking off the thumbs of customers who reached too eagerly for their packages." Yet it still must have rankled the young Maxey, already dreaming of professional possibilities, to read the destiny given to him by his classmates. He was destined to be a chauffeur.

With that, Maxey was sent forward into the world.

4

WALKING RIGHT INTO TROUBLE

M axey and his classmates graduated into a world at war. Pearl Harbor was bombed in the middle of their senior year, and by graduation day the country's armed forces were gearing up for a long, arduous ordeal. Maxey and all of his fellow graduates knew that they would take the brunt of it, and in their youthful enthusiasm and naiveté most of them welcomed the chance. Carl, for one, had dreams of being the most daring kind of warrior, a combat fighter pilot. For a brief few months after graduation, Carl also attempted to nurture two other dreams. One was to be a dentist, which was one of the few professional jobs open to an ambitious black man, if only for practical reasons. Many white dentists, even in the Northwest, wouldn't work on a black patient, so black communities needed to supply their own. Spokane in 1942 still had no black dentist.

His other dream was to become a college football player. Maxey later said that he received partial scholarships that summer from Washington State University, Gonzaga University, University of California–Berkeley, and University of Oregon, "mostly for track and basketball." But football apparently still burned inside of him, so that summer Maxey and his football comrade, Nick Scarpelli, headed fifteen miles down the road to Eastern Washington College of Education (now Eastern Washington University) in the small town of Cheney and attempted to make the team as walk-ons.

They walked on, all right, and walked right back off. The problem wasn't with the coach, or the team, or even the college. The problem was with Cheney itself, which was just about the least sophisticated college town imaginable. Cheney was essentially a wheat-farming village that had somehow landed a college. The biggest building in town was the grain elevator. Downtown consisted of one street. And some of the people, apparently, had just rolled in off the hay trucks. In Scarpelli's words, "These people just didn't know the right thing to say to Negroes." When Scarpelli and Maxey walked downtown, people called Maxey names and made other racial comments.

At first, Maxey and Scarpelli just let it slide. Carl, who smiled when a rake was broken over his head as a child, pretended it didn't hurt. He never said anything back. It was Scarpelli who couldn't stand it anymore, especially after it happened two or three days in a row: "I said, 'This is ridiculous. You don't have to put up with this stuff. Let's leave and forget about it and go back to Gonzaga University.'" So after a grand total of four days at Eastern Washington, Maxey and Scarpelli went back to Spokane. In the end, they enrolled at Gonzaga on basketball scholarships, but Carl's basketball career didn't last much longer than his Eastern Washington College football career.

The problem, once again, was that some people didn't know the right thing to say to a black man. Or possibly in this case, some people knew exactly the perfect thing to say, if the purpose was to offend. This time it was his teammates—the two cocaptains—who started muttering racial slurs, slipping in innuendoes, making good ol' boy wisecracks, just loud enough for Carl to hear. Gonzaga was not accustomed to black athletes and wouldn't be until the 1950s. In 1942, the football team had no black players either and had never, according to Maxey, done anything to encourage any. If the intent of the basketball cocaptains was to discourage their only black player, it worked, even on someone as well-armored as Maxey.

One day, hearing one too many racial remarks, Maxey stormed out of a practice, never to return. When he walked out the gym doors, he kept right on going, upstairs to boxing coach Joey August's office. There he planted himself in the doorway and announced, "I want to box."

He stood there expectantly, awaiting a reply. The crusty boxing coach stared at him hard for a few moments, and said, "Okay, kid, let's see what you got." He handed Maxey a pair of gloves and put him in the ring with one of the team's reigning heavyweight hotshots. Maxey, a skinny six feet one, weighed in at about 170 pounds. His opponent significantly outweighed him and had far more experience, and Maxey hadn't boxed since DeSmet. But while the coach and the whole team watched, Maxey proceeded to beat the tar out of that hotshot. August stood there flabbergasted. "Okay," he finally said. "You're on the team."

That was the beginning of the legend of King Carl, as his teammates soon called him. (Apparently, he had been promoted from Count.) It was also the beginning of an extraordinary journey for both Maxey and the team, which would end at the highest pinnacles of the collegiate sport. But not right away. First there were other battles to be fought. On December 9, 1942, Maxey did what hundreds of thousands of other eighteen-year-olds had done—he joined the Army Reserve. He boarded a train to Fort Douglas, Utah, where he was inducted as Private Carl Maxey. He went through basic training and then was sent back to Gonzaga to continue his studies.

He took premed classes, because the young Maxey had settled on his life's work—he was going to be a dentist. In fact, the dentistry program at Tufts University in Medford, Massachusetts, had already accepted him, with the proviso that he could guarantee the annual one-thousand-dollar tuition. To Maxey it was a frightful sum, but he thought with his connections in the City Club he could raise a loan. He set about trying to assemble what amounted to a consortium of investors. "I went to many influential persons I had met while working at the City Club and asked them to help finance my education," he said in a later interview. "But I couldn't find enough people who felt my future was worth investing in. So I went on active duty in the Army." He hadn't even completed a full year at Gonzaga yet, but like so many graduates of the high school class of 1942, he felt it was not only the right thing to do financially, but also the right thing to do patriotically. Maxey may have even had more reason than his white schoolmates to enlist. "The right to fight," as black leaders were calling it at the time, was seen as a crucial advance against a nationwide system of discrimination.

Maxey had dreamed of enrolling in officers' candidate school so that he could become a fighter pilot. He had avidly followed the news accounts of the Battle of Britain, in which the jaunty Royal Air Force fighter pilots had turned back Hitler's air power and almost certainly saved Britain. Winston Churchill, who growled the stirring words that year—"never in the field of human conflict was so much owed by so many to so few"—had become Carl's biggest hero. Saxophonist and combat pilot—those were the two things Maxey had always wanted to be, he would confess later to his wife Ninon. A lack of musical talent prevented the first, but segregation prevented the other.

In the period right before Pearl Harbor, antiblack sentiment in the army was stronger than at any time since the Civil War. An army of a half million soldiers contained only 4,700 black enlisted men and two officers. The Army Air Corps did not include a single black man. Secretary of War Henry Stimson probably spoke for the military establishment when he said, "Leadership is not imbedded in the Negro race yet, and to try to make commissioned officers to lead the men into battle is only to do disaster to both." After Pearl Harbor, these attitudes began to change under the pressure to create a massive, unified striking force, but the change came slowly.

At the time Maxey entered, army bases were still segregated. The Army Air Corps had just started training black pilots in a program known as the Tuskegee Experiment, but they still were not allowed into combat. Moreover, that program was hard to get into unless you were from one of the elite black colleges in the South. Even highly educated and trained black professionals were learning that they wouldn't yet be allowed to fight for democracy. In the book *No Ordinary Time*, author Doris Kearns Goodwin recounted the story of an experienced black pilot from Minnesota who applied for the Army Air Corps in 1940. He was told it was useless to even complete the application: "There is no place for a Negro in the Air Corps."

The inexperienced Maxey's chances, of course, were even slimmer.

So when he joined up, his destiny was that of the vast majority of black recruits: he became an enlisted man assigned to a black unit. Private Carl Maxey was trained for a noncombat role in the army's medical corps. Actually, he was not Private Carl Maxey, he was Private Leonard Carl Maxey. While lined up for induction, he noticed that all of the other inductees had three names. He had never had a middle name, not that he knew of, so he decided to make Carl his middle name and pick a new first name. On impulse, he picked Leonard, after his new hero, Winston Spencer Leonard Churchill. Churchill, with four names, could certainly spare one. On various official papers from then on, Maxey was known as Leonard C. Maxey, but he never actually went by Leonard, not even around his new army buddies.

One of those army buddies already knew Carl from childhood. Robert D. "Bob" Gibson, from Tacoma, Washington, had met Carl in Spokane years before while visiting Ross Houston, Carl's mentor at the City Club. They had become good friends. When Maxey was sent to Camp Crowder in Missouri early in his army stint, he was delighted to find Gibson there too. This was not as unlikely as it sounds. Most black troops went into a relatively few black units, most of them being trained for noncombat. So they both ended up in a medical battalion, learning to assist the (white) doctors in operating rooms and field hospitals. Maxey later said he was one of the few people in his outfit who could read and write. About 75 percent of all black recruits were from the southern and border states, and 80 percent had not finished the fourth grade. For a college student like Maxey, this was an eye-opener.

The rampant segregation in the army was another eye-opener for Maxey. He'd encountered his share of racism in Spokane, but he was appalled by what he discovered during his time at Fort Lewis, a huge army base just outside of Tacoma. "When I first went to Fort Lewis, I couldn't go to the main base canteen," said Maxey. "I couldn't go to the main base theater. They were bringing in some German prisoners and Italian prisoners from the North Africa campaign. They had more rights over in Fort Lewis than the blacks."

He was learning what thousands of other northern blacks were learning. Blatant Jim Crow regulations had been enacted, aimed at keeping the white troops away from the black troops. When one black soldier found that he had to sit in a colored-only chair at an army dental clinic, he was quoted in an army memo as saying, "That's the kind of democracy we are fighting for? It's so foolish it makes me laugh most of the time. I can't sit in a dental chair that a white man has sat in or will sit in the future!" Maxey learned about some of these rules the hard way. Once, he walked onto a bus to take him into camp. He sat down and waited. He was the only one on the bus. He waited, and waited, and waited, and still the bus didn't leave. The driver just sat there and stared straight ahead. The night grew on. "When is this bus gonna leave for camp?" Carl finally asked. "When you sit in the back of the bus," the driver replied.

Maxey later said that his "social awareness was born in the outrageously segregated army" and in the City Club. Yet he and his two best army buddies—Private Gibson, who went on to become associate vice-chancellor of the University of California Medical Center in San Francisco, and Private Joe Black, who became a star pitcher for the Brooklyn Dodgers—knew better than to try to make any waves. "In those days, you knew what you could do and what you couldn't do," said Gibson. "I wasn't particularly one to go out and get myself busted for doing some dumb thing, and neither was Carl. We stayed most of the time in camp, going down to the USO, which was a segregated USO."

Gibson, like Maxey, had dreamed of becoming an officer, but that dream was dashed early on. "I tried to get into Officer Candidates School, but I had trouble with that for the same reason as Carl," said Gibson, who had already spent a year at the University of Oregon on a football scholarship. "Shit, I had more education than the officers that were commanding my battalion. All of the officers in our battalion were white, and that frosted me. But that's the way times were then."

Maxey, Gibson, and Black all spent a great deal of time in sports competitions at the various bases where they were stationed, competing with teams from other units. Carl won several track competitions, and it was in the army that his skill as a boxer began to set him apart. "He was well liked and well respected," said Gibson. "He was a good athlete and a good boxer, and that was something that was prized in the black community back then."

These three strong, handsome young men did get into one scrape. During a leave, they decided to go to Tulsa, Oklahoma, for no other reason than to "see what Tulsa was like." They were standing on a street corner when three black women in a convertible pulled up. The men waved, the women smiled, and the next thing they knew they were riding in that convertible out to a juke joint, way out in the country. "Nobody was there except the bartender, the three girls, and the three of us, and boy, we thought we had things made for the evening," said Gibson, laughing. They put some money in the jukebox and began to dance. Suddenly, three glowering men burst through the door. They pointed out in a most unfriendly manner that these three women were their wives. The husbands were much smaller than the soldiers, but they had an equalizer, a "pistol that looked like a small cannon," said Gibson.

They backed the three soldiers against the wall, while their wives were screaming, "Don't! Don't!" Gibson reached up behind him and tried to unlatch a window to make a quick getaway, but the man with the pistol cracked him on the wrist. "I thought we were gonna die," said Gibson. In Gibson's version of the story, the men harassed them for a while and finally realized they were posing no threat to their wives and told them to get out. In Maxey's version of the story, the three husbands began laughing so hard watching these "three fools" trying to escape out a window that they finally said, "Oh, to hell with it." In any case, the "three fools" found themselves in the middle of the boondocks, with no way to get back to town. They finally walked and hitchhiked their way back to Tulsa, where they immediately caught a bus and headed back to the safety of the base. This incident cured them of any more curiosity about Tulsa.

Sometimes these three friends were separated when one was sent off to another camp or even overseas, but they always ended up getting back together. Gibson distinctly remembered going down to the

bus one time to see Carl off for an overseas stint. Gibson was planning to head to the baseball diamond after waving goodbye to Carl,
so he had a baseball glove on one hand and a baseball bat on his shoulder. Five months later, Gibson was walking along the same street, glove
on one hand and bat on his shoulder, when a bus pulled up. Out walked
Carl. He looked at Gibson and said, "You been waiting here for me
all of this time?" And they both burst into laughter.

Carl had been overseas, but not in combat as he had wished. He
was sent to Hawai'i, and he said sardonically of his time there, "I picked
pineapples and worked in a leper colony." What he actually did was
serve five months as a surgical technician in a hospital unit. According to his army record, his job was to prepare patients for operations
by administering hypodermics, by administering general anesthesia,
and by handing instruments and bandages to the surgeons. He also
administered first aid on his own, and dressed minor wounds. His discharge papers noted that he had "excellent training in physiology,
malaria-medications and operating room procedures, has given all types
of vaccinations and has worked in a pharmacy mixing all types of med-
icines from doctor's prescriptions."

It was honorable work, yet it still rankled Maxey. For one thing,
the living conditions of the black medics were appalling. He said the
housing was on stilts over a sewage lagoon, which the troops sarcas-
tically called Lake Louise. For another thing, it wasn't combat. Until
his discharge from the army on March 24, 1946, he never went anywhere near the war zone in his three years, three months of service.
"Overall, the experience was heartbreaking, because he wanted so
badly to fight," said Lou Maxey.

Yet he did get something out of it. He had begun to help some of
his fellow soldiers with counseling. He decided that he liked helping
people solve their problems, especially those who most needed help.
"It was really fulfilling," he later said. "I lost all interest in pulling
teeth." He also began to see a change in racial attitudes in the army
and in the rest of the country as well. In 1942, the *Pittsburgh Courier*,
one of the most influential black newspapers in the nation, had
launched what it called the Double V Campaign—Democracy: Vic-

tory at Home, Victory Abroad. The goal was to urge America to end segregation at home at the same time it was defeating fascism elsewhere. The campaign spread beyond the black community. Former Republican presidential candidate Wendell Wilkie was photographed wearing a Double V pin.

In the armed services, the change began at about the middle of the war and slowly gathered momentum. In 1943, the War Department ordered all army bases to stop segregation of theaters and other post facilities by race. Later that year, the Tuskegee airmen finally were sent into combat in North Africa and then to Italy and Germany, where they shot down 111 enemy planes and won one hundred Distinguished Flying Crosses. When the Battle of the Bulge in late 1944 required huge numbers of fresh troops, the War Department finally sent black troops to fight beside whites. The white soldiers were not convinced of the wisdom of this at first, and a survey showed that 64 percent of them were skeptical about their new black comrades. But three months of hard combat later, 77 percent of the white soldiers looked on the black soldiers favorably.

To the twenty-one-year-old Maxey, coming home to Spokane on the bus, it seemed as if the war had finally taught the whole nation about equality. On his visits back home on furlough, it even appeared that his own Inland Northwest was feeling these sweeping changes. With thousands of black troops stationed near Spokane and in northern Idaho, even places like Natatorium Park began to welcome all colors. "With so many black soldiers, they didn't dare try to enforce it [segregation]," said Maxey. But when he finally rolled into Spokane at the end of the war, his duty to his country discharged, he was in for a quick reminder that the world hadn't completely turned around. As he got off the bus, in full uniform, he walked into the bus station cafeteria and was denied service. "He told me that story a hundred times, and he told it in public too," said Lou Maxey.

This incident fit in all too well with the larger situation for black soldiers in Spokane. A few months after Maxey's return, two frightening racial confrontations rocked the region. On July 17, 1946, a boxing match at Geiger Field, an army air base a few miles west of Spokane, turned ugly. A white boxer had been declared the winner over a black boxer in a fiercely disputed decision, according to historian Dwayne Anthony Mack. About two hundred angry black soldiers hooted at the decision and milled around the ring afterward "looking for trouble," according to one army report. At one point, shocking news circulated among the crowd: a black soldier had been found dead, from blunt trauma to the head, on the street only about a hundred yards from the match. The angry black soldiers moved en masse into the area where the white soldiers were housed and began throwing rocks. Military policemen met them there, fired shots over their heads, and dispersed the crowd with tear-gas canisters. When the smoke cleared, fifteen soldiers suffered injuries, none serious. An investigation failed to find the soldier's killer—a car may have hit him, said authorities. In ensuing days, emotions cooled down surprisingly quickly; the rioting soldiers were not punished and the authorities ordered an increase in recreational facilities for the black soldiers.

Then, in October 1946, about twenty-five black soldiers raided an armory at the nearby Seven Mile Camp, fired off some weapons (without hitting anything), and then ran into the nearby woods, according to Mack. The soldiers were apparently protesting the arrest earlier that evening of four black soldiers who had disarmed a black military policeman in a scuffle at a downtown café. The soldiers who raided the armory were soon arrested without any injuries, and the disturbance never spread to the surrounding neighborhoods. Yet Spokane went on high alert: police closed all businesses that catered to blacks that night and set up roadblocks at the city limits to prevent an incipient attack from black rioters.

So despite the fact that the nation had just fought a war to uphold the ideals of democracy, and despite the fact that black soldiers had served their country honorably, there was still plenty of work to do in Spokane when it came to racial harmony. Slowly the question began to form in Maxey's mind: what about the law? He saw the law as a powerful tool of social change—certainly much more powerful than dentistry—so he decided to continue his undergraduate studies with that goal in mind. Now he had the GI Bill on his side, and once again he used his athletic prowess to get where he wanted to go: the University of Oregon in Eugene.

Exactly how he arrived there is a matter of some conjecture. According to one story Maxey used to tell, he received a track scholarship to the University of California. He was on the way to Berkeley when he passed through Eugene, saw the green and mossy University of Oregon campus and said, "I've never seen a more beautiful place." He didn't go a step farther. Somehow he wangled a track scholarship at the university and got admitted. Lou Maxey considered this story to be perfectly plausible for Carl, especially the young and impetuous Carl.

The more likely story is that he had decided on Oregon long before, for two reasons. First, Maxey had his sights on being a track star and the University of Oregon had a record of nurturing black track stars. Mack Robinson, Jackie Robinson's brother, had come out of the university and won a silver medal in the 1936 Olympics. The second reason, and maybe an even bigger one, was that Bob Gibson was planning to reenroll at Oregon.

He and Carl remained the closest of friends after they were discharged from the army. Carl went to Tacoma several times to visit Gibson and his sister and father. He bunked in their home and stayed up late into the night, talking, talking, and talking. The fatherless Maxey got along especially well with Gibson's father, a mechanic for Greyhound. "My dad just loved the guy," said Gibson. "Carl was good at relating to everybody, but he was especially close to my dad." Gibson said it was during these late-night sessions that Maxey decided to join Gibson at the University of Oregon. Gibson had already put in a year before he entered the army and was heading back on a football scholarship. They became roommates during the spring semester and summer session of 1946 and then again during the 1946–47 academic year, which turned out to be Maxey's last year at the University of Oregon.

That year and a half had a tremendous impact on Carl's path, both in terms of his intellectual life and his personal life. The University of Oregon had a reputation as a liberal bastion. In those heady years after the triumph of democracy over fascism, the campus was particularly giddy with liberalism. Wayne Morse, later to become Oregon's maverick U.S. senator and a fierce critic of the Vietnam War, was the dean of the law school and an influential force for many students, including Maxey. "It was great just listening to him speak," said Maxey. "He expressed concerns about people and the world, and it was sort of my advent in both law and politics."

Maxey joined the One World Club, dedicated to liberal ideals and social justice. The school brought the great black actor, singer, and activist Paul Robeson to campus, at a time when such an invitation was practically a radical act in itself (Robeson's passport was revoked in 1950 because of his friendship with the Soviet Union). The university also had a much more tolerant policy toward black athletes than many schools of the era, which is one reason why Gibson and many other out-of-state black athletes gravitated there.

Maxey's track career at the university never panned out, partly because of some nagging injuries and partly because of a clash with the coach, who was from Texas and was considered by Maxey to be a racist. Yet Maxey's academic career progressed steadily, if not spectacularly. He was B and C student, with an occasional A thrown in when he took a course that really captured him, such as U.S. history. Yet the drive that Father Byrne noticed ten years prior was now in full flower. Gibson remembered that Carl methodically set out to make himself into the kind of speaker, and the kind of man, that he wanted to be. "He used to memorize a new word every day and try to use it in his daily language, so he would have that in his vocabulary," said Gibson. "He used to tell me, if you're going to be a lawyer, you need to have the words."

Even while his athletic aspirations stalled, his romantic aspirations flourished. Not long into that first (and last) academic year, he met Ninon King, a senior from Ashland, Oregon, a small town nearly on the California border. Ninon was beautiful, talented, and brilliant. She also happened to be white. Her mother had brought up Ninon after her father died when she was three. Her mother was a cultured, educated woman herself, and she taught Ninon to love music, history, and theater. Ninon especially loved Shakespeare; as a teen, she had played small parts in Ashland productions.

When Ninon came to the University of Oregon, she first had her eye on a history degree so that she could become a teacher. "But I got scared at the thought of teaching kids, and I figured I really wasn't ready for that," she said. "So I changed my major to psychology and I was going to get my masters in psych. I had just been accepted into the graduate school at the University of Oregon." That plan never quite worked out. This Phi Beta Kappa scholar had other things on her mind that year, and it all started when one of her girlfriends brought some friends over to the dorm. "There was a bunch of us gals who lived in the same dormitory, and we all ran around together," said Ninon. "And one was named Harriet, a big red-headed girl from Coos Bay, Oregon. There was a black girl living in our dorm too, and Harriet got to know her, and got to know some of her friends, who were these guys who were there on football scholarships, black kids from Portland."

One day, Harriet brought Carl over to the dorm. Ninon was standing on the lawn, out in back of the dormitory, when Harriet walked over and introduced her to Carl. Ninon was immediately taken with this tall, athletic young man who seemed to be so strong, so sure of himself and so well put together. "When I met him, he already came equipped with all of those things that he had later, the social conscience, the ethical strength," she said. "He had already developed quite a sense of what was fair and what wasn't. It was a time when people were thinking that they were going to change things a lot, and I think he was eager to be in the forefront of that. And he was eager to be appreciated for what he was, rather than for anything else."

Ninon certainly appreciated him right away. She and some of her girlfriends began to circulate socially with Maxey's crowd, which included Gibson and Bobby Reynolds, a football player from Portland who was, in Ninon's words, "making a lot of ink, as they say, at the time." He was one of the stars of the team. "So we all started running around together, and of course that caused quite a stir," said Ninon. "But it was a wonderful time, the best of times and the worst of times. It was right after the war, and everybody was in a hopeful mood about *everything*, and anybody could do *anything*, if they had the chance. So by that time, Carl was the kind of person and Gib [Gibson] was the type of person, who would just not take a back seat to anybody over anything. And they were strong and clever enough to—well, if there was going to be trouble, then Carl was going to walk right into it."

He walked right into it as soon as the two began dating. Even on the enlightened University of Oregon campus some people couldn't handle the prospect of mixed couples. After all, Oregon still had an antimiscegenation law on the books, which meant that a marriage between Carl and Ninon would have been a felony (the law wasn't repealed until 1951). The law didn't prohibit them walking together, but even so, guys in the dorms would yell insults—"the same old words," according to Ninon—yet Carl and Ninon just kept walking. Most of the "trouble" was much more subtle than slurs yelled from windows.

For instance, Ninon had been elected the president of her "living group," a dorm leadership position. When she started going out with Carl, the implications were considered serious enough that the group held another vote. Should a girl with that kind of . . . reputation . . . be allowed to stay in office? They did vote to let her stay, but it wasn't long before there was another crisis. Carl had asked her to go to the house dance, which was like a prom for the dorm. Some girls in the dorm raised the question, would he be allowed to escort Ninon to this dance? The idea had simply never come up before. A mixed couple at the *house dance*? Could this happen? These students, in the most advanced seat of learning in the state, debated this question every night into the wee hours. The quandary was eventually kicked all the way upstairs to Genevieve Turnipseed, head of the dorms and also a friend of Ninon's older brother. She finally ruled that yes, Carl could escort Ninon to the dance. "He had to borrow a suit from another guy," remembered Ninon with a laugh.

The dance was wonderful, and no one gave them any guff. Some of the school authorities probably wished silently that these two would grow tired of each other and find more suitable sweethearts, but it didn't happen. Finally, the dean of women herself decided to take a stab at resolving this problem. "She sort of made veiled threats to me about what she would do if I kept this up," said Ninon. "I had made Phi Beta Kappa in my junior year, and she was sort of implying that I should not be setting such a bad example."

The dean never made good on that threat, and Ninon remained in Phi Beta Kappa. With the self-confidence of youth, she saw these victories as confirmation that the world had changed and that a rosy future of reason and equality lay ahead. She felt she and Carl were blazing a trail, showing the whole school that the days of petty interference in people's lives were over. Yet deep inside, Ninon wasn't nearly so brave and confident. The dean of women had also made a threat that chilled Ninon much more deeply than the fear of being kicked out of Phi Beta Kappa. She threatened to call Ninon's mother.

The dean never followed through on that threat either, but Ninon knew that someone would eventually have to tell her mother and that someone would have to be herself. That's because, as the school year waned, the relationship had deepened so much that she and Carl had decided to get married. As Ninon's graduation approached in the spring, she and Carl mapped out a plan for the future. Carl decided that he was going to law school. Ninon typed out letters and applications for him to various schools in the West, including the University of California Law School and Gonzaga University School of Law. He would enter law school and she would join him wherever he enrolled, and they would be married. Her plans for a master's degree were put aside.

When school got out, Carl returned to Spokane to dig ditches for the City of Spokane Water Department and await word from the law schools. Ninon returned to Ashland for the summer and became involved in another theatrical project in this small but artsy little Oregon town. A man named Angus Bowmer had started up a Shakespeare project before the war with the slightly eccentric dream of turning Ashland into the Stratford of the West Coast. In the summer of 1947, he decided to revive it and Ninon, who had always had a flair for acting, became one of his lead actresses. She was in four plays that summer for Bowmer's Oregon Shakespeare Festival. "Playgoers are still exclaiming over her perfection in the part of Ophelia," gushed the *Ashland Daily Tidings*. "Believe me, we were amateurs, totally," she said. "Angus Bowmer did a great job with very little material." Today, the Oregon Shakespeare Festival is one of the most respected theater festivals in the United States and a major tourist destination for culture lovers up and down the West Coast.

When fall of 1947 came, Carl enrolled at Gonzaga University School of Law, and Ninon took a job on the support staff of the psychology department at Southern Oregon College in Ashland. Meanwhile, she and Carl corresponded all summer, continuing to pledge their love for each other. Their plan was still in force, except for one problem. Ninon's mother didn't know that Carl existed. Ninon still hadn't broken the news to her. "I was scared to," said Ninon. Finally, she had to break down and tell her, and none too soon. Ninon planned to go to Spokane in January and marry Carl. She steeled herself and said the words— and it was just as traumatic as she was afraid it would be.

"My mother begged me not to do it," remembered Ninon. "She had never been a prejudiced person. She couldn't really beg me on those grounds, because she had always been a very intelligent, unprejudiced person. But she just said, 'Oh, you don't know what you're getting into. You shouldn't do this.' Well, she had never met Carl. If she had met him, she might not feel quite so bad, you know." Even if she had, she might not have changed her basic message, which was that Ninon had no idea how hard this would make her life. Yet Ninon was not to be dissuaded. She still believed that the world was changing, *had* changed, and that mixed couples would be accepted and welcomed in this new world. Besides, Ninon was in love with Carl, and that was that. Fortunately, Washington's antimiscegenation law had been repealed in 1887.

So Ninon quit her job, said goodbye to her merry band of Shakespearean players, and headed to Spokane. On January 9, 1948, she and Carl were married in the Holy Trinity Episcopal Church, the same church where Carl used to light the furnace every morning on the way to school. Did her mother finally relent and come to the wedding? "Oh, heavens to Betsy, no," said Ninon. "She sent me all kind of letters and warnings, and she was right on the brink of disowning me. But not quite." The mother and daughter relationship continued to be tense for years. They spoke and they wrote to each other, but tersely. "She was not the kind of person who would be overtly rude," said Ninon. "She was a real lady. But she was never too happy with what had happened."

All of that came in the future. When bride and groom walked down the aisle, neither with a parent in attendance, two forces already dominated their lives. One was law school, and the other, which was already making Carl a local celebrity, was boxing.

5

KING CARL WINS THE CROWN

Gonzaga University School of Law in 1948 was not like law school today. It was strictly a night school—a tradition that began when the law school was founded in 1912 and the faculty consisted of volunteer lawyers with daytime practices. Many law students, like Carl, did not have undergraduate degrees. Others were taking undergraduate courses during the day and law courses at night. Also, in those days law students were eligible for the school's National Collegiate Athletic Association (NCAA) athletic teams. This played a significant role in Carl's decision to come back to Gonzaga for law school. Boxing coach Joey August wanted King Carl back and was willing to give him a scholarship.

According to one newspaper account, August and Father Dussault, the school's athletic director, planned the whole thing back in 1943, just before Maxey went into the army. At the time, Maxey was suffering a bout of what was thought to be tuberculosis. But it turned out to be a minor malady, cured by simple rest. When they heard the good news, August and Dussault gathered around his bedside at the Edgecliff Sanitarium, where the three of them huddled and "laid plans for postwar boxing at Gonzaga." If this ever actually happened, Maxey must have forgotten, because after the war he immediately enrolled at the University of Oregon. But he may have remembered those dreams when it came time to go to law school. He later said that one reason he went to Gonzaga was the promise of boxing. "Athletes got jobs at school," he said.

Between the GI Bill, his boxing scholarship, and his day job as a janitor and stocker at one of the downtown Washington State Liquor Stores, Maxey cobbled together enough money for tuition. His schedule was brutal: he worked mornings at the liquor store, studied the law books in the afternoon, worked out in the ring from 3:00 to 5:30 P.M., and went to law classes from 7:00 until 10:00 P.M. And then he'd wake up the next morning and do it all over again. Clarence Freeman, another young black Spokane man, worked next door to Maxey's liquor store as a bellhop at the Ridpath Hotel. The two became good friends, and often passed the time on slow days. One day, Carl rapped on the window and got Clarence's attention: "Clarence, we're not going to be doing this all of our lives." But for the time being, it was all they could find.

Meanwhile, Carl was worried about a more mundane employment issue: getting some extra income to supplement his meager wages. He told Ninon, "Hey, you'd better get a job." She found one at the *Spokesman-Review*, one of Spokane's two daily papers. She started out as a typist but soon was doing research for the paper's farm-news publication. She stayed there for a year, and then switched to bookkeeping for the Girl Scouts. With her strictly liberal arts background, she found bookkeeping to be an uncomfortable match. She had never taken a bookkeeping course in her life. "So about this time there were a lot of law students working daytimes with the state welfare department," said Ninon. "And someone suggested that since I had a degree in psychology, and they were hiring people with psych degrees to do casework, I ought to try there. So I got a job . . . there, which was much better."

Carl was struggling with the intricacies of tort law and contract law and was not having an easy time of it. In his first year, he earned four Bs, six Cs, and three Ds. He earned only one A: significantly, in public speaking. Gonzaga's Scholarship Committee issued warnings to Maxey after each of those first two semesters. In the first, they recommended that he improve his written English, "particularly construction of sentences and expression." In the second, they suggested that the reason for his low grades was "too much outside activity," meaning boxing. The next year, they said he must not let these outside activities "interfere, in any way," with his law school work. Whatever he did, he had to get that grade point above the bare minimum of 2.0.

Maxey was having a much easier time mastering the intricacies of punching and counterpunching. He rapidly developed into the kind of intelligent boxer who relies on timing and finesse over brute strength. Although neither did he lack for muscle. "He was a very smart boxer, but he could hit, too," said Eli Thomas, one of his teammates and a frequent sparring partner. "I worked out with him probably 70 percent of the time in his last year, and believe me, he could hit." When he was a freshman, before the war, the *Spokane Daily Chronicle* ran a picture of him in a Joe Louis pose, biceps bulging, with the caption, "Carl Maxey, one of the hardest hitting of the Boone Avenue scrappers." Thanks to three-plus years of army training, Carl was now even stronger and more formidable. He moved up one weight class, from the 165–pound division to the 175–pound division, equivalent to light heavyweight.

In his first boxing season, his biggest problem was finding quality opposition. He went undefeated in all of his matches and was frequently ordered to "carry" a boxer, in other words, to go easy on him. "There were a number of fights I had when I was instructed not to try to beat the guy up," Maxey told a *Spokesman-Review* columnist in 1983 on the day he was inducted into the Inland Empire Sports Hall of Fame. "There were mismatches, but that was good experience, too—from a discipline standpoint. Nobody ever thinks about that part of it—not knocking somebody out who you're clearly superior to. That's a far more decent deed than trying to addle somebody's brains. It taught you some integrity about what you were doing—and some of the dangers, too."

His goal that first year at Gonzaga, and one that appeared eminently attainable, was to make the 1948 Olympic boxing team. Yet as the date approached for the Olympic trials in June, Maxey was having trouble getting into proper fighting trim. Nobody his own size would get in the ring with him. "Carl Maxey, Gonzaga University's top-notch Negro scrapper is finding it hard to get ready for a shot at the Olympics," wrote a Spokane sportswriter after one particularly dispiriting bout. "Maxey was matched against San Jose's Don Schaeffer, a full-grown heavyweight in a three-rounder billed as an 'exhibition.' Exhibitions are all right but not much good when it comes to preparing for tougher battles ahead. And all Maxey has been permitted to fight thus far have been exhibitions and nothing more."

So Maxey kept it reined in during the first round, but in the second he decided to show off his firepower. "He belted Schaeffer from pillar to post much to the delight of the near-capacity crowd," according to the story. "Coach Dewitt Portell, who apparently doesn't like to see the crowd happy if it meant that his big heavy was being belted around by a guy 20 pounds lighter, rushed across the ring at the end of the second heat and demanded that coach Joey August put a leash on his battler. Joey did, and the third round was another cream-puff affair. But the crowd was happy. They had seen Maxey cut loose for one round and for the first time this season."

August had been selected as the coach for the Inland Empire's sub-regional Olympic team, Inland Empire being the grandiose term that Spokane had invented for its huge (in square miles if not population) sphere of influence in eastern Washington, northern Idaho, and western Montana. Maxey was an automatic member of the team after blazing his way through all of his collegiate competitions. In fact, he was considered one of the favorites when the team embarked by train for the regional Olympic trials in San Francisco.

Yet the lack of quality competition had taken its toll. In the first bracket, he ran into Fred Lambert of Utah. Lambert, a converted southpaw, stunned Maxey with a flurry of fierce punches from both hands in the first round, and Maxey ended up flat on his back before he even made it to the second round. Lambert had taught Maxey the first hard lesson of his boxing career. "I remember seeing some stars above my head," remembered Maxey. "That's about all." He also saw his Olympic ambitions evaporate.

It was his first defeat ever, and even though it didn't count on his collegiate record, people began to wonder, sometimes in print, whether Maxey was overrated. He did what he could to quash these whispers during the 1948–49 collegiate season, when he remained undefeated and practically unchallenged. At the regular season's end, in March 1949, he and the rest of the Gonzaga team, with a record of 6 wins, 2 losses, and 1 tie, were on their way to the Pacific Coast Intercollegiate Tournament in Sacramento. Once again, Maxey was favored to win. Once again, that optimism was tempered by a fear that he had not faced any serious rivals most of the season. Ted Diehl of the University of Idaho was the most respected competitor in his weight class, but he and Maxey had not been matched in the regular season. Everybody knew Diehl would be waiting in Sacramento. Would Maxey once again learn a hard lesson?

Both boxers scored relatively easy victories in their semifinal bouts. Maxey scored a technical knockout (TKO) over Jack Lamke of the University of California. Diehl scored a TKO over Fred Ross of San Jose State. The stage was set for a Maxey-Diehl bout for the Pacific Coast tournament, and this time Maxey learned a much happier lesson. Here's how the *Chronicle* sports editor, Herb Ashlock, reported the story:

"Carl out-punched his home-area rival cleverly and won a decision, plus the Coast championship. In this tournament, the winner gets to keep his gloves. Naturally, these are highly prized. After the scrap, Carl strolled across the ring, slapped Ted on the back, and said, 'Hey, Diehl, you take these gloves. They belong to you. You deserve 'em for a good fight.'

"We're particularly happy for the tall, quiet Maxey. His Coast title means much to him, very much. Carl has been almost too good as a 175-pounder—and for that reason has fought almost more exhibitions than bona fide bouts. His career has thus been partially stymied.

"We well remember the day Maxey fought his bout in San Francisco during last year's regional Olympic trials . . . The loss was a surprise and a blow. And there were those who wondered then, if this Maxey was as good as he had been rated. Well—Carl showed 'em last night."

Maxey and three other Gonzaga boxers—Bill Macey, Jim Reilly, and Maxey's good friend Eli Thomas—were invited to compete in the National Collegiate Boxing Championships in East Lansing, Michigan. But the Gonzaga fighters turned down the invitation reportedly because of "the press of class work." Money might have also had something to do with it. Gonzaga didn't have the budget to fly four boxers to Michigan. And in Carl's case, at least, the press of class work was a nine-hundred-pound anvil. Maxey had managed to bring his grade point average up to about 2.5, which was a little safer but not exactly stellar. He could not afford to slip back. He already had three Ds on his record, and those warning letters were still sitting in his file, smoldering.

So he spent the rest of the spring concentrating on his classwork and on one other project: fatherhood. Ninon became pregnant near the beginning of the school year and in May of 1949 gave birth to William Carl Maxey. Carl finally had a true family to call his own. "Carl loved being a father," said Ninon. "He loved it right from the beginning. He played with Bill, tossed him around, showed him off. He was always a great father." The little family lived in a tiny apartment in Victory Heights, one of the new tossed-together housing projects for veterans that sprang up after the war. It was in a low-rent area of Spokane, hard by Hangman Creek. People called this dirt-road section of town Vinegar Flats because of the fragrant aroma from a vinegar plant. The neighborhood's ambience was more Appalachian mining town than burgeoning northwestern city. "We had to cook on a coal stove because they still had a coal room heater in that place," said Ninon. "I didn't know how to cook at all, much less on a coal stove. But I learned."

As the 1949–50 boxing season approached, King Carl continued to rule. With Jim Reilly and Eli Thomas also back on the squad, the team was clearly the best in Joey August's ten-year tenure as coach. August praised the talent he had to work with, but most of the boxers, and especially Maxey, gave August all the credit. The relationship between Maxey and August went beyond athlete-coach and became more like a kinship. Once again, Maxey had found a father figure, this time in the form of a short, tough Italian kid who had come up the hard way.

Joey August was the son of Augustagua Nicoletti, from Bari, a town in southern Italy on the Adriatic Sea. Nicoletti had packed up his young family in 1913 and embarked on a crowded immigrant steamer to the United States. Unlike many Italian families who ended up in Manhattan's Lower East Side or Boston's North End, this family had an unusual destination: the Hillyard area of Spokane. Lured by some cousins who were already established, the family made their way to this blue-collar neighborhood that had already become a kind of mini–Little Italy. The Italian immigrant population of Spokane was substantial, most of them having arrived in the previous ten or fifteen years to work in the railroad yards of Hillyard (literally, Hill's Yard, after Northern Pacific Railroad tycoon James J. Hill) in northeast Spokane. Nicoletti found a laboring job almost right away, and when the foreman asked his name the newcomer said, "Augustagua Nicoletti." The foreman made him repeat it one or two times, and then finally just shook his head and wrote down "Nick August," because at least he knew how to spell it.

The newly named Nick August bought a horse and wagon and began peddling fruit in south Spokane. Before long he had a small grocery store and six kids to feed. Joey was born two years after the family's arrival, and it didn't take long for him to start contributing to the family finances. He was a newsboy at the corner of Post and Main, one of downtown Spokane's busiest corners. "A guy could walk in and try to take your corner away," Joey once said. " I had to fight for my corner every night for awhile. After a while you get a reputation."

He channeled that pugnacious energy into organized sport at Gonzaga High School, about ten years ahead of Carl. By the time he was seventeen he was in Madison Square Garden, boxing in the national Amateur Athletic Union championships as a 112–pounder. He knocked out one opponent, defeated a second by decision, but lost in the quarterfinals. He boxed for the University of Idaho for two years, won several regional titles, turned pro in 1937, and went 14–1. When he finally hung up the gloves, he became a nationally known boxing referee and then, in 1939, the coach of Gonzaga University's boxing team. Coaching was strictly a labor of love. His day job was bartender and proprietor of Joey's, a popular student tavern in the Gonzaga district.

A Herb Ashlock column from 1952 gives some insight into the profound effect August had on the athletes he coached and trained. For one thing, he not only coached them: he boarded and fed them. That year, six of the nine boxers on the team actually lived in August's home. "I find it's a pretty good arrangement, having my boxers live in my home," August was quoted as saying. "I can keep an eye on 'em, help with their studies and be sure they observe the proper hours. The first year in school is generally tough for the frosh. They get lonesome. Often as not, they'll come up in the kitchen and talk to my wife. They discuss their problems with us and we give all the help we can."

Maxey, married with a child, did not live with August, but Maxey undoubtedly spent his share of time sitting at that kitchen table, talking to the man he ranked with Father Byrne as one of his most important influences in his life. August was the opposite of the redneck coaches Carl despised. Maxey later said he learned more than good defense and a good jab from August. He learned discipline, individualism, and integrity. "I've found out you have to be a coach's friend to perform well for him," Maxey told columnist John Blanchette more than thirty years later. "And I think he has to be the athlete's friend, too."

So as the 1949–50 season got underway, everybody wanted a part of Joey August and the Gonzaga boxing team. That fall, a *Chronicle* headline blared, "60 Ringmen Go Out for Irish Team." The paper continued, "The veteran ring mentor said that his squad will work out in a newly constructed and modernly equipped boxing room," tripping only slightly over its own adverbs. "'The facilities now available in Gonzaga's training quarters compare to the finest in the Northwest,' August said. 'We now have much more space in which to work and have added several new pieces of training equipment to handle the large boxing turnout.'"

When the regular season began, King Carl pulled on the gloves and went to work. None of his opponents in the regular dual-match season came close to beating him, and once again Carl had to use much of his art in *not* beating an opponent into submission. "With dynamite in both hands, King Carl has blasted the opposition again and again, but the fans will also remember the numerous occasions when he could have knocked a rival into oblivion, but instead elected to box just hard enough to win and not injure a less experienced boxer," said the program notes for one match. "It is men of Maxey's caliber who are placing college boxing in its enviable position in college athletics."

His exemplary conduct may have been partly due to what has become known as the Jackie Robinson principle. When Jackie Robinson broke the color bar in baseball in 1947, Branch Rickey told Robinson that he not only had to be good at baseball, but he had to be Saint Jackie as well. His behavior and demeanor had to be above reproach both on and off the field. When provoked, no matter how crudely, he had to remain calm. In every situation, he had to be a gentleman. So this may have been in Carl's mind as he gently dispatched weaker foes or when he handed his gloves to Ted Diehl.

Yet there was more to Maxey's behavior than that. In a way, this was just Carl. He knew the value of respect and dignity, not having received enough of it in his early life, so he believed in doling it out to others when he could. He tried to treat people the way he himself wished to be treated. This earned him a reputation for sportsmanship that was noticed outside the sport as well as inside: "Two Inland Empire college presidents, J. E. Buchanan of the University of Idaho and J. R. Nichols of Idaho State College, congratulated Carl on his gentlemanly conduct in the ring after he had defeated representatives of their schools," reported the *Spokesman-Review* in 1950.

Meanwhile, Maxey's reputation for sheer talent and power grew with every bout. By the time of the last collegiate home match of 1950, the local press was practically worshipful, and so was Coach August. In a story headlined, "Zags' King Carl in Local Finale," August couldn't praise his light heavyweight enough: "Coach Joey August . . . said today that Maxey is the best collegiate fighter he has seen during his many years of coaching and officiating at local, West Coast and national collegiate boxing tournaments," reported the *Spokesman-Review*.

"'Carl is definitely the finest collegiate boxer it has been my pleasure to coach here at Gonzaga,' August said today."

Maxey won his bout in that home finale, running his collegiate boxing record to 26–0. From there, Maxey and the rest of the squad headed to Sacramento one more time for the Pacific Coast Intercollegiate Boxing Tournament. The Gonzaga team was not a favorite, despite having two returning champions. The *Sacramento Bee* picked the University of Idaho, the regional powerhouse, to successfully defend its title. Washington State University coach Ike Deeter thought his team had a chance to eke out a victory too, although he told the *Bee* that he had lost several boxers to injuries and that "some of the athlete's girl friends have made them quit the sport," adding, "that is what really burns me up." He went on to say that Idaho, San Jose State, and UCLA should be considered the favorites. As for little Gonzaga, they were favored to win nothing except the light heavyweight division, with Maxey. "I don't think anyone on the coast can beat Maxey," said Deeter.

He was right. Maxey once again plowed his way through the field, defeating Ted Diehl in the preliminary rounds and then meeting Don Schaeffer of San Jose State in the finals. This was the same Don Schaeffer that Maxey had toyed with two years earlier in that exhibition bout. Schaeffer had gone on to make the NCAA national tournament twice, appearing in the heavyweight finals the year before. He was no pushover, but Maxey didn't have any more trouble with him this time than he did in his exhibition. Maxey defeated him handily, and he became the Pacific Coast champion for the second straight year.

The Gonzaga team as a whole surprised everyone. The team finished third, behind Idaho and San Jose State, and won three champions out of the eight divisions: Jim Reilly in the 130–pound class, Eli Thomas in the 155–pound class, and Maxey. All three were invited to the National Collegiate Boxing Championships in State College, Pennsylvania, and this time August was determined not to miss it. This time "the press of class work" was not cited, even though in Carl's case this was a more urgent problem than ever. His grades had gone south again in this glorious year, and he had earned another pair of

Ds to go with long list of Cs. He had received an extremely stern letter in early March, right before the Pacific Coast tournament: "The Faculty Council has met and has recommended that you be warned very strongly that your work for the past semester has been unsatisfactory. The faculty agrees with you considerably in the judgment that much of your difficulty is caused by the lack of a good grammar school foundation, and it is my earnest suggestion that you greatly increase your efforts to remedy this defect as it well could be an insurmountable problem to you unless substantial improvement is made."

But boxing frenzy had descended on the school, and August was determined to take his team to the national championships no matter what. First he had to scare up some money, and fast. The Ringsiders, a recently formed boxing booster club, went feverishly to work on an instant fund-raising drive, perhaps sensing that this could be Gonzaga's best shot at glory. Gonzaga had never won a national championship in any sport. The plane was scheduled to leave at midnight on March 28, 1950, but at noon that day the Ringsiders still hadn't come up with enough money. "Fund Is Still Short as Time Nears for Leaving," reported the *Chronicle*. The Ringsiders worked the streets furiously, begging, borrowing, and calling in favors. They also wrangled a few more dollars out of Gonzaga's sparse athletic budget. Some way, somehow, when that flight took off from Spokane's Geiger Field at midnight, the "Boone Avenue scrappers" were on it. "None of the wives went, of course," said Ninon, who was just as happy to stay home with little Bill. "Gonzaga was paying the freight and they didn't want us along."

Once again, Gonzaga was a severe underdog. The tournament consisted of fifty-six boxers from sixteen different schools, including strong contingents from the perennial boxing powers, the University of Wisconsin and Michigan State. Those schools had five contestants apiece, and two schools, Syracuse and defending champion Louisiana State, had six. With only three contestants, little Gonzaga simply didn't have the depth to be a threat. From the first bell, however, this tournament defied expectations. Several of the reigning champions were defeated in the first two rounds. Ten unbeaten boxers started the tournament and several were lopped off right away. Meanwhile, all three of Gonzaga's boxers won their first-round matches. Maxey had little trouble with Jack Bolger of Penn State. Maxey knocked him out in the first round, despite being exhausted from the Pacific Coast tournament the previous week and seriously underweight.

Next he faced Don Schaeffer again, and it looked as if Schaeffer might have finally discovered a Maxey-beating formula. "Maxey had a little trouble with Don Schaeffer of San Jose State at the outset, but soon overcame the Californian's efforts to disconcert him," reported the Associated Press (AP). "After finding the range, Maxey jolted Schaeffer time after time with short rights to the head. Strictly a counter puncher, Maxey only waded in to trade punches a couple of times, but he brought blood from Schaeffer's nose in one exchange." Maxey won the bout easily on points, and the victory put him into the finals against Chuck Spieser of Michigan State, a former Olympic boxer and the tournament favorite.

Overall, Michigan State, one of the favorites, was sitting at the top of the standings due to consistent performances from its boxers in the lower weight classes. Meanwhile, Maxey's teammates had defied the odds and put Gonzaga within reach of the top. Reilly had lost in the semifinals, but in getting there had earned important team points. Eli Thomas was marching through the 155–pound division, thrashing Bucky Ennis from Catholic University in the semifinals and "punching away almost at will," according to the AP. Then Thomas pounded his way to victory over Pat Heims of Penn State in the finals. "To be honest, three of the easiest fights I had all year were in the nationals," said Thomas, years later. "I kind of peaked at the right time." In *The Six-Minute Fraternity*, a book about NCAA tournament boxing, E. C. Wallenfeldt wrote that "Thomas proved to have too much muscle and ring savvy for the courageous but inexperienced Heims. The Gonzaga boxer's aggressive tactics, strength, and excellent body punching were overpowering and he won a clear decision over the surprising Heims."

So as if the stakes weren't high enough, when Maxey and Spieser shook hands and came out fighting on April 1, 1950, the NCAA title, as well as the individual championship, was on the line. If Spieser won,

Michigan State would win the team championship outright. If Maxey won, Gonzaga had a chance to tie for its first ever NCAA championship. Adding to the pressure, both boxers were undefeated in their college careers, Maxey's sole loss being outside of collegiate competition. As the two boxers warily approached each other from their corners, each carried the weight of his career, his ambition, and his entire team. That burden weighed especially heavy on Maxey, who had been worn down and wrung out over the past two weeks. He was down to 164 pounds, 11 pounds under the limit. He knew he had the battle of his life on his hands.

August, in the corner, must have decided that the best way to get Maxey's adrenaline flowing was to put a scare into him. "When [Spieser] is advancing, he's like a hungry tiger!" barked August. "When he's retreating, he's like Tony Zale [pro middleweight champ]. He's about the best college boxer in the nation. Now—go out there and get him!" What happened in the next six minutes was remembered by Gene Rankin, one of the tournament referees, as "the most masterful piece of boxing" he had ever seen. In the early going, both men circled and attacked, circled and attacked, displaying all of their skill and defensive savvy. Neither was able to break through and cause any decisive damage. Through the first two rounds, the two men fought to a virtual draw.

As August toweled Maxey off before the third round, Maxey realized that the next two minutes would mean everything. "I haven't trained all of these years for nothing, Joey," he later recalled telling his coach just before the third-round opening bell. "I'm going out there this round and win." As he stepped out to meet Spieser, he let loose with his characteristic counterpunching attack. "[Maxey] clipped Spieser three or four times and was quick to follow up this advantage with flurries of body punches," according to the AP.

Still, when the bell clanged to end the bout, the decision could have gone either way. The three judges huddled over their ballots; the boxers stood in their corners, their Gonzaga and Michigan State teammates looking on nervously. "We knew if Maxey won, so would we," said Thomas. Finally, the referee beckoned both boxers to the center of the ring. The referee grabbed each by a wrist. The announcement blared over the loudspeakers in the State College gymnasium. The referee thrust Maxey's glove toward the sky. "Maxey provided the biggest upset of the evening when he earned a decision over Spieser by about the slenderest possible margin, one point," reported the AP. "Two judges gave him one-point margins, while the third voted the other way. It was the tall Gonzaga Negro's short, accurate counter punching in the third round that swayed the decision."

The jubilation was complete when Michigan State's heavyweight boxer lost in the tournament's final match, thus ending Michigan State's bid for first place and thrusting Gonzaga into a first-place tie with its rival just sixty miles to the south, the University of Idaho. Gonzaga and Idaho had snatched the NCAA collegiate boxing championship right out from under boxing's big eastern and midwestern powers. Spokane's sportswriters were so overwhelmed with excitement that they could only compare it to consummated love.

"Like the last page of a romantic novel, the NCAA boxing tournament at Penn State provided the happiest of endings for Inland Empire fight fans," wrote George O'Connell in the *Spokesman-Review*. "The Gonzaga-Idaho tie was almost poetic, for most fans in the Northwest were rooting hard for both of these clubs. Gonzaga, with only three men in the tournament, was considered an almost hopeless underdog. Although they were figured to win at least one championship, team balance will usually decide the title, and they simply didn't have it. In fact their entry hung fire for several days while the Ringsiders club scraped—and president Jimmy Keefe says they really had to scrape—up the money to insure the necessary finances for the trip. They were strictly a Cinderella entry, but unlike the fairy tale, their coach didn't turn into a pumpkin at the stroke of midnight."

The entire city of Spokane, starved for any kind of national sports recognition, responded as if their city had just won a World Series. When the team's flight touched down at Geiger Field, one thousand students and alumni waited on the tarmac. The *Spokesman-Review* described the crowd's demeanor as "frenzied," and that was no exaggeration: "There was a touch of hysteria about this crowd, which broke past the restraining lines of state patrolmen and surged like a tidal wave toward the Northwest Airlines Stratocruiser which brought them home from Gonzaga University's greatest athletic triumph," said the *Spokesman-Review.* "The patrolmen had kept the crowd back as the huge plane taxied to its parking strip, but when the engines were stopped, they broke toward the plane and surrounded the ramp, setting up the chant, 'We want the champs.'"

"The team, led by coach Joey August, emerged and were mobbed by the enthusiastic Bulldog followers, hoisted atop various shoulders and paraded to the airline's waiting room. Their hands were wrung by hundreds of well wishers. The Gonzaga pep band furiously played 'Bulldogs of Gonzaga,' and almost no one heard. The waiting room was a madhouse as they received congratulations from all sides. A noisy motor cavalcade was organized to take them to the Gonzaga gym where a victory rally brought out some 500 students and friends to hear from the champs the story of the championship."

"I didn't realize it was that big of a deal until we got to the airport and it was loaded with all of those people," said Thomas. "Carl was a little older [by five years] and probably understood it better than I did. They took us to a big rally and I just thanked everybody and said I appreciated their prayers. When I sat down, Carl said, 'It's a good thing he can fight better than he can speak.' Carl made a long speech, a good one. He was a good speaker, very thorough." After Maxey presented his account, he received a "rising ovation," according to the paper. This was one of the first public speeches Maxey ever made and was probably his first standing ovation. But the biggest cheers were reserved for the Reverend Francis Corkery, Gonzaga's president, who made a deliriously received announcement: all students could take the next day off.

Meanwhile, one of Gonzaga's student managers, Tony Vetre, was thrilled to be invited to a victory dinner held by the boxers. Vetre, who was known as the "official second" of the boxing squad, showed up at the dinner to discover no place setting at his spot at the table—only a razor and scissors. It seems that before the boxers left for Pennsylvania, Vetre had said that if they won the championship they could give him his next haircut. As he sat at the table, the boxers grabbed him and took turns shearing Vetre like a sheep. The *Spokesman-Review* reported that Vetre had to resort in the next few weeks to wearing hats to cover his bald pate. "Bulldog boxers seem to make sure that his latest chapeau disappears," noted the paper dryly.

One further honor awaited Maxey that spring. The Ringsiders Club held their first annual banquet at the Desert Hotel in Spokane, with August and all of the student boxers as the guests of honor. "But the largest and most unanimous hurrahs went to Carl Maxey, 175–pound Pacific coast and national champ, captain of the Bulldog team and outstanding law student," wrote Don Smith of the *Spokesman-Review*. "To him went the first presentation of the new, annual and perpetual J. J. Zappone, Sr., Inspirational Trophy." The award was in the memory of the first commissioner of boxing in Montana and a vice president of the Amateur Athletic Union boxing board. The criteria were "inspiration, sportsmanship and ability," and it was awarded by vote of the entire Gonzaga team.

The unwanted orphan child was now the toast of Spokane. The *Spokesman-Review* profiled him for its Sunday magazine in a story headlined, "Carl Maxey—Gonzaga's 'Great.'" He had gone 32–0 in college boxing. He had given his school a championship. He had snatched the national crown. And to top this off, he did something quintessentially Maxey-like: he announced that he was quitting boxing. "He said, this is my last year, and I'm going to devote myself to school," said Lou Maxey. "He had such a developed sense of purpose." He was also in deep hot water with the faculty council over his slipping grades—his GPA was hovering back around the 2.0 mark—so he may not have had much choice but to quit.

This decision certainly made Ninon happy. From the beginning, she had refused, whenever she could, to watch Carl box. "I didn't like boxing and I still don't like boxing," said Ninon nearly fifty years later. "I had to go, of course, some of the time. What I hated most about it was the crowd, the viciousness of the crowd. The things people were saying in the stands. Carl did not beat anybody up. He boxed; he did not slug. People would scream at him, to egg him on. They wanted blood, and he didn't want that."

Carl's opinion of boxing was, like so many other things in his life, an agonizing mix of emotions. He knew his law studies were more important than boxing, yet a part of him yearned to turn pro. He was so gifted in the sport he couldn't help but wonder how he would stack up against the best. "He had a chance to turn pro and I did everything I could to keep him from doing that," said Ninon. "I think he was smart enough to see that that was not the thing to do, and the future did not lie in that direction. I think he wanted something better than that . . . Boxing was a sort of a 'show' business, not a totally ethical place." As Lou Maxey remembered, "I'm telling you, people wanted him to turn pro so bad. But he didn't even consider it. He once heard this big promoter from Seattle making incredible fixes and deals. He just couldn't stand that. And he couldn't stand the stuff he saw happen to his idols, like Joe Louis. It wasn't for him, although he was *so* good at it."

There was the rub. Because the truth is, Carl loved boxing and hated it at the same time. "Like everything else in his life, there was a lot of joy connected with it, because he was good at it and he loved the discipline," said Lou. "And he loved the way he said it could be like a ballet. But he had to do some things that were just so reprehensible. He had to carry so many guys. He said, 'That beats the hell out of beating their brains out.' But the fact that he had to do it took some of the honor away from the contest." He later said that boxing "is a treacherous, prejudiced sport full of all of the hazards of the real world." This, of course, was one reason why it was so important for him to triumph. Winning at boxing was a powerful and direct symbol for winning in the real world.

Maxey had one other reason for being ambivalent about boxing. He had never, not once, stepped into the ring with a black boxer. "I must make the observation that in four years of collegiate boxing I never fought a black guy and never saw one in a major tournament in my weight class," Maxey wrote in a passage printed in *The Six-Minute*

Fraternity. "The year I won the nationals, they still had the CIAA [Colored Intercollegiate Athletic Association]; that says it all." Maxey was wrong about the details—there was another black boxer, whom he didn't meet, in his weight class at the 1950 NCAA tournament—but he was right about the general atmosphere of sports at the time. And this rankled Maxey all of his life. "He said, 'I never fought a white guy I didn't like,'" said Lou with a laugh. "That was his line." Yet in typical contradictory fashion, Maxey loved boxing partly because of the way it rendered race irrelevant. When the bell rang, it was one man versus one man. Period. "Once in the ring, I knew we were very, very equal. I've tried to insist on that ever since," he told John Blanchette in 1983.

Even if he had loved boxing unconditionally, the practical truth was that it would have been insanity to try to box and finish law school at the same time. So as he entered his last semester, he wished the team well and hit the law books harder than ever. It was as if he decided to embark upon his adult life, his real life, in earnest. He wanted desperately to be the first black graduate of Gonzaga University School of Law and the first eastern Washington black man to pass the bar exam. And that wasn't all. He had decided that he wanted to change the world, or at least this particular corner of it, and he had settled on a law practice as the best springboard for achieving it. Here was a man who was not going to be anybody's chauffeur. "He had a vision not only of practicing law but of making law," said Lou. "It was a path by which good things could be accomplished. He believed that, and he knew he could do it."

So when the NCAA boxing tournament rolled around in March of 1951 at Michigan State, Carl was back home in Spokane. Yet his image, at least, was ubiquitous in Michigan. The cover of the 1951 official NCAA tournament guide featured Maxey, last year's star, climbing out of the ring, wearing his Gonzaga trunks and a charismatic smile. Maxey was proud of that cover. He later gave one of his copies to Joey August, with the inscription, "This book is from your team, and all those you helped, [signed] Carl and Lou."

August remained Gonzaga's boxing coach until the mid-1950s, when boxing ceased to be a collegiate sport. He soon parlayed this tavern business into the biggest beer-and-wine distributorship in Spokane. His Joey August beer trucks became a familiar sight all over Spokane, and his name was even better known because of the status he held in Spokane's sports world. He continued to spend his spare time as a coach, trainer, and benevolent supporter of every sport from Little League baseball to NCAA basketball. By the time he died in 1995 he had been elected to five different regional sports halls of fames and was one of the most beloved figures in the Spokane sports community.

As for Maxey, the *Spokesman-Review* sent him off into his law career with this generous prediction: "If his law battles are waged with the success his ring battles were, his future is secure." His fight was just beginning.

6

EASTERN WASHINGTON'S FIRST BLACK LAWYER

L ater in life, Maxey came to believe that his Gonzaga University School of Law class was somehow anointed. He was fond of pointing out how many important judicial positions were filled by his classmates, all the way up to chief justice of the Washington State Supreme Court. When he graduated from law school, however, Carl knew only that his classmates were the best group of friends he had ever had. They accepted him for his mind, his sense of fair play, his character, and his accomplishments. All of them were white. "We just didn't seem to make as many black friends as we did white friends. He moved in an all white world and he just seemed to be hitting it off with all of those law school buddies, and that's who we partied with," said Ninon Schults. "His law school friends became an important part of everything he did. I might add that Carl made friends quite easily." Lou Maxey commented, "He became very close to them, and not only that, he became very close to their fathers."

Maxey, even at age twenty-six, still had a need to seek out father figures. He was particularly close to the father of his best friend William H. "Bill" Williams. "Bill Williams's dad would talk and talk and talk about politics, and he would talk to Carl about stuff that maybe Billy didn't have all that much interest in," said Lou. "History, poetry, subjects like that. Carl would sit and listen to them. Almost every one of his good friends, he was very close to all of their parents. He learned a lot from them."

Bill Williams had grown up in Hillyard, the bluest of Spokane's blue-collar neighborhoods. When Williams transferred to Gonzaga University School of Law after one year at the University of Idaho Law School, Maxey found they had plenty in common. Williams had been a boxer too, winning the Pacific Coast championship title as an Idaho student in 1942. Then he went off to war, serving as a B-24 pilot in bombing missions out of England. When he was discharged, he continued his undergraduate work at the University of Idaho. One day, the Idaho football coach saw him tossing long bombs for his intramural team and recruited him for the varsity squad. Williams became the team's quarterback and earned the nickname, the Hillyard Rifle.

Maxey and Williams even spent their law school summers together, humping shovels for the Spokane Water Department on a ditch-digging crew. While these two budding lawyers were mucking around in the bottoms of those ditches, they passed the time solving the world's problems. "Carl was especially interested in politics," remembered Williams, after he retired as chief justice of the state supreme court. "He loved to talk about current events. And here's the other interesting thing about Carl. He would recite poetry while we were working." Ever the Anglophile, Carl was particularly partial to Rudyard Kipling. Someone walking past a water main project in those days might have heard a voice from down below, bellowing out lines from one of Carl's favorite poems: "Though I've belted you and flayed you / By the living Gawd that made you / You're a better man than I am, Gunga Din!" The bond between Maxey and Williams was made manifest at the birth of Carl's first son. William Carl Maxey was named after his best friend, combining the two friends' names for the next generation.

As Carl neared graduation in the winter of 1950, he and Ninon and little Bill were still living in the small apartment at Victory Heights. Carl was still working days at the state liquor store downtown, and Ninon by this time was working as a caseworker at the state's welfare department. During the day, Ninon left Bill with Thelma Carpenter, the wife of Carl's high school pal and role model, Kenny Carpenter. Meanwhile, Carl continued to struggle in law school, even after he quit boxing. As he entered his final year his grade point average was only 2.08, just barely above the minimum. Cs dominated his transcript; Ds weren't unusual.

As his final semester approached, in fall of 1950, he was still operating under an official academic warning. The registrar had sent him another ominous letter that summer: "The faculty council having reviewed your work feels that it is definitely unsatisfactory. I explained to them your personal problems and they, therefore, are willing that you continue in Law School. However, in view of the grades you have received, it is suggested that you make an appointment to see me so that we may discuss your situation with a view to insuring a successful conclusion to your studies." Prodded by that threat, Maxey did better, but only slightly, in his final semester. He earned an A in administrative law, but his final grade point average was still only 2.25.

He sat through his final law-school class on Christmas Eve, 1950, and graduated in January of 1951. He immediately started cramming for the Washington State Bar Exam, a test that looms large for any law graduate, but that had more than the average import for Maxey. If he passed it, he would be the first black person from eastern Washington to do so. Plus he had another incentive. "He had been told by a law professor that he would never make it through the bar exam," said Lou. Maxey must have been filled with a sense of vindication, not to mention relief, when he passed on the first try. Imagine, for a moment, how thoroughly gratifying this must have been for him. What were the odds that the little boy at the Spokane Children's Home would graduate from high school, much less law school? And now, he had become the first and only member of Spokane's black professional class. Spokane still did not have a black doctor, dentist, or teacher. But it had a black attorney.

The lack of black legal representation in the region had been particularly glaring just a year before, when the nationally known singer and actress, Hazel Scott, the wife of the U.S. representative from Harlem, Adam Clayton Powell Jr., was denied service at a Pasco, Washington, restaurant while on the way to a Spokane concert. Scott sued the restaurant for $50,000, and the suit was heard in federal court in Spokane in 1950. Scott and Powell hired local attorney Max Etter, prompting Thurgood Marshall, then special council for the National Association for the Advancement of Colored People (NAACP) and later U.S. Supreme Court justice, to express concern about Etter's qualifications (which turned out to be exemplary) and Etter's official connection with the local NAACP (which turned out to be nonexistent). Etter withdrew from the case without explanation and was replaced by another white Spokane attorney, Willard J. Roe, who won the case. Yet it was a mixed victory, according to historian Dwayne Anthony Mack. The jury awarded Scott only $250. If this trial had taken place a year or two later, the results might not have been any different. Yet nobody would have debated which lawyer to hire.

Maxey, even before he passed the bar in 1951, had already established himself as one of the leaders of Spokane's black community. That spring, he was elected president of the Spokane chapter of the NAACP. The chemistry was somewhat volatile—the fiery, idealistic young law graduate landing like a hot coal in the middle of the dry Spokane black establishment, which had been spending most of its energy on internal squabbles. According to Ninon, Maxey was exactly the spark that the group needed. "Here was this young orphan upstart, in the midst of the fairly settled black community," said Ninon. "I would say that the NAACP was rather in the doldrums, and he got in there and got it moving. He gave it a speaking voice, made it into a group that paid attention to what was happening and was concerned. He mobilized them a little bit more than they were before."

The settled black community didn't necessarily want to be mobilized. Many of them had become well established in the city, many had steady jobs, a few had small businesses and they "didn't want anybody rocking the boat," said Ninon. In the era of the Red scare and McCarthyism, even pointing out that a problem existed was increasingly dangerous. Seattle historian Quintard Taylor noted his book, *The Forging of a Black Community*, that Spokane state legislator Albert F. Canwell "spoke for many Washingtonians" when he declared in 1949, "If someone insists that there is discrimination against Negroes in this country, or that there is inequality of wealth, there is every reason to believe that person is a Communist."

Carl wanted members of the black community to keep what they had, but he also wanted to show them what they *didn't* have. Yes, they had friends and homes and a relatively comfortable status quo, but they did not have social equality, legal equality, and housing equality. And especially, they didn't have economic equality, as evidenced by a 1950s NAACP survey. "There are no regularly employed Negro mechanics in any major auto agency, no chefs in any major restaurant or hotel, no employees with any of the airlines, no repairmen, meter readers, collectors and so on," reported James M. Sims, one of Spokane's black leaders. "There are no tellers or clerical employees in the banks or savings and loan agencies. There is not a single regularly employed elevator operator in the Spokane area." The situation was that bad—a black man couldn't even get a job as an elevator operator. The vast majority of black workers in Spokane were in custodial, laboring, and service positions, similar to the jobs that Clarence Freeman and Maxey had held at the hotel and liquor store.

And even if some black residents had carved out comfortable niches for themselves, one notorious incident involving jazz legend Louis Armstrong illustrated how backward Spokane remained in 1950. Armstrong, already considered one of America's premier goodwill ambassadors, was booked to play the Spokane Armory on March 4, 1950. When he and his band arrived at the Davenport Hotel, the fanciest hotel in town, the hotel manager told them, sorry, he had no record of any reservations. Nor did he have any rooms available. He offered to get Armstrong and his group rooms in another hotel. Satchmo, who had been rejected and slighted by many hotel clerks in his long career, was in no mood to believe this was an innocent mistake. He immediately turned around and "left in a huff," according to the *Spokesman-Review*.

He didn't just leave the hotel—he left town. The next thing the concert promoters knew, Armstrong was on the train back to Seattle. Jazz fans were in a frenzy; the concert scheduled for the next day was in peril. As soon as he arrived in Seattle, the promoters called and begged him to come back to Spokane. He balked. Why return to a city that had just insulted him? The promoters reminded him that thousands of ticket holders had already paid to see him. Yet Armstrong still resisted. Only when the promoters said they had made reservations for him at the Spokane Hotel—another of the city's top hotels, but with a longstanding reputation for tolerance—did he relent and get on a plane back to Spokane. The city gave Satchmo a welcome befitting a president, as if to make up for his treatment. "Three shining new cars donated by the Utter Motor Company met him at the airport," said the *Spokesman-Review*. "A caravan of Washington State Patrol wagons and police cars screeched a siren escort into town for him. A line of photographers flashed their cameras when he strode into the Spokane Hotel lobby."

Spokane's black residents knew better than to accept the Davenport's official line that there had been an innocent mix-up. The Davenport had been off-limits to blacks for decades. A young unknown entertainer named Sammy Davis Jr. had discovered that the hard way a few years earlier when he visited Spokane as part of the Will Mastin Trio. According to his autobiography, *Yes, I Can*, Davis tried to book a room at a Spokane hotel that, from the description, sounds a lot like the Davenport (Davis called it only "the whitest goddamned hotel in town"). He marched into the lobby, asked for three rooms, and was rebuffed by the desk clerk and thoroughly humiliated by a bellhop, who called him a "nervy nigger." Davis lost his temper and threw a punch. In the ensuing fight, the bellhop emerged the victor. The next thing Davis knew, he was on the ground, clutching a broken nose, trying not to bleed all over his shirt. He and the rest of the trio spent the next few nights sleeping on tarps on the floor of their dressing room.

These incidents laid bare the unwritten rules that Spokane's black residents lived with every day. Another example could be found every week at Spokane's own center of black culture, the Harlem Club, a raucous dinner-and-dance establishment patterned after Harlem's famous Cotton Club. Spokane's 365–seat nightclub was owned by a black entrepreneur, Ernest J. Brown, and featured a black jazz orchestra called the 13 Black Cats. Brown's own daughters performed a tap-dance routine every night. Despite this, the clientele was, like at the real Cotton Club, mostly white. "In those days, the white people didn't want to associate with the colored people," Berneice Adams, one of the 13 Black Cats, told the *Spokesman-Review* nearly sixty years later. "Well, the man [Brown] had to make his living. So the white customers had six nights a week and we had one night." Or two nights. On Sunday and Monday nights, Brown invited in the black community for what he called "dance specials." His daughter, Doris Mae Aaron, remembered those nights as the best nights of all. "I had lots of friends at those," she said.

Even if the older black establishment was wary, the younger black community was ready to make some progress. Carl brought with him the promise of change through legal action. Even the most staid members of the black community could see the advantage of having a lawyer of their own. "At first I wasn't so sure that they were so glad that this black lawyer came with a white wife," said Ninon. "But that wouldn't be fair to say that, because I can't read anybody's mind." Yet Ninon, clued into nuances, could tell that her reception was slightly cool. Carl apparently didn't waste much time worrying about this, though. He waded right into the city's racial politics and started using his new legal clout. At his first NAACP banquet as president, in March 1951, he publicly hammered the Washington State Liquor Control Board, his former employer. He said that the board had been issuing some oddly worded licenses to black applicants, licenses that "restricted the licensee to the sale of liquor to Negroes." Maxey said he was personally aware of such a license being issued to a black tavern owner in Spokane.

"This is clearly a violation of the law," he told NAACP members. "In this way, the board could use its authority as a means of controlling the location of Negro-owned businesses. The solution to this problem seems to be a matter of reacquainting the liquor control board with existing laws and educating the people that Negroes do not live in a colored district by choice, but by compulsion." Maxey made it clear that he considered the license contrary to the state's newly passed fair employment practices legislation. He then requested a hearing before the board for the purposes of "clarifying" the purpose of this license. With that salvo fired over its bow, the liquor control board quickly backtracked and said that the license in question was never intended to deny the owner the right to serve white people. Instead, the board said that the license was meant "only to exclude unattended, unescorted white women," a statement that perhaps revealed an even more complicated form of bigotry.

Maxey was not mollified, and he filed suit against the liquor control board. The board, apparently sensing the weakness of its argument, settled the case before trial and quietly dropped all restrictive licensing language. "We are happy to see the board has seen fit to avoid the unpleasantness and animosity which sometimes arises from court action," Maxey told the *Spokane Daily Chronicle*. Thus, Maxey launched his career as a civil rights lawyer. He must have been gratified at how easily this first victory came. Maybe he needed merely to aim a spotlight on inequity and people would see the light. Would it all be this easy?

He opened his practice on March 1, 1951, in a downtown Spokane office with Victor J. Felice, the son of an Italian immigrant, another former Gonzaga boxer and another of Carl's favorite law school buddies. "They weren't partners, that was very clear," said Ninon. "They just rented office space together. They each had their own practice." The *Chronicle* announced the fledgling law practice with a story headlined, "Ex-Boxers Plan to Practice Law." The story noted correctly that Maxey was "the first eastern Washington Negro ever to pass the state bar examinations" and noted incorrectly that "he was the first Negro to practice law in Spokane since the early 1900s." No evidence exists that there had ever been another black lawyer.

The article included an alarming exaggeration of Maxey's college record, saying that in addition to being a Gonzaga University School of Law grad Maxey had "graduated from the University of Oregon in 1947 with a bachelor's degree in political science." In fact, he barely had attained junior status there. This mistake probably resulted from a reporter's less-than-careful reading of Maxey's résumé. Someone, presumably Maxey himself, called the paper to correct it, because in a later edition on the same date the story simply read, "Before attending Gonzaga, he was a University of Oregon student." But the mistake lived on and was repeated a year later when Maxey announced his candidacy for a state office.

It was one of two mistakes that persisted in print, the other being that he had earned a battlefield officer's commission in World War II. That mistake originated in the flattering Sunday magazine profile of Maxey at the height of his boxing career in 1950 and was repeated as late as 1994 in the book about collegiate boxing, *The Six-Minute Fraternity*. When that book came out, Maxey immediately wrote a letter to author E. C. Wallenfeldt, pointing out the mistake and explaining how the error had originally made its way into print. "When the [original] interview was being conducted, he [the reporter] asked me what I wanted to say about the Army," wrote Maxey. "I told him I wished that I could tell him that I had such a celebrated career that I had been commissioned in the field, but such was not the case. He took the jest and put it in the article. I immediately tried to remedy the situation, but it never got corrected. I did not want anybody to think I was anything but a Private First Class in the service and proud of that."

In any case, when Maxey hung up his shingle at the Mohawk Building in downtown Spokane, he and his law school friends soon found that past accomplishments were of little consequence. They were all struggling, all sitting in their offices praying for a good client to walk in. Lawyers were forbidden by ethical rules from advertising or from actively pursuing cases. "Lawyers just had to sit there," said Ninon. "It was free enterprise at its purest. You know, you really couldn't chase ambulances. It was strictly word of mouth." Maxey soon discovered that he was laboring under a handicap that would have been comical if it hadn't been so serious. "His phone number got mixed up with the Bon Marché," said Bill Maxey, referring to one of Spokane's leading department stores. At first, this was a minor disaster for the new lawyer. But then he talked the Bon into answering their phones, "Bon Marché or Carl Maxey's law office," thus getting free advertising at one of the most-called phone numbers in town.

Maxey must have toyed at some point with leaving Spokane after law school and heading for Seattle, San Francisco, or anywhere else where the black population was larger, the opportunities for a black professional were greater, and the struggle for acceptance would be less lonely. Yet Maxey apparently never seriously considered practicing anywhere except Spokane. Carl had connections in Spokane, and a lawyer needs connections above all. Also, Carl's roots were in Spokane, and for an orphan roots are not yanked up blithely. Maybe, too, Carl felt a sense of mission when it came to Spokane. Other cities, *every* city, needed civil rights reform, but other cities already had black lawyers. Carl may have looked around his hometown and said to himself, if I don't stick around here and try to fix things, who will? So he began the long slow process of not just establishing a law practice, but of proving himself to an entire community. The first thing he had to prove was that he could make a living.

"I knew if I were to be successful in a rather provincial community, I'd have to represent everybody and provide a service I knew was something different," said Maxey in a 1975 *Spokesman-Review* interview. "As a result I worked awfully hard in the field of criminal law and domestic relations." For "domestic relations," read "divorce cases." His clients were mostly white, of course, since the city's black population was still less than 2 percent. "My road was a little tougher than the rest of them [the white lawyers] because I had to educate a community to come to a black professional person," he said in a 1981 *Chronicle* interview. He remembered his first years of law practice as only slightly more lucrative than digging ditches for the Spokane Water Department: he brought in only forty dollars one month and nothing at all during another. "I used to go to the jail and the courts and beg to be appointed to defendants," said Maxey. "Getting accepted in court was no problem and, in fact, the judges were just great in appointing me to cases. They kept me from starving."

His bank account wasn't the only thing that suffered. So did his idealistic principles, his plans to use his law career to help those in need. "There was one time where he had to serve some papers on someone on Christmas Eve," said Ninon. "And if he hadn't done it, there would have been no presents for us. He felt kind of . . . wry . . . about that, because the other person's sorrow was going to be our Christmas." Maxey always had a "special interest" in Christmas, and in making a good Christmas for his young family, according to his son Bill. "He always went out of his way to make sure that there was plenty, as plenty as there could be, under the tree." Patrick Stiley, one of Maxey's later law partners, said he once asked Carl why he was so hung up on Christmas. When Maxey answered, he did not answer as the big, tough lawyer he had become. He answered as the little boy he once had been: "You know, Pat, you have to grow up without ever having had a Christmas to appreciate the way I feel about it . . . it's important to me."

When Maxey wasn't trying to put food on the table, he plunged into any case of discrimination he could find, whether it paid or not. These were the moments when Maxey, even at an early age, was at his most ferocious. "He was ready to take on anything," said Ninon. "Carl was not afraid of anybody, he would not be deterred. Nobody could scare him away from a case by saying it was useless, or it would just cause trouble. That was like waving a red flag."

He found exactly one of these cases in the person of Eugene Breckenridge, a man who applied for a teaching job with the Spokane School District in 1951. By any measure, Breckenridge was an accomplished and highly educated man. He had served four years in World War II and had emerged a technical sergeant. Like Maxey, he went to college on the GI Bill. He earned a bachelor's degree with a major in chemistry and a minor in biology and then went on to graduate work in sociology and education at Whitworth College, a private liberal arts college nestled in the ponderosa pines on the northern edge of Spokane. He had been named outstanding student teacher in Whitworth's education program earlier in 1951 and was now the proud recipient of a master's degree in education. Yet he was deemed unqualified to teach mathematics and science to the seventh and eighth graders of Havermale Junior High School in Spokane. Breckenridge had applied for the job in the fall of 1951, but he lacked one key qualification: white skin.

According to Spokane School District custom, being black was disqualification enough. The school board was perfectly content having no black teachers in the district. There had been a black teacher once, but only for one year. In 1936, Helen Dundee, a distinguished graduate of Spokane's Lewis and Clark High School and Washington State College (later to become Washington State University) had been hired to teach at a Spokane high school. But Dundee left a year later for unknown reasons, and since then the district's teaching corps had been lily-white. The board's reasoning was this: We've never had any racial problems in this district. Why create any? Not that there weren't black applicants. Just a few years earlier, a qualified black woman applied. The superintendent, John Shaw, was inclined to hire her, but he encountered too much resistance from the school board, which was timid at best. The board put pressure on Shaw to drop the applicant.

With Breckenridge, however, a new player entered the debate. Maxey caught wind of the Breckenridge case and immediately went to Shaw's office and smothered him with a mix of friendly persuasion, principled argument, and legal threat. Maxey believed that the principled argument is what carried the day. "John Shaw was an Indian, a fellow Indian as far as I was concerned," said Maxey, who always identified strongly with the Coeur d'Alene Tribe from his boyhood. "He found some morality in my argument." What carried the day with the school board, however, was the legal threat, as Maxey had bandied the word "lawsuit" about. In any case, Shaw summoned the courage to finally stand up to the school board and insisted on hiring Breckenridge. The board wasn't keen on the idea of adding black teachers to the system, but finally relented and hired Breckenridge, or in the words of the *Chronicle*, "allowed" Shaw to hire Breckenridge.

Later that 1951–52 school year, the *Chronicle* checked in on Breckenridge to see how this daring social experiment had turned out. "Breckenridge has won the confidence of students, parents and his fellow teachers during the seven months he has been on the Havermale Junior High School staff," said the *Chronicle*. "Breckenridge himself feels it has been a privilege to be the first of his race to assume the responsibilities of a teacher." Breckenridge told the paper, "I came here feeling like any other normal human being, never have mentioned race or creed to my students and I know of no incident that has given anyone cause for embarrassment. My classes have been conducted as I believe any other teacher would conduct them. I've been very pleased with the attitude of everyone around me. I was given an opportunity to work in the profession for which I had prepared myself. I believe I have been no better nor worse than any other teacher with the same qualifications. In some instances I might have been looked upon as a curiosity. I have treated these boys and girls as ladies and gentlemen. I have tried to teach them to respect one another and they have shown respect for me."

Superintendent Shaw and the Havermale principal spoke of Breckenridge in words that Maxey must have identified with in his own situation as the first black lawyer. Shaw said that Breckenridge had done a fine job in a situation "which carried with it the added burden that always must be borne by the man who happens to be first in any particular line of endeavor." Apparently, the Jackie Robinson rule applied to teachers as well as athletes.

Maxey never had to file that threatened lawsuit, and his work behind the scenes on this case never made the papers. Yet it was the biggest triumph of his fledgling legal career. Breckenridge turned out to be one of the smartest hires the district ever made. He taught fourteen years at Havermale and then at Shadle Park High School, and he won the Washington Education Association's highest honor in 1965, the Educator-Citizen of the Year Award. Later that year, he was hired away by the Tacoma School District, where he went into administration and became the district's social studies director. In 1969, Whitworth College bestowed upon him an honorary doctorate in education for the "distinguished and exceptional manner in which Mr. Breckenridge served as a leader in the field of public education." His hiring opened up the Spokane teaching ranks for good—by 1969, the district had sixteen black teachers.

Maxey performed a similar kind of "opening-up" service in other areas of Spokane life, including in restaurants. Many Spokane restaurants would not serve black patrons, as the cast of *Carmen Jones* had discovered in 1945 and as Emmett Holmes and his family had discovered in 1900 at Natatorium Park when they were refused service and lost the subsequent lawsuit. Around 1911, an appeal to conscience had produced somewhat better results. The Reverend Emmett Reed, a black minister with the Calvary Baptist Church, made a list of every restaurant in town with a "No Colored Patronage Solicited" sign, and he paid them all a visit. He asked the proprietors to take the signs down and many did. But some of them soon put up new signs that said, "We reserve the right to refuse service to anyone," which the black community took as code for "No Colored Patronage Solicited." So even into the 1950s, black residents knew which restaurants welcomed them and which didn't.

This problem was not exclusive to Spokane by any means. The South had erected a virtual wall of Jim Crow laws that barred blacks outright from white establishments. Meanwhile, every city in the North had its share of restaurateurs who believed that they could simply make their own laws when it came to who sat at their tables. Prudent black travelers, when in a strange town, didn't just trust to luck when it came to restaurants or hotels. They bought NAACP travel guides, which listed welcoming restaurants and hotels in every region, including Spokane. Of course, Maxey and the other black residents of Spokane didn't need to consult the Spokane part of the booklet. The knew that information by heart. They went to the Fern, the Coney Island, and the splendid Oasis Room of the Desert Hotel. They stayed away from the elegant Davenport and dozens of other less-than-elegant spots. They didn't need the humiliation.

Yet black Americans all over the country were chafing under these restrictions. Many had served their country in the war; they were tired of having to live by these unfair rules. So when black customers found themselves denied service in Spokane in the early '50s, they discovered they didn't have to just sit back and take it. They could take it to Maxey. "I can name three or four restaurants that I brought action against," said Maxey in a 1997 interview. "I don't really need to name them now; they've changed their habits since then. But believe me, we started to open them up with litigation."

During one such lawsuit in 1951, the owners of a downtown Spokane restaurant were accused of refusing to serve a black janitor and his friend. They said they had ordered a cup of coffee and then sat and sat. No coffee ever arrived and the waitress testified that the owner told her not to serve the two men. When the men went to the cash register to say they had been waiting thirty-two minutes, the owner was blunt. "She told me they didn't serve colored people . . . they didn't serve niggers nothing in here," the janitor later testified, according to *Spokesman-Review* accounts of the trial. Maxey took the case, and during the trial the restaurant's attorney suggested that the judge and attorneys inspect the restaurant so they could better understand the layout of the counters. Maxey immediately retorted, "I'm not sure I could get in there, your honor."

"That's an uncalled for remark," snapped the restaurant's lawyer, who had been arguing that Maxey's client had been refused only because of his behavior. Maxey then said it was "a matter of principle" for him not to go into a place accused of refusing to serve blacks. The judge reprimanded the rookie lawyer Maxey, telling him to put his client's interests ahead of his personal feelings. Maxey did not win this suit, but from then on the restaurant began serving all races.

Sometimes, all it took was the threat of a lawsuit to prod restaurants to integrate. In the mid-1950s, Spokane's black residents discovered that they could patronize more and more restaurants, although they remained perfectly aware which ones accepted them only grudgingly. Jerrelene Williamson recalled that even after the Davenport Hotel was forced to accept black patrons in its restaurants in the '50s, "we always felt uncomfortable, because we knew we weren't wanted there before." Black residents preferred to give their business to the Spokane Hotel and the Desert Hotel, places that had always been friendly.

Most of Maxey's work involved small-time criminal charges. But one case in 1954 turned into a big-time triumph for the young lawyer. Stanley C. Olsen, age twenty-four, was arrested for carrying a pistol in his car without a license and also for possession of burglary tools. Olsen was sentenced to ten years in the state penitentiary at Walla Walla on the gun charge and to one year, suspended, on the burglary tool charge. Maxey and Felice took on his appeal, arguing that the state's

Uniform Firearms Act was unconstitutional because it prescribed different punishments and degrees of punishment for the same act. The case eventually went to the Washington State Supreme Court. On March 22, 1956, Maxey was in Sacramento judging for the Pacific Coast Intercollegiate Boxing Championships when the ruling came down. An associate sent him a Western Union telegram that read, "Olsen case reversed as unconstitutional. Olsen ordered released. Congratulations." Maxey saved that telegram all of his life. It was his first successful state supreme court appeal.

Throughout his early law career, Maxey was also working toward his other ambition: politics. This was the Carl who had said that he didn't want to just practice law—he wanted to make law. He and Ninon soon got involved in new and idealistic liberal groups, one of which was the Americans for Democratic Action (ADA), a national liberal organization started in 1947. Carl and Ninon joined shortly after a Spokane chapter formed and they not only debated issues of the day with like-minded people, but found a new social circle that accepted the couple for who they were. "That's another place where we met so many of our friends," said Ninon. "We met various people from all walks of life, all of them liberals." The group had a pro–civil rights, pro–economic security agenda that fit just right with Carl and Ninon's idealistic views. However, as the McCarthy era progressed, some labeled the ADA as radical, even subversive, although the group specifically rejected Communism. Membership in the organization proved exhilarating, but not necessarily useful for someone with practical political aspirations. For that, the Democratic Party was the ticket.

Carl and Ninon both dove into the Democratic Party at the precinct level, attending caucuses and working doorbells at election time. Ninon became a precinct committeewoman, and it didn't take long for Carl to throw caution aside and declare himself to be candidate for office. His first attempt was fairly ambitious for a twenty-eight-year-old right out of law school: the state House of Representatives. Maxey filed for the Democratic nomination for the Seventh District in July 1952, just a year and a half after he passed his bar exam. The *Chronicle* wasted no time in announcing this as historic. "Attorney Carl Maxey, a former national intercollegiate light heavyweight boxing champion, today became the first Spokane Negro to announce his candidacy for a state legislative office," said the *Chronicle*. "It was recalled that the late F. A. Stokes ran for city commissioner many years ago, but Maxey is believed to be the only member of his race from Spokane ever to run for a state office."

The state legislature had only one black representative at the time, Charles Stokes of central Seattle, and Stokes was the first since 1889. Yet running for office seems to have been contagious among Maxey's class of recent law graduates. His pal and office partner Vic Felice had also filed for a Democratic state representative nomination in a different district, and at least three of his law school buddies were running in various other primaries. Maxey had already figured out that running for office was good advertising at a time when lawyers couldn't advertise. "Carl used to tell me, 'Pat, run for office. It's the only ethical way to get your name out there. It doesn't matter whether you win or lose. You get your name on signs all over town,'" said Stiley during an interview years later.

Maxey, still in the flush of idealism, believed that with the right message and the right issues the white voters of Spokane would vote for the right man for the job—even if it wasn't the white man for the job. And Maxey believed passionately in his message, which boiled down to something not necessarily calculated to resonate with Spokane's conservative voters: no tax cut! He believed that a tax cut would punish those who most needed society's help. "I will campaign against that element in the Republican administration and those 'dissident' Democrats who have formed an alliance to cut taxes by depriving the children of the educational advantages they deserve," Maxey was quoted as saying. "It is not possible to cut taxes at this time, but we can be wise in our spending. We do not need more taxes but an equitable distribution of tax money. First things must come first, and that means our schools and social security program. Many people are suffering because of the arbitrary administration of Initiative 178, which is an example of the Republican conception of fair play."

Initiative 178 was a recently passed statewide measure that cut back the amount of public assistance for welfare recipients. A later story, just before the primary election, distilled the Maxey platform even more concisely: "Revise tax structure by replacing sales tax with a graduated net income tax with a pay-as-you-go collection system; repudiation of Initiative 178; write a good social security act, fairly administered; expansion of school program." Washington State had no state income tax. The main tax source was the sales tax, which Maxey believed was regressive and hurt those most who could least afford it. With this compassionate, looking-out-for-the-little-guy platform, Maxey hoped to defeat the other two Democrats in the primary, Edward J. Reilly and William L. Bennett.

Carl spent the rest of that summer knocking on doors, which no doubt must have alarmed at least a few white residents of Spokane. Yet he probably dispelled a few ingrained prejudices with his articulate manner and his personal charm. In the long run, however, a candidate running on a no-tax-cut platform faced an uphill battle, even if that candidate *wasn't* twenty-eight years old and black. On September 9, 1952, when the votes were tallied, Maxey came in dead last of the three Democratic candidates. And since all three Democratic candidates finished behind the two Republican candidates, Howard T. Ball and C. A. Orndorff Jr., Maxey finished fifth in a field of five. The vote totals were Ball, 2,812; Orndorff, 2,683; Reilly, 1,779; Bennett, 1,221; Maxey, 1,149.

These totals bounced Maxey right out of the general election, of course, but in a way, the results were somewhat encouraging. He had started from scratch and ended up with over a thousand votes. His showing was strong enough to convince him to try again two years later, in a local race. This time, the position was justice of the peace, what might be called an entry-level municipal judgeship for the city of Spokane. According to Ninon, Maxey filed for this open spot because it was a job he felt qualified for and because he was "ambitious," both in his legal and political career. But he also had a more pragmatic reason for coveting this job. It was a steady and secure post compared to practicing law. "Most of these young lawyers were living hand to mouth," said Ninon. "They were strapped just like all of us were. Most of the wives were working, of course, and so they were interested in anything that looked like a job where you could get a steady income without having to worry about who might or might not come through the door. A judgeship paid like a regular job, and that's one reason lawyers were interested in those things. That was one of Carl's motivations. Of course the other motivation was that he wanted to try everything."

Again, he knew it was an uphill battle, especially when he found out who one of his opponents would be: Kathryn Mautz. "Woman Throws Hat in Contest!" trumpeted a headline in the *Spokesman-Review* in July 1954. The story continued: "A young woman entered the race for Spokane Justice of the Peace yesterday, insuring the five other candidates a run for their money. Kathryn Ann Mautz, S. 507 Howard, is an attorney as are all candidates required to be. She is also pretty enough to have been an aspirant for the Miss Spokane title last fall; orator enough to be named 'Toastmistress of the Year' in 1953 as a member of the Spokane Toastmistress Club, and talented enough to be a pianist as well as a tap and ballet dancer."

Mautz reaped almost all the publicity for this relatively lowly judicial contest. Maxey's entrance into the race didn't even merit a story. Consequently, he went about campaigning with a cheerfully pessimistic, nothing-to-lose mentality and so did his law school friends, particularly Bill Williams and Henry Opendack, who helped out. "All of those buddies of his, they just made a game out of it," said Ninon. "They had a big lark out of it. They went out door to door ringing bells. But they ended up really putting their heart into this thing."

It was hard to compete with someone who had the Miss Spokane Pageant on her résumé. This became especially clear by the eve of the primary, when even more flattering stories came out about the attractive Miss Mautz. "Normally, candidates for Justice of the Peace attract little more attention than candidates for precinct committeemen," said the *Spokesman-Review* the day before the election. "But this campaign is an exception, for one of the candidates is a young woman, Miss Kathryn Ann Mautz, a practicing attorney in Spokane for two years. For the first time in the political history of Spokane, a woman is seeking a judicial office." The story went on to call her "this talented Portia," and noted that although the campaign was nonpartisan, "it is no secret that she is an active member of the Young Republican club in Spokane."

As for the first black candidate ever to seek a judicial office in Spokane, he received only a small capsule story, like the other three candidates for this particular position. Apparently, the novelty of a black candidate had already worn off. The terse story noted only that he was an orphan and former boxing champion and then went on to give his platform: "I believe the office of justice of the peace is of fundamental importance in our legal system. Seventy percent of all legal problems receive judicial disposition in justice court. Therefore the office should be filled by men who can bring integrity and experience to it."

Was that word "men" a deliberate slap at Mautz? That would seem uncharacteristic of the equality-minded Maxey, but in the heat of battle he may have decided to use any weapon at hand. In any case, it didn't work. When the primary results were counted, Mautz rolled easily past all four of her male foes. Maxey came in second, more than 1,000 votes behind. Still, it was a victory for Maxey, because he and the other three men received just barely enough votes to keep Mautz from gaining a plurality and winning the position outright. She missed by only 27 votes, thus forcing a run-off in the general election two months later against all four of her opponents.

So Maxey and friends went to work again. But it was impossible to swim against what looked like a Mautz infatuation, at least among the press. Just before the general election, the *Spokesman-Review* reported that the campaign had "attracted attention throughout the state and as far away as San Francisco." The paper noted that a member of San Francisco's Board of Supervisors, who happened to be a law school friend of Mautz's, wrote a letter on her behalf saying that "here in California we have many successful and capable ladies in judicial positions." When it came out that Mautz was supplementing her law income by working as a cashier at her aunt's cafe, the campaign might as well have been declared over. Mautz was not only pretty and bright, she was a regular gal!

The general election results were predictable: Mautz, 18,468; Maxey, 13,225. The three other candidates finished below Maxey, none of them garnering more than 8,000 votes. In Mautz's victory statement, she said, "I believe the citizens of Spokane will profit by having a woman on the justice court because women have a faculty for seeing and evaluating both sides of a story. Women pay attention to detail and temper justice with mercy." As for Maxey, he came away pleased that he at least finished second, and he also came away a little bit more savvy about political reality. Spokane voters were ready for a female candidate, but were they ready for black candidate? Maybe they were, but only if the black candidate outworked everyone else and chose his opponents wisely.

So Maxey threw himself back into making a living and also into making a life for his family. He and Ninon had recently discovered what seemed to be a gap in little Bill's education. "We were driving down Third Avenue and Bill said, 'What's that on top of that building?'" recalled Ninon. "It was a steeple. He was looking at the Presbyterian Church. We looked at each other and said, 'Well, I guess we'll have to do something about this. He needs to know about the Judeo-Christian heritage.'"

Soon after, some friends took the Maxeys to their church, the Unitarian Church. Carl and Ninon discovered that the Unitarian style and philosophy fit their open-minded, liberal bent perfectly. Spokane had several black churches, two of which—the Calvary Baptist Church and the Bethel African Methodist Episcopal Church—were centers of the city's black community life. Yet apparently those did not fit Maxey's style. Neither did Catholicism, even though Carl had been immersed in it for fifteen years of his youth. In the Unitarian Church, Carl and Ninon found a denomination that matched both their personalities and their politics. Before long, both became deeply involved in church activities. Ninon became the Sunday school superintendent; Carl played Santa Claus every year at the church Christmas party. "Me and my contemporaries, we'd always see a white Santa in a department store or somewhere and we'd say, 'No, that's not the real one. Santa's black,'" said Bill Maxey.

Santa was not Carl's sole foray into the performing arts. In early 1955, he made his stage debut. The Spokane Civic Theatre, the city's major community theater, was preparing for *The Hasty Heart*, John Patrick's World War II drama about a group of soldiers in a British army hospital in Southeast Asia. The producers wanted to accurately portray the diversity of British colonial forces, so they needed at least one black actor to play a Bantu in a supporting role. A black actor was not easy to find. The city's theater community and the city's black community moved in two different worlds. "They were desperate to find someone black to do it, and who could do it with grace," said Ninon. "A neighbor down the block was active in the Civic Theatre, and he talked Carl into taking the part. He was delighted to do it."

When *The Hasty Heart* opened, Carl received his first and only rave theatrical reviews. "One of the more difficult roles was most capably handled by Carl Maxey, as the dark-skinned Blossom, one of the patients," said the anonymous reviewer in the *Spokesman-Review*. "Since Blossom speaks no English, the role is a largely silent one. At times, simply by standing immobile, face passive, Maxey stole the scene from his more active companions."

Shortly after this, Ninon decided that she wanted to take part in theater again. In a few years she was so deeply involved with the Civic Theatre that she considered it "as sort of a nonpaying job." As for Maxey, he enjoyed the cast parties and the camaraderie, but he remained unbitten by the acting bug. Maxey never took on another role, although there were those who considered his later courtroom performances to be Oscar-worthy. He was often accused of using theatrics and melodrama in the courtroom—but never again of standing silently immobile.

Just before this, around 1954, Carl and Ninon were getting restless in their Victory Heights apartment. It was tiny and getting tinier by the minute with a little boy bouncing off the walls. Plus, the ambience could best be described as Early Housing Project. One of Maxey's oldest friends from high school, John Bogle, told Carl that there was a house for sale on Eighth Street, in an established middle-class, mostly white section of Spokane's upscale South Hill. The situation looked perfect to Ninon, because Marian Braune, the wife of another law school friend, had become a regular babysitter for Bill and the Braunes lived in the same block. In fact, Marian had become "like a mother to Bill," said Ninon. So somehow the Maxeys scraped together enough money to buy the house at 976 Eighth Avenue.

The situation was ideal for a working mother, but as soon as the Maxeys moved in they found that some of the neighbors were not quite so enthralled. "We sort of busted into that neighborhood, much to the dismay of some of the neighbors," said Ninon. "There was a Japanese American family around the corner, but it was an all-white neighborhood except for that. The neighbor next door was so bitter about it. They complained to all of the other neighbors and they wouldn't speak to us when we first moved in. The one next door ended up trying to be real good friends, but by that time I didn't really care to meet them."

Life for an interracial couple was complicated, but it had its lighter moments too. Sometimes, these moments came courtesy of the naiveté of youth. One day, young Bill, a first grader with an interest in toy soldiers, decided that he wanted his mother to make him a Civil War uniform. "I liked those uniforms," said Bill. "I asked her to make me one of the grey uniforms." Stifling a laugh, she went ahead and did it. When Carl came home he and Ninon shared a chuckle over their smiling young Confederate. Bill had no idea what his parents thought was so funny.

Father and son shared an interest in history, especially military history. Carl helped Bill amass a small collection of toy soldiers, the little metal ones, mostly from the Napoleonic era and the Civil War. They spent many hours together, setting up historic battles. Bill remembered his childhood as stable, happy, and loving.

Once, early in Carl and Ninon's marriage, an envelope arrived in the mail, a letter out of Carl's forgotten past. An insurance company was writing to inform him that his adoptive father, Carl Maxey, had died and had listed him as the beneficiary. Inside was a small check, less than five hundred dollars as Ninon remembered it. As Carl stared at the letter and the check, an amazed Ninon asked him if he wanted to find out more about his father and the circumstances of his death. A stoic Carl replied that he had "no interest in inquiring any further." He cashed the check, and that was that. He could not muster any feelings toward the man. Carl had considered himself an orphan for more than twenty years, and the fact that he was now one in every sense of the word made no difference.

Carl had apparently been aware of the whereabouts of his adopted father for at least five years. When he applied to Gonzaga University School of Law, he had mysteriously listed his father as "Leonard Carl Maxey," a fifty-five-year-old Catholic railway mail inspector who had graduated from both high school and college. What's more, he indicated that this "father" was living at 122 NE Schuyler in Portland, Oregon. Yet the young man who had spent the better part of the previous fifteen years seeking out father figures had apparently never tried to find the man who legally was his father. And now, here in this envelope was evidence that Carl's adopted father had given some thought to his child's welfare, at least at some point in his life. The child was unmoved.

7

STIRRINGS FROM THE SOUTH

As America moved through the mid-1950s, the civil rights movement began to stir nationwide. In March of 1956, it touched Spokane in the person of a small but stubborn woman from Montgomery, Alabama. "Woman to Tell of Bus Boycott," trumpeted a headline in the *Spokane Daily Chronicle*. "Mrs. Rosa Parks, the Montgomery, Ala. woman whose refusal to give up her seat on a bus touched off a boycott of the Montgomery Bus Lines, will speak here Friday."

Maxey and the new Spokane NAACP president, James E. Chase, had learned that Parks was speaking to the Seattle NAACP, so they prevailed on her to come across the state to address their much smaller group. Maxey had stepped down from the chapter presidency several years earlier—he had only served one year—but he remained the NAACP's legal counsel. Chase, who ran an auto body business and who would become Spokane's first black mayor, explained why the group was bringing Parks to town: "To give Spokane people of all races an objective report on an incident that has taken on international importance."

Maxey was quoted as explaining that the bus boycott began when Parks refused to slump her way to the back of the bus and stand in the aisle just because a white teenage boy said he wanted her seat. This was a simplification, but was more or less accurate. As the local NAACP group learned when Parks told her story from the pulpit of the Calvary Baptist Church, she had been returning from a shopping trip in Montgomery on December 1 and had boarded a city bus. The bus was crowded. All seats for black riders were occupied, so she sat in one of the seats in the middle, considered no-man's-land, one row behind the white section. Soon all seats in the bus were filled, and the driver noticed a white passenger standing in the aisle. The driver ordered the black passengers in Parks's row to get up and stand in the back so the white passenger wouldn't have to stand. Three of the women dutifully got up. The fourth, Rosa Parks, said she wasn't in the white section and wasn't going to move. The driver threatened her with arrest. She still wouldn't budge. The driver summoned the police, who arrested her. She was convicted of violating Alabama's bus segregation ordinance and sentenced to fourteen days in jail. As she stood in that Spokane church, she was free on bail pending appeal.

As the audience learned, her tiny act of civil disobedience had mushroomed into a movement that was changing the balance of power between whites and blacks in the South. In the four months since Parks had been arrested, virtually every black citizen of Montgomery had refused to ride the city buses, nearly bankrupting the bus line. The white community's refusal to accept the simplest compromise—they had rejected a modest proposal to allow black riders to sit in the middle of the bus if the back section was full—had caused the controversy to escalate far beyond Parks. It was turning into an international cause célèbre. A twenty-seven-year-old Montgomery minister named Martin Luther King Jr. had emerged as the boycott's leader and had become a national figure. King had already been tossed in jail briefly—for "speeding" while driving blacks to work in a car pool—and had just been arrested and convicted on another charge: inciting an "illegal" boycott. In January, his home had been bombed while he was speaking at a boycott rally, although no one was injured. The most momentous development however, came when King and the other NAACP leaders in Montgomery finally decided to challenge Montgomery's segregationist bus ordinances—and by extension, segregation itself—in a federal court of appeals.

So when Parks gave her talk to the small Spokane NAACP group, she represented not only personal bravery and determination, but also a movement that would have repercussions everywhere in the United States, even in this northwest corner of the country. Within three months of Parks's appearance in Spokane, federal judges struck down the bus segregation ordinances and seven months later the U.S. Supreme Court affirmed the decision. The South's Jim Crow laws had been breached for the first time and civil rights was suddenly front-page news all over America.

For Maxey and the other Spokane NAACP members, Parks's speech must have been exhilarating. Maxey was beginning to admire King and his tactics of forcing change through nonviolent protest. Maxey was a born fighter, no doubt about that. Yet he was convinced that equality would be better achieved through the law and social change. King would soon lay out the tenets of his principles in words that surely resonated in Maxey's soul. "This is not a method for cowards; it does resist," wrote King in a February 1957 article in *Christian Century*. "The nonviolent resister is just as strongly opposed to evil . . . as is the person who uses violence . . . It is nonaggressive physically but dynamically aggressive spiritually."

At the same time, the Spokane audience must have found Parks's message a bit sobering. The NAACP was finally beginning to effect some serious legal change both nationally and locally, but where would it all lead? Even King confessed in 1956 that he had "no idea where the movement is going." Spokane's civil rights leaders did not have Alabama's reactionary bus laws to worry about—Spokane's black bus riders had always been allowed to sit where they pleased—but there were plenty of local segregationist problems to worry about in 1956. It wasn't long before Maxey confronted one of these problems personally, while standing at the door of a nightclub with the most powerful man in the state.

It all began earlier that summer with a political campaign. Maxey had been working on the campaign of Albert D. Rosellini, the Democratic gubernatorial candidate. Maxey and his other law school pals, especially Bill Williams and Jack Dean, had long been fans of Rosellini. He represented the liberal wing of a Democratic Party, which was sharply divided between old-line conservatives who had no interest in pushing for civil rights reform and the younger, more progressive Democrats who were fighting for social change. This split would grow much wider in the 1960s—with Maxey neck-deep in the middle of it. But in 1956, Rosellini had united the party behind his campaign, and Maxey became an important part of the local Democratic machinery as it tried to get the vote out among its core constituency. "We needed someone like him [Maxey] to represent the minorities of the district," said Robert Dellwo, a Democratic activist and attorney who later became a Spokane City Council member. Maxey became one of Rosellini's most visible spokesmen.

After Rosellini won his hard-fought election in November, he came to Spokane to celebrate with the workers who had contributed so much to the cause. A small group, including Maxey, headed out to see a sensational young entertainer who was making a name for himself as a singer, dancer, and Broadway star: Sammy Davis Jr. By this time, Davis had left the Will Mastin Trio and his nose was, presumably, all healed up from his visit years before. Now, Davis was headlining his own act at the Greek-American Club, one of many private clubs that dominated the city's social life. The place had a big nightclub upstairs that brought in national acts and attracted audiences far beyond its membership. But, as a private social club, it was free to make its own rules about who was permitted on the premises. No black citizens were allowed, except, of course, the ones who could sing and dance and draw big white crowds.

When the proprietors of the club saw Maxey at the door, they informed him that he was not allowed in. Governor Rosellini told them that Maxey was with his group, but it made no difference. They still wouldn't let Maxey in. So the whole group, including the governor, walked out. "They threw him out, too!" Maxey recounted with some glee in later years. "They threw out the governor!" At the time, Maxey was angry at being denied access to an event because of his race. He was also heartened that the most powerful man in the state stood by him. Overall, the incident pointed up how powerless even the governor could be in the face of long-entrenched rules and customs. Nobody in 1956 could force a private club to accept a black patron. "If they wouldn't serve you, they wouldn't serve you," said Maxey.

Opening up the city's social clubs became one of Maxey's crusades over the next ten years. This was a matter of no small importance because, as one Asian American woman was quoted in the newspaper as saying, "This is a club town. And most all bar members of minority groups." This incident at the Greek-American Club didn't even make the news. It was just business as usual in a city that was busy watching the news from Montgomery, Alabama, and probably feeling morally superior. No Jim Crow bus laws *here*.

Governor Rosellini couldn't get Maxey in to see Davis perform, but he did come through with some statewide appointments for his young Spokane supporter. In 1957, Maxey was named to the Spokane advisory council of the Washington State Board Against Discrimination, a new board organized in response to the growing prominence of civil rights in the nation's political discourse. This would be the first of several civil rights boards Maxey would sit on throughout his life. Two years later, Rosellini appointed Maxey to another advisory council, this one dealing with Maxey's second-favorite passion: sports. The Washington State Sports Advisory Council was founded to promote "major league sports in Washington." Another ten years would elapse before Seattle would land its first major league franchise, the hapless Seattle Pilots.

Meanwhile, Maxey was attending to other social concerns as he made speeches throughout the region, apparently in his capacity as an increasingly prominent attorney. At a speech before the rural Lincoln County unit of the Washington Education Association, he addressed an issue that had suddenly become a kind of national hysteria: juvenile delinquency. This was the year of the movie *Rebel Without a Cause*, and parents all over the country were scaring themselves with the thought that their cute little Bobbies and Billies would turn into cigarette-smoking, motorcycle-riding James Deans. Maxey told the teachers that too many parents were abdicating their parental responsibilities and shoving the problem off on educators, law enforcement agencies, the Boy Scouts, and other groups. Maxey, a man who had grown up without benefit of parents, said that no agency or school can ever substitute for parental responsibility. And then he went on to give a lecture about responsible parenting and responsible citizenship.

"Some of the problems are traceable to the tendency of parents to set a double standard, one for themselves and one for the children," the *Chronicle* quoted Maxey as saying. "They delegate the responsibility of raising children to a 'do as I say, not as I do' attitude. Respect for the rights of others, which is the basis of true democracy, should begin with the family at home. Love of country is simply an extension of the love of home and community. Patriotism is more than the waving of the flag and the marching of feet. It is an awareness of individual responsibility and it should begin at home." These words resonated with the passion of a man who was still grappling with a childhood scarred by the complete absence of parents, much less parental authority. He was in no mood to let parents off easily.

At home, he was doing his best to live up to those sentiments. His second son, Bevan Maxey, was born in June of 1957. Carl tried to be an involved and loving father to his two boys and, according to Ninon, succeeded. Bill remembers that he and his father both shared a love of football and they would often "play hooky" from church to catch the only games that they could pick up in Spokane, the San Francisco 49ers or the Los Angeles Rams. Y. A. Tittle, quarterback for the 49ers, was their particular favorite. They would also indulge their love of Western movies together, and Bill vividly remembered the time when some loudmouth in the back of a Spokane movie theater looked at Bill and guffawed, "Hey, there's a nigger with red hair! I never seen a nigger with red hair." Maxey stormed up the aisle, grabbed the man by the shoulders and told him to shut his trap. The man, cowed, didn't say another word.

When Bevan was born, Ninon was able to achieve that '50s ideal of quitting her job and staying home with her children. Carl had slowly built up a practice that was approaching the level of lucrative. The civil rights cases certainly weren't the ones paying the bills. He took most of those on a pro bono basis, at no charge. His divorce cases were far more profitable, and he had even developed a canny strategy for landing more of them. "He once told me, 'As long as we're in the divorce-domestic law business, you get a bartender or hairdresser as a client, we do not charge them what we charge other people,'" said Pat Stiley. "He said, 'We charge them at cost. Those are the best source of referrals we could ever have.'"

His business clients, however, were the best paying of all. Maxey had become the counsel for Majer Ford, one of Spokane's big car dealerships. Not only did this provide a steady source of income, but it also enabled Maxey to get discounts on cars. He had a special weakness for big cars. Bill remembered that his father would get a new car almost every year, and he was particularly partial to Lincoln Continentals and Thunderbirds. That relationship with Majer Ford had another aspect too, almost a symbolic aspect. "Here you have the first black lawyer ever to represent a business in this area," said Bill. "That was significant to him."

It signified acceptance. With money in the bank account and a new baby at home, the family began looking around for another house in 1957. A nearly new one, in a recently developed subdivision on Spokane's west side, practically landed in their laps. One of Carl's friends told him about a man who was desperate to sell his big sprawling house on F Street because of financial troubles. "Also, his neighbors were mad at him for parking too many cars in the drive," said Ninon. "He wanted to get even with them, so he sold the house to us."

Ninon laughed about this years later, but it was not entirely funny at the time. Once again, the mixed Maxey family was not met by a welcome wagon. "Clarence Freeman lived at one end of the street, and a couple of Japanese families lived in the neighborhood too," said Ninon. "So it wasn't as if they [the neighbors] hadn't acclimatized. But they made things a little tough. The neighbors were very cold and unfriendly for quite a while, but eventually they began to get used to the idea."

"I don't know if this was a matter of race or not, but I do know that within days of moving in there, I had to fight the neighborhood tough guy," said Bill. "I think we were kind of baited into it by others. He turned out to be great—we became classmates and friends."

8

THE HAIRCUT UPROAR AND A PERFUNCTORY
EXECUTION

In 1960, Maxey joined up with Spokane lawyers Leo Fredrickson and Robert Bell to form the law firm of Fredrickson, Maxey, Bell and Allison Inc. This partnership stayed strong for more than two decades. "That was a match made in heaven," said Lou Maxey. "They all got along forever." Pat Stiley, who joined the firm in the 1970s, actually said that "Bob Bell and Carl were a strange marriage. Bob Bell was just as conservative as could be. As straight a straight arrow as you would see. Bell wore polyester blue suits and shaved around the ears. What the hell they were doing together, made no sense at all. But they loved each other—*loved* each other."

The firm had one distinctive trait from the beginning: it was committed to devoting 20 percent of its time to pro bono work or, as Maxey later phrased it, "free law to people who cannot afford, but need, legal services." Maxey always felt this policy set his firm apart. "I wish more lawyers would fight for rights and liberties with the same enthusiasm they do for money," he said. "He was never interested in just making money off of people," said his longtime legal assistant, Marsha Dornquast. "He gave away 20 percent of his practice and he'd represent people for free to the point where I'd think, 'Carl! Knock it off.'" Lou agreed: "He used to say, 'There will always be more money.' He made money and gave it away like it was lunch."

One of his most prominent pro bono cases came in 1963, with an event that the Spokane newspapers labeled "The Haircut Uproar." This incident seems mild compared to the news coming out of Alabama that spring and summer—massive civil rights demonstrations in Birmingham, hundreds of arrests, attack dogs tearing into lines of marchers, and fire hoses trained on children. Yet it sprang from the same impulse that was sweeping through much of America—an increasing conviction that it was time for segregation's barriers to be toppled wherever they were found—even in a Spokane barber's chair.

One October day, a Gonzaga University exchange student named Jangaba A. Johnson, a Fulbright scholar from Liberia, walked into John M. Wheeler's downtown Spokane barbershop. There Johnson sat, waiting patiently for over an hour, until Wheeler finally came out of the back room and told Johnson to get out of the chair. Wheeler informed Johnson that he did not cut "colored hair." Johnson walked out, embarrassed and hurt, and went to a black barbershop that the shoeshine man in the shop recommended. Johnson, the son of Liberia's minister of culture, later said that in his country he had been "barbered by both colored and white shop owners and I assumed the same situation existed here." Johnson went back to his Gonzaga dorm and told his fellow students what had happened. Dan O. Dugan, the prefect of Robinson Hall, said he could tell right away that Johnson was stung by the incident. Dugan and some other Gonzaga students, mostly white ones, decided that they had to do something about it. "We felt the best way to prevent recurrence of such a situation was to bring the matter to the attention of the residents of Spokane in an orderly fashion," Dugan told reporters.

First, they wrote a letter of protest to the barber, signed by student body president John Villaume, asking for assurance that such an incident would not occur again. The barber gave them no such assurance. In fact, Wheeler was quoted in the paper later that week as saying, "I believe I have the right to accept or reject any person." The seventy-six-year-old barber told a reporter that it had always been his policy "not to serve colored people, because you cannot mix trade in a barbershop and keep your customers." He added that Johnson had been "very understanding and simply walked out."

So the students organized a protest the next Saturday, October 19,

1963, outside of the barbershop. A total of thirty-five students, twenty-nine of them white, showed up with signs, one of which read, "Prejudice Prevents Progress: Help Spokane Grow." Dugan and the students took great pains to avoid the appearance of provocation. Dugan said, "The whole thing was organized as a closely controlled demonstration with one purpose. We want to make our point and then we are finished. And we do not want to do anything that would reflect badly on the university." Yet this small protest made big news, showing up on the national broadcast of the CBS News the next day. The *Chicago Tribune* ran the wire service story on its front page.

The students also contacted Maxey, who immediately went to work for Johnson. Maxey filed an official complaint with the Washington State Board Against Discrimination, which had been set up several years before. His argument was simple, the same one that was being used to open up lunch counters in Mississippi and Alabama: The law provides that places of "public resort and accommodation" may not refuse service because of race. A barbershop, he said, "clearly comes under that classification."

Wheeler, however, proved unrepentant. "I have operated shops in Spokane for 45 years and it is my policy not to serve colored persons," he told reporters. "This personal service is somewhat different than selling merchandise. I have refused to serve many people, including both white and Negro, but there has never been any trouble because of that policy." Now he had all the trouble he could handle. The incident soon mushroomed into a rancorous political debate. A Spokane Republican state senator, A. O. Adams, defended Wheeler, announcing that he was certain that the citizens of Washington would never condone a situation that "takes away from majority groups their civil rights under the guise of protecting the civil rights of minority groups." He also suggested that the barber might have somehow been the victim of "planned entrapment." In other words, he suggested that Johnson was a plant, sent there strictly to cause trouble.

Maxey issued an outraged rebuttal. He said that Johnson was a "shy, sensitive student from Africa," not a civil rights militant, and that "there is not the shadow of suggestion of entrapment in this case."

He accused the senator of disrupting the "very sanctity" of the upcoming hearing by issuing prejudicial public statements. Following Maxey's complaint, the chief investigator of the State Board Against Discrimination arrived and tried one more time to get Wheeler to relent and sign a conciliatory letter saying that he would not discriminate in the future. Wheeler again refused. So, in November 1963, Wheeler was hauled before a meeting of the board's tribunal. A crowd of three hundred people jammed the Spokane County Public Health Department auditorium. By this time the case was making not just national headlines, but, as Maxey commented in his remarks to the board, international headlines.

Maxey represented Johnson. Each side stipulated to the facts of the matter, which were that Johnson had walked in seeking a haircut and had sat in the chair for over an hour, until Wheeler finally came out and told him to leave. Nobody was going to argue that. The tribunal's chairman tried to thin out the crowd by saying that the hearing would not include witness testimony and would consist strictly of dry legal arguments. "If you are expecting some kind of show," said the chairman, "you might as well leave." No one left, noted the *Spokane Daily Chronicle*.

The legal arguments weren't so dry after all. Michael J. Hemovich, representing Wheeler, managed to come up with a novel argument: He maintained that forcing Wheeler to perform a personal service constituted "involuntary servitude." Therefore, it violated the Thirteenth Amendment of the U.S. Constitution—the same amendment that abolished slavery in America. Maxey probably didn't know whether to laugh or just shake his head. When his turn came, he scoffed at the very notion that Wheeler chose to "crown himself" with the protection of *that* particular amendment. Then, perhaps spurred to extra eloquence, he launched into his case.

"The eyes of the world are on Spokane and on a small barber shop," he began. "But the issue is not small. We face the decision of whether a man with a public license can say on his own, 'I cannot or I will not serve you.'" With a tone of controlled outrage, Maxey pointed out that this sort of behavior had been banned decades ago. In 1909, the state criminal code made it a misdemeanor to discriminate in public places. The position of the federal government was made clear in the Fourteenth Amendment, enacted after the Civil War and that proclaimed all citizens entitled to equal protection of the law. "Yet 100 years later," he said, "we are arguing whether or not a Negro has the right to public accommodation." Finally, Maxey noted that a barber's license is a privilege, not a right. A barber cannot, under the law, arbitrarily refuse service to a customer because of his race.

The tribunal deliberated less than three minutes before ruling against Wheeler. Wheeler was ordered to cease refusing service because of race. He was ordered to write a letter to Johnson saying he would henceforth be served in his shop. And he was ordered to put up a poster for a year stating that all persons would be served "regardless of race, creed, color or national origin." Wheeler refused once again to comply. He immediately appealed the ruling, saying he would seek to overturn the state's public accommodations law. Two years later, a superior court judge upheld the board's ruling, writing that a barber who opens a shop "thereby invites every orderly and well-behaved person" into his place of business for service. "The statute will not permit him to say, 'You are a slave or the son of a slave; therefore I will not shave you,'" said the judge. The judge who issued this ruling was William H. "Bill" Williams, Maxey's closest friend from law school.

Wheeler still wasn't finished. He eventually took his appeal all the way to the Washington State Supreme Court. In May of 1967, the justices ruled 9–0 against him and termed his arguments "without merit." Wheeler, stubborn to the end, never did comply with the ruling. He chose to retire instead.

Meanwhile, Maxey found himself in the middle of another headline-making civil rights case, this one reflecting even more directly the tensions boiling over in the South during the summer of 1963. In August of that year, the FBI arrested a twenty-six-year-old black man, Charles Will Cauthen, on a farm in Warden, Washington, one hundred miles southwest of Spokane. Cauthen had been found guilty of murdering a white service-station operator in Pike County, Georgia, four years earlier. Yet, a few days before his scheduled execution, Cauthen had escaped from jail and hopped a freight to Washington State, where he had been laying low ever since. When the FBI found him, they took him to the Spokane County Jail to await extradition back to Georgia— and the electric chair.

As he sat in jail, details of his former imprisonment and life on the lam began to come out. Cauthen had been convicted on February 23, 1959, and had been jailed in Spalding County, Georgia, awaiting execution. He later said his white jailers routinely stopped at his cell to taunt him by explaining gleefully what a man looks like when he dies in an electric chair, how "he wiggles and strains and screams for mercy." Those jailers must not have been paying enough attention to their jobs, because on March 26, 1959—three days before his execution date— Cauthen managed to break a lock and escape. He headed for the railroad, where he jumped on of the first freight train he saw. He had no idea where it was going. He didn't get off for more than twenty-five hundred miles, until he was in Quincy, Washington, not far from Warden. He then hitched a ride with a truckload of farmworkers and wound up at John Zirker's farm, where he was hired as a laborer under the name of Bob Williams. He never left. He was still on the farm when a phalanx of FBI agents closed in on him and arrested him on August 15, 1963. The people of Warden were shocked. Williams, a.k.a. Cauthen, was, in Zirker's words, "the best man I ever had on my farm."

Georgia authorities wanted Cauthen back so that his sentence could be carried out. For this to happen, Washington governor Albert Rosellini would have to agree to extradition, a routine step in fugitive cases. Yet the Cauthen case was turning out to be anything but routine. Cauthen had an alarming tale to tell about his Georgia capital murder trial. He said that his trial had lasted less than a day; the jury was all white; relatives of the murder victim were on the jury; Cauthen's court-appointed attorney was trying his very first case; that attorney had repeatedly told Cauthen he preferred music to the practice of law; and that attorney had not called a single witness for the defense. Cauthen's explanations might not have found such a willing audience in Washington State a decade or two previously. But in 1963, with images on TV every week of baton-wielding policemen beating protesters in Selma and Birmingham, Alabama, Cauthen's story confirmed a growing northern suspicion that a lynch mob mentality ruled the South.

It was also becoming evident that Cauthen, who was being held on a hundred-thousand-dollar bond, was a respected and even beloved member of his dusty little Columbia Plateau farm town. More than four hundred residents of Warden, nearly half the population, immediately signed a petition asking Rosellini to deny extradition. "We've trusted Bob with everything from our property to our children," neighbor Charles Clyde De Graff told reporters.

When Cauthen appeared before Spokane justice of the peace Ellsworth C. Gump, Gump told him he needed a lawyer. Gump immediately arranged for Maxey to see Cauthen in jail. After interviewing Cauthen, Maxey smelled something rotten in the Georgia conviction. In a September 10 newspaper interview, Maxey said that Cauthen's "trial was held in an atmosphere free from the restraint of judicial process." He said that in Spokane County a murder trial would take at least several days and that "we spend more time on a petty larceny charge than was spent in this murder trial." In one memorable phrase, Maxey termed the entire affair "a perfunctory execution."

Cauthen himself denied that he had ever confessed—as Georgia authorities contended—to robbing, beating, and strangling Melvin Perkins, the white service-station attendant. In fact, Cauthen said he had been riding in a car with Perkins when people in another car pulled up and attacked them both. Cauthen also raised the specter that the arrest and trial had been conducted in a lynch mob atmosphere. He said that when he was arrested four days after the murder, officers told him that a mob was forming and that he would be lynched if he didn't confess. He said that he had been moved four times from jail to jail because of lynching threats. Maxey believed that these threats of coercion were enough to taint the case. "I don't know whether Cauthen is guilty or not," Maxey told the *Chronicle*. "I do know that a fair and impartial atmosphere is needed when a man is on trial for his life."

During a September 12 hearing on a motion to reduce bond, Cauthen was cheered by the sight of thirty Warden residents crowded into the courtroom. Zirker, Cauthen's elderly employer, told onlookers that he had "never had a man who would take ahold as [Cauthen] did." A neighbor told Cauthen, "You know, you've helped us when we were down. It'd be pretty bad if we did any different for you." The *Chronicle* noted that "only two of the crowd were Negroes; one was Japanese, the rest Caucasian." Warden residents also obtained the services of Warden attorney C. E. Hormel. Cauthen took the stand briefly to say that he was not a flight risk. In fact, staying in Washington was his "last hope." In Georgia, on the other hand, he had been given no other choice but to run. "I don't think there's no man who wouldn't run from death if he had a chance," reporters quoted Cauthen as telling the judge. "Up here, I have another chance besides running. I spent four years of nervous tension. I just got all the running out of me."

Georgia authorities vigorously disputed many of Cauthen's contentions. The solicitor general for the Griffin, Georgia, judicial district, who prosecuted Cauthen, arrived in the state capital of Olympia to make the case that Cauthen's trial had been fair and impartial. For one thing, he denied that the victim's relatives were on the jury. That, he said, would have been illegal. But Maxey painted a different picture. At a September 17 extradition hearing in Olympia, Maxey called Cauthen's murder trial the most "pitiful" he had ever heard of. He said it was definitely established that Cauthen's trial lasted less than a day and that the jury deliberated for less than fifty minutes—less time, he said, than for a typical drunk-driving case in Washington State. He said that the Georgia trial transcript—which Maxey complained was only a partial transcript—showed that fifteen witnesses testified for the prosecution and that the entire defense case consisted of only one unsworn statement from Cauthen. Maxey accused Cauthen's original defense attorney of "inaction"—an understatement.

Maxey's arguments were convincing enough for Governor Rosellini to announce on September 25 that he was at least going to delay a decision on extradition. Rosellini said he wanted the federal courts to rule, first of all, on the constitutionality of Cauthen's conviction. If the conviction were overturned, extradition would be moot. If not, Rosellini would at least buy some time to acquire more information on what was becoming an increasingly high-voltage case. By September 24, twenty-six hundred people had signed petitions asking Rosellini to deny extradition, and these signatures weren't just coming from Warden. A Seattle couple sponsored these new petitions. Also, the case had become a "possible issue in the 1964 gubernatorial race in Washington . . . A ruling either way by the governor could sway the heavy black vote in King County and it could influence the votes of the liberal wing which has espoused Cauthen's cause," said the *Spokesman-Review*.

Maxey and several other local attorneys embarked on a fact-finding campaign. Samuel W. Fancher, a friend of Maxey's and another Spokane attorney working pro bono for Cauthen, went to Zebulon, Georgia, and dug up some information that made the case even more sensational. For one thing, Cauthen's court-appointed attorney hadn't just been trying his first case. He had also been trying his last case. Fancher discovered the man had clearly meant what he said when he had told Cauthen he preferred music to law. Almost immediately after the trial, the attorney had retired from the practice of law and was now happily practicing his new profession: electric organist in Miami Beach.

Fancher also confirmed a fact that was considerably less surprising: the Cauthen trial indeed had included no black jurors. The superior court clerk in Pike County told Fancher no black person had ever served on a jury in at least the forty-five years he had been clerk. In fact, the county hadn't had a black juror since Reconstruction—and this was a county with a substantial black population. Fancher interviewed a Pike County Superior Court judge, who said that blacks were not "culturally ready" for jury service. Fancher did dispel one of Cauthen's charges: Fancher found no evidence that the jury had included any of the victim's relatives—although the original jury panel may have included a few.

These revelations prompted a new outpouring of sympathy for Cauthen. The Reverend Francis Conklin, a Jesuit priest and Gonzaga University School of Law professor, filed a writ on behalf of the American Civil Liberties Union, an organization that Maxey was now connected

JUST KIDS...*But*

Your Gift to Your Community Chest

Helped 3462 of Them Last Year!

•

Some of them were babies...orphans ...kids from broken homes...some were sick...but all of them say... THANK YOU for your help.

Life could be cruel for the orphans at the Spokane Children's Home, but the public wouldn't know it from this undated fund-raising brochure, used to drum up money. The children are not named, but decades later Milton Burns identified the child fifth from left as Carl Maxey. If so, this is the first existing photo of Maxey. Northwest Museum of Arts and Culture/Eastern Washington State Historical Society, Spokane, Washington.

Orphans and "charges of the county" play on the grounds outside of the Spokane Children's Home in this photo taken just a few months before Maxey arrived at the home in 1930, at age five. Northwest Museum of Arts and Culture/Eastern Washington State Historical Society, Spokane, Washington.

Milton Burns relied on his best friend, Carl Maxey, throughout their years at the Sacred Heart Mission school at DeSmet, Idaho. The smaller and more timid Burns stands behind the big, outgoing Maxey, whom Burns considered his protector. Northwest Museum of Arts and Culture/Eastern Washington State Historical Society, Spokane, Washington.

Father Cornelius E. Byrne, the lanky Jesuit priest who ran the Sacred Heart Mission school, was the most important figure in Maxey's life. Byrne rescued Maxey from the juvenile detention center and gave him the confidence and the rigorous academic grounding he needed. Byrne was far ahead of his time when it came to his belief in racial justice and equality. Northwest Museum of Arts and Culture/Eastern Washington State Historical Society, Spokane, Washington.

The Gonzaga University boxing team licks its chops for a meal of cougar, evidently in preparation for a match with the Washington State Cougars. Joey August is depicted as the chef. Maxey wears no. 7 in this circa-1942 photo, taken before Maxey went off to war. No. 3 is Vic Felice, who later shared Maxey's first law office. Gonzaga University Archives, GUA43:3.

The young Maxey shows off his form in this early 1943 photo from his first stint with the Gonzaga University boxing team. He joined the army and returned later to make his mark, once and for all, on the collegiate boxing world. *Spokesman-Review* Photo Archive.

Boxing coach Joey August was another influential father figure for Maxey, guiding him all the way to an undefeated collegiate record and a national collegiate championship. *Spokesman-Review* Photo Archive.

Maxey tries out the sophisticated, pipe-smoking look in this formal studio portrait, probably from his days at the University of Oregon in the late 1940s. Lou Maxey collection.

The star of the 1950 tournament graced the cover of the 1951 NCAA boxing tournament guide, even though Maxey was not there in the flesh. After his 1950 championship, he retired from boxing to devote himself to his law studies. Northwest Museum of Arts and Culture/Eastern Washington State Historical Society, Spokane, Washington.

Delirious fans carry the victorious Gonzaga University boxing team off the tarmac when the team arrives home at Geiger Field in Spokane in 1950. From left, Eli Thomas, Jim Reilly, Joey August, and Maxey are hoisted above the throng. It was the first NCAA championship of any kind for Gonzaga. Gonzaga University Archives, GUA43:5.

(Facing page, top) Father Francis P. Harrington, Gonzaga University's dean of men and "athletic moderator," cradles one of the NCAA trophies as Maxey looks on in this 1950 photo. *Spokesman-Review* Photo Archive.

(Facing page, bottom) Maxey studies in Gonzaga's law library in this 1950 photo taken for a newspaper profile. He quit the boxing team after his national championship to devote full attention to improving his grades. *Spokesman-Review* Photo Archive.

Eugene Breckenridge broke the color barrier for teachers in the Spokane School District, largely through the efforts of young lawyer Carl Maxey. Breckenridge went on to a distinguished career as a teacher and administrator. *Spokesman-Review* Photo Archive.

Ninon Maxey sings Christmas carols in this undated photo. She was married to Carl from 1948 to 1972 and is the mother of both of his sons. *Spokesman-Review* Photo Archive.

★ ★ ★ ★

A REFERENDUM ᶠᵒᴿ PEACE

The ballot for the 1970 Washington State Primary Election includes the opportunity to cast your vote for peace and equality NOW.

Although there is no resolution that offers the chance there is a man who does.

Carl Maxey, a black man who has spent his life fighting war, racism and poverty, is a candidate for the U.S. Senate. He is running on the Democratic Party Platform—the platform that has been rejected en toto by every party chief.

Incumbent Henry Jackson is worried about the Maxey challenge. His office has been all but uncontested for years and a strong anti-war opposition is not all he could hope for. Indicative of the dilemma, Jackson was nowhere to be seen at the recent party convention— the same convention dominated by Maxey and his supporters.

Maxey's Campaign is attracting nation-wide attention. Eugene McCarthy will be heading a pro-Maxey rally in Seattle on September 10th.

But Maxey needs more than McCarthy and friends. Maxey needs you. He needs your support as well as your vote. With your help the Primary Elections will say Washington State wants NO MORE WAR.

VOTE & WORK
FOR
CARL
MAXEY

To volunteer to help end war and racism, contact your local Maxey office.

SPOKANE
S. 105 Stevens
(509) TE 8-5121

SEATTLE
4406 N.E. 50th
(206) LA 2-1800

ᶠᵒᴿ PEACE... ᶠᵒᴿ U.S. SENATE

PAID POLITICAL ADVERTISEMENT

This 1970 campaign flyer presents the case for Maxey in his race against Senator Jackson, ending with the words, "NO MORE WAR." Northwest Museum of Arts and Culture/Eastern Washington State Historical Society, Spokane, Washington.

This 1970 newspaper ad—a parody of Scoop Jackson's concern for the environment—outraged the Jackson campaign. The ad was designed by Merrie Lou Douglas, soon to become Lou Maxey. Northwest Museum of Arts and Culture/Eastern Washington State Historical Society, Spokane, Washington.

(*Facing page, top*) Maxey, as the antiwar and anti-Scoop Jackson candidate in the 1970 Democratic Senate primary, flashes the peace sign on the floor of the Washington State Democratic Convention. Northwest Museum of Arts and Culture/Eastern Washington State Historical Society, Spokane, Washington.

(*Facing page, bottom*) Former presidential candidate Senator Eugene McCarthy appears at a news conference with Maxey during Maxey's quixotic Senate run in 1970. The signed inscription reads, "Thanks for a good try, Carl Maxey." Maxey would later be listed as McCarthy's vice-presidential running mate on the 1976 Washington State ballot. Northwest Museum of Arts and Culture/Eastern Washington State Historical Society, Spokane, Washington.

no deposit . . . no return

Is Vietnam Henry Jackson's idea of conservation?

vote for Carl Maxey (Demo) U. S. Senate for human conservation

Paid for by Veterans for Maxey, Greg Kreshel, chmn.

Six members of the Seattle Seven strike a defiant and irreverent pose in
1970 in front of the U.S. Courthouse in Seattle. They had just been charged
with damaging that courthouse and with conspiracy to incite a
riot during an antiwar demonstration and melee. Maxey was one of their
lawyers in the subsequent trial, which he later called a "riotous, disgraceful
courtroom event." From left are Joe Kelly, Susan Stern, Michael Lerner,
Michael Abeles, Chip Marshall, and Jeff Dowd. The seventh member,
Roger Lippman, had just been arrested in California. Copyright Alan
Lande, 1970.

The Maxey family in 1975, a year after Carl and Lou were married. Bevan is on the left and Bill is on the right. *Spokesman-Review* Photo Archive.

Lou and Carl Maxey were married from 1974 until Carl's death in 1997. Lou Maxey collection.

The walls of Maxey's law office in 1981 were festooned with an intimidating array of weapons, a puzzling decorating choice for this lifelong advocate of nonviolence. *Spokesman-Review* Photo Archive.

Ruth Coe, on trial in 1982 for ordering a hit on a judge and prosecutor, was one of Maxey's highest-profile clients. She was found guilty, but, due to Maxey's advocacy, was given a remarkably light sentence. *Spokesman-Review* Photo Archive.

Maxey in 1982. As his career progressed, he was increasingly lionized for his unceasing work toward racial and social justice. *Spokesman-Review* Photo Archive.

Every day, Gonzaga University School of Law students walk by this bust at the entrance to the law library. The man who was told he would never pass the bar exam is now one of the school's most-honored graduates. Photo by the author.

with, asking for Cauthen's release. Cauthen's Warden neighbors organized a community fund-raiser: a benefit hootenanny. Hootenannies—essentially folk-music concerts—had become a fad in the early 1960s, a time when Top 40 radio rang with the sound of banjos, dulcimers, and "If I Had a Hammer." The Warden hootenanny featured a lineup of five Spokane-area folk performers; it was later pronounced a foot-stomping success.

The next legal test came at the end of December when federal district court judge Charles L. Powell heard arguments on a petition for a writ of habeas corpus, which was a request that Cauthen be immediately freed because he had been denied due process in his original trial. Maxey advanced the now-familiar arguments about the trial's deficiencies, but also came up with some colorful new images. Returning Cauthen to Georgia, he told the court, would be like "leaving a lion to guard the roast." Washington State's assistant attorney general Steven Way represented the other side in this hearing, since it was essentially a request that Cauthen be released from state custody. Way maintained that the federal courts in Georgia should at least be allowed to review Cauthen's conviction before Washington released him. "Georgia is capable of correcting its own errors," said Way. "I cannot reconcile myself that justice has been abandoned in Georgia."

Yet that was precisely what many northwesterners feared had happened in that opposite quadrant of the country. An argument used by one of Maxey's fellow lawyers in the hearing was that Cauthen's trial had taken place in a "backward county." In fact, the Cauthen case was being played out against an ever-expanding backdrop of unrest in what many northwesterners considered the "backward" South. Two days before Cauthen's extradition hearing, a Birmingham church was bombed, killing four small black girls who were preparing for Sunday school. Riots flared throughout the city; young white men raced through the Birmingham streets, flying Confederate flags; two young black boys were shot to death; and five hundred National Guard troops were on alert. In the rest of the country—certainly in the Northwest—the South was increasingly seen as barbaric and indifferent to justice.

Ten days after the hearing, Judge Powell issued a ruling against

Cauthen—he refused to order him freed. Maxey seemed unperturbed—this was hardly a fatal blow. "I'm not complaining," said Maxey. He said he was just grateful that Powell had "graciously granted us an afternoon for arguments." The ruling said only that a federal court in the "asylum state"—Washington—should not pass judgment on the constitutionality of the prisoner's incarceration. Powell said Cauthen could raise all of the same questions before the federal court in Georgia—if he was extradited. Powell did not take a position one way or the other on extradition. The ruling essentially cleared the field for a yes-or-no decision by Governor Rosellini. "I have not lost hope," Cauthen told reporters. "But I'll admit, I'm scared."

The wait was excruciating. January and February of 1964 came and went. The petition drive on Cauthen's behalf ballooned to five thousand names. Rosellini allowed that it "was a most difficult decision to make." He came to Spokane and conferred with Maxey and Cauthen's other lawyers. Then, on March 16, the governor made his announcement. He set Cauthen free. When Maxey walked into the Spokane County Jail to give Cauthen the news, Cauthen replied with words from an old Negro spiritual, "Thank God almighty, now I'm free." Rosellini said that he denied extradition "because there is serious doubt as to [Cauthen's] guilt . . . I feel that the best ends of justice are met by denying the application for his extradition . . . If there is reasonable doubt as to his guilt, I am bound by the law and constitution of this state to find in favor of the accused." Rosellini's only condition: that Cauthen remain under the jurisdiction of the state parole board and make periodic reports to a parole officer.

Maxey was deeply gratified by the ruling. "To me, this is one of the finest days for justice in the Northwest," he told reporters. "I wish to thank the governor for his humanitarian disposition of this case . . . This case shows that at least Washington State will not turn its back on the accepted standards of judicial procedure. This will serve to let the rest of the states know that due process must be followed if our legal system is to be preserved." It was a personal triumph for Maxey as well. This thirty-nine-year-old Spokane lawyer had performed on a statewide stage and won. And he was particularly proud that he had taken the case "without fee and worked nearly a year."

Georgia authorities were outraged. "I know of no reason why Cauthen should not be returned, since he was tried in a Georgia court of respect and esteem, " said Georgia governor Carl E. Sanders. "The burden of Cauthen's guilt rests now upon the state of Washington. It is they who must assume responsibility of the actions of a man who in court admitted murder and then escaped to flee the imposition of justice as decreed by the court." The Associated Press pointed out that Sanders was stretching the facts: Cauthen had never admitted to the murder in court. The Georgia court transcript quoted Cauthen as saying, "All I can say is, I did not kill Mr. Perkins. But I don't have any proof of it. I don't have anything to back up my story. All I know is I am not guilty."

J. A. Riggins, the Pike County sheriff who arrested Cauthen, was nearly red-faced in his rage. He called Rosellini's decision "one of the dirtiest deals that has ever been handled in the United States." He said that he himself had recovered Cauthen's pistol at the scene. Riggins expressed the fervent wish that "every hoodlum or outlaw and gangster in the country will end up in Washington State."

If Georgia authorities thought that Washingtonians would reap some kind of harvest of evil, they were sadly disappointed. After returning to Warden, Cauthen legally changed his name to Bob Williams, got married, had kids, moved to Spokane, and became, in Maxey's words, "a good citizen of the state of Washington."

9

FREEDOM SUMMER IN THE TAIL END
OF AMERICA

After the Cauthen case, Maxey was one of the best-known black attorneys in the state. With that came some problems. His son Bill, who turned fourteen in 1963, remembered that the family would occasionally get a phone call at home, "someone spewing some profanity and name-calling and some threats." His father was uncowed. "It was kind of like, 'Come on, if you want to,'" said Bill.

One hate letter arrived in 1965, along with a pamphlet titled, *Martin Luther King and his Civil Rights Urinators*, which claimed that blacks forced their way into southern restaurants in the name of desegregation and then urinated in the sugar bowls. "You niggers are all the same," the letter said, in spidery handwriting. "Niggers like you make it bad for the good colored people who are good. You will pay for what you are doing some day. [signed] S.O.N." Bevan Maxey recalled a harrowing phone call when he was young and still naïve: "Somebody called and said, 'Is your dad home?' and I said no. 'Is your mom home?' and I said no. I was probably about ten and too young to know how foolish my answers were. He said, 'Well, I'm going to come over and I'm going to get you.' I hid outside in the bushes until somebody came home." After another such threat, Bill remembered standing in the lower level of their house, watching out the window with "my baseball bat ready." But he never had to use it.

On balance, both Bill and Bevan remember their home life as happy. The family took a vacation to Europe in the early '60s (leaving little

Bevan with a close friend). Bill remembered his father taking him to see Napoleon's tomb and to a French war museum where they both marveled over the miniature recreations of famous battles. Even Ninon's mother went along on this trip. "My mother had never really gotten over this [the marriage]," said Ninon. "She was polite and she certainly accepted the trip to Europe, which she had always wanted to see. But I must say, she was not totally reconstructed. But the trip was great. I was an Anglophile, and so was Carl. We spent most of our time in England. Carl rented a car and driver and we were chauffeured through England, Scotland, and Wales." Most summers, Ninon took the two boys to Ashland to see her mother. "I don't remember my dad going down there with us, though," recalled Bill with a laugh.

By the early '60s, Maxey was in demand as a speaker. In the fall of 1963 he was invited to Washington State University in Pullman to speak to the student YWCA organization, which had a race relations committee. Merrie Lou Douglas, age eighteen, was one of the committee's heads. It was, as she recalled, a surprisingly radical group for Pullman— she jokingly called herself "Little Miss Bolshevik." They grilled Maxey on the state of racial relations in the United States and Douglas even remembered "attacking" Maxey for not being enough of an activist. However, after the speech, a friend of Douglas's introduced her to Maxey, saying she thought "you two will get along." This proved to be prophetic, because Merrie Lou Douglas ended up marrying Maxey eleven years later.

Meanwhile, a momentous bill had passed the U.S. Congress: the 1964 Civil Rights Act. Many of the principles at the core of the civil rights struggle, including those of equal accommodation and the right to vote, were now encoded in federal law. Maxey, as the state chairman of the Washington State Advisory Committee to the U.S. Commission on Civil Rights (to which he had been appointed by President John F. Kennedy in 1963), went to a convention in Washington, DC, in late June of 1964 to learn how the Civil Rights Act would be implemented. Maxey told the *Spokane Daily Chronicle* that Washington State already had a stronger civil rights bill than the new federal one. After his experience in the Cauthen case, Maxey was more concerned with how the new federal law would be enforced—and with what kinds of judges would be enforcing it. "There will be serious discussion at the convention concerning the judges and jurors who belong to organizations that are, at one extreme, hate groups, or at the other, a fraternal or private organization that discriminates in membership," Maxey told the *Chronicle*. "It goes without saying that a person couldn't socially practice discrimination at night and treat all persons equally in the daytime."

Then, just days after returning from the DC convention, Maxey embarked on a trip that would put him at ground zero in the nation's increasingly volatile civil rights movement. He and two white Spokane attorneys, Samuel Fancher and Thomas F. Lynch, volunteered for Freedom Summer, the 1964 Mississippi voter-registration drive sponsored by the Student Nonviolent Coordinating Committee (SNCC) and Martin Luther King Jr.'s Southern Christian Leadership Conference. Many of the more than nine hundred Freedom Summer volunteers were northern white college students. They joined thousands of local black activists to demand voting rights for unregistered black Mississippians. The movement's leaders realized that those thousands of activists and volunteers would need plenty of legal representation, certainly far more than Mississippi lawyers could provide. As Maxey dryly remarked, most Mississippi lawyers were simply "not available" for civil rights cases. He said that out of two thousand lawyers in that state, only three would touch a civil rights case.

The three Spokane lawyers, sponsored by the National Lawyers Guild, raised money for the trip through the Unitarian Church in Spokane. They left on July 11, 1964, in the middle of one of the most highly charged and violent months of the entire civil rights struggle. Just three weeks earlier, a local black civil rights activist, James Chaney, and two white Freedom Summer volunteers from New York, Michael Schwerner and Andrew Goodman, had disappeared in Neshoba County, Mississippi, after being picked up by a local sheriff for speeding. In a by-then familiar ruse, the sheriff had released them from custody—straight into the hands of waiting Ku Klux Klansmen, who had somehow been notified. The three civil rights workers had not been heard from since.

The investigation had been hindered, if not completely blocked, by the mistrust and hatred that many Mississippi whites had for this influx of civil rights volunteers. The newcomers were considered trouble-makers and outside agitators, if not card-carrying Communists (in fact, there were charges that the National Lawyers Guild had Communist sympathies). This almost pathological mistrust was revealed by one particularly defensive speech on the U.S. Senate floor. Senator James Eastland of Mississippi stood up and insinuated that the entire disappearance was a hoax. He said the three civil rights workers were just as likely "voluntarily missing" and that it was all just a publicity stunt pulled off by the agitators themselves to make the state look bad. This speech was delivered nearly a month after the men had disappeared.

Other Freedom Summer workers were harassed, beaten, spit upon, and cursed on a nearly daily basis. This was the atmosphere that awaited the three Spokane lawyers when they landed in Jackson, Mississippi, and it only became worse while they were there. In three weeks, they counted up two hundred incidents of harassment and assault among the workers they were serving. The hostility had become so blatant that many of the college students were ordered home by their parents following the disappearance of the three volunteers; the students who remained were scared to death.

As for Maxey? "Carl said he was petrified," said his old friend and fellow civil rights lawyer, Kenneth A. MacDonald of Seattle. Maxey told him that one day he was riding in a car with some other civil rights workers when a Mississippi State Patrol car pulled up beside them, lights flashing. Nothing came of the incident, but Maxey knew that it could have turned ugly. "He told me he wore a dark suit the entire time he was there, so he would look like a U.S. marshal," said Lou Maxey. "He thought that might give him some protection."

Maxey was never physically harmed, but he ended up in the middle of one of the more harrowing incidents of the summer. On July 16, the Greenwood SNCC and its young, charismatic district director, Stokely Carmichael, organized a Freedom Day at the Leflore County Court-house in Greenwood, Mississippi, a city of twenty-five thousand in the heart of the Mississippi Delta. The city was already known as a center of the civil rights struggle; on several previous Freedom Days, masses of black citizens and volunteer picketers had descended on the county courthouse and demanded to register to vote. The activists knew from experience that the county would refuse to register them. Leflore County was 65 percent black, but only whites could register to vote. The SNCC leaders also knew from experience that the police would arrest them. The original purpose for these Freedom Days was to clog the jails with so many people that the legal system couldn't handle them.

Sometimes, though, the demonstrators got rougher treatment than they bargained for. Following an earlier Greenwood Freedom Day in 1963, Willie Rogers, age seventeen, described his arrest and incarceration to Howard Zinn of *The Nation* magazine: "The [police] chief said, 'I'm asking you all to move on.' We said that we were just there to get our folks registered. So he said, 'I'm asking you all to move on, you're crowding the sidewalk.' The sidewalk was clear—we walked up the courthouse steps so as not to block the sidewalk . . . So he started placing us under arrest, one by one . . . "

"We stayed in jail for about two hours before the trial came off and the judge sentenced us to four months and $200 fine for refusing to move and about an hour later they came and took us to the penal farm . . . Without us knowing, they had sentenced us to the Mississippi State Penitentiary, Parchman, Miss. Two boys and I, he put us in the hot box. We stayed in the hot box two nights. It's about five foot nine inches square, which is why they call it the hot box . . . There's no openings for light or air—there was a little crack under the door but you couldn't see your hand in front of your face less you get down on your knees . . . They hand you the [food] tray through a little door which they close—and then you can't eat unless you get down on your knees by the light comin' in the door." Some boys were left in the hot box for more than a week at a time; when they were finally released, after two months of legal maneuvering, many were physical wrecks.

By the summer of 1964, the atmosphere in Greenwood had worsened. In his autobiography, *Ready for a Revolution*, Carmichael described the hate-filled atmosphere that July, when the passage of the 1964 Civil Rights Act inflamed the rougher elements of the white population. "See, once that bill got close to passing, you began to see even more carloads of white men, guns bristling, cruising the city," wrote Carmichael. "Some were flat-out Klan. Some were supposed to be deputized, armed 'auxiliary' police. You couldn't tell the difference. People said they recognized Byron de la Beckwith [the man later convicted of murdering Medgar Evers, and a notorious Greenwood resident], armed and riding as an 'auxiliary' policeman."

Some people in the movement were now questioning the wisdom of Freedom Days, with their mass arrests and terrifying jail sentences, but the young black citizens of Greenwood were in no mood to back down and the SNCC leadership felt the need to reinvigorate the movement in Greenwood. So on July 16, Carmichael and the other SNCC leaders devised a plan for a few volunteers, but not a mass of people, to be arrested at the courthouse. As Taylor Branch described it in his book *Pillar of Fire: America in the King Years, 1963–65*, it didn't turn out that way. The situation at the courthouse escalated, tensions rose. and finally nearly everyone present, including the movement leaders, joined an improvised call to "fill all the jails." A total of 111 people were arrested at the courthouse, including Carmichael and 13 Freedom Summer volunteers. Maxey was one of the lawyers brought down from Jackson to try to get them out of jail.

Peter Orris, one of the arrested volunteers, described the scene in an interview conducted for the Center for Oral History and Cultural Heritage at the University of Southern Mississippi. "There were about eight of us, I think, white males in our cell," said Orris, a student from New York. "And we were thrown in with a bunch of other guys that were already in there, which proved a bit tense for a while, too. There was a guy—most of the prisoners were very friendly—there was one guy who was very angry, both that he was in there and then at us. And, in fact, [he] took out a handmade knife and on one occasion tried to stab this minister from Michigan who was with us. He was calmed down by everybody concerned, and so other than a small cut, nobody was particularly hurt. But once again that was quite tense.

And then we decided to do something that at the time seemed to be a good idea—but I'd never do it again—and that is that we decided to go on a hunger strike, because we were sure that a hunger strike protesting this injustice would be heard round the world. In fact, nobody had any idea we were hunger striking except us. There was some reporting on it, but that convinced me [to] never choose the tactic that's harder on yourself than the other side."

They were in jail for six days before they were bused back to the courthouse for a trial. Their jailers told them that their attorneys "didn't show up," which didn't any make sense to Orris. In fact, Maxey and the other attorneys were very much in the picture, working hard to get the cases removed to federal court, where the charges would almost certainly be dropped. But meanwhile, the Leflore County authorities were trying to get what Orris described as "one more crack at us" with a series of quick trials. Maxey showed up at the courthouse later that day and described the trials as "conducted in the most hostile environment imaginable." In a later summary of the event, Maxey wrote that "hundreds of angry Ku Klux Klan members, including the man later convicted of killing Medgar Evers, surrounded the courthouse."

Those angry residents weren't just surrounding the courthouse—they were inside it as well. "The room was jammed with people who were all very white and very hard-faced and very angry and some had guns on," said Orris. "I think they were cops maybe, I don't know . . . So it was a little bit of a tense situation. And then they swore in the witnesses and all these folks standing around the room, about twenty of these people standing around the room who were very—they looked very angry, and I felt very unsafe. They all raised their hands as witnesses (laughter) . . . So in rather short order I was convicted and sentenced to 30 days in Parchman penitentiary and then put back on the bus, and they did this with everybody."

Maxey recalled that the bus was just about to roar off to the dreaded Parchman farm when news arrived that the lawyers had succeeded in getting the case removed to federal court. The defendants were immediately released. The charges wound their way through federal court for a while, but were eventually dropped. Orris and his fellow defendants never had to experience the hot box.

Maxey's three harrowing weeks in Mississippi did include one moment of pure inspiration: his first and only meeting with the Reverend Martin Luther King Jr. King flew in to Greenwood on July 21, the day the prisoners were released. According to a story the next day in the *New York Times*, King and his entourage showed up unannounced at a small billiards hall called the Van Pool Room. A group of utterly astonished black youths put down their pool cues and listened. "Gentlemen, I will be brief in what I have to say, but I hope you will take it seriously," said King. "In the state of Mississippi today, officials have consistently, ruthlessly and at points violently denied Negroes the right to register to vote. We must make it clear to everybody in the world that Negroes desire to be free and to be . . . registered voter[s]." King then walked down the street, stood atop a wooden bench at the Savoy Café, and delivered a similar speech to a street-corner crowd. He told them that "every Negro has worth and dignity" and that Mississippi had "treated the Negro as if he is a thing instead of a person."

About a thousand people jammed a Greenwood meeting hall that night for a mass rally in which King attacked Barry Goldwater, the Republican candidate for president, for giving "aid and comfort to the segregationists." The *New York Times* reported that, during the meeting, a small airplane without lights flew over the building and dropped leaflets referring to King as the "Right Rev. Riot Inciter" and vowed that if violence erupted, it was the "moral obligation of the white men in Leflore County to restore law and order." The leaflets were signed "The White Knights of the Ku Klux Klan in Mississippi." When someone brought a leaflet inside and read it to the crowd, the people responded emotionally, chanting, "Freedom! Freedom!" When the rally ended, a defiant crowd formed in the street and began marching downtown, only to be dissuaded by movement leaders after a few blocks.

King went on to Meridian, Philadelphia, and Jackson (where Maxey was based) during his five-day Mississippi visit. It was evidently in Jackson that Maxey had the opportunity to meet King. "I had the privilege of knowing the man and walking the backwoods and city streets in Mississippi with him," said Maxey in a later speech commemorating Martin Luther King Jr. Day. "I saw the blood of Medgar Evers on his steps," meaning apparently the steps of Evers's home in Jackson. Maxey never left a detailed account of meeting King, suggesting that he probably didn't have a one-on-one conversation with the civil rights leader. But Maxey was at least in the man's presence and heard him speak, which meant an enormous amount to Maxey. He had embraced King's philosophy of nonviolence since the Rosa Parks days and had never ceased to admire the man.

"Carl regarded Dr. King as almost a saint," said Lou Maxey. "There was a lot of division in the movement at the time about tactics and personalities, but there was never a time when Carl had any philosophical disagreements, or any other kind of disagreements, with Dr. King. His *Letter from the Birmingham Jail* [King's famous 1963 manifesto and statement of purpose], Carl regarded that as almost a way of living." King's *Letter* contains the following passage: "One day the South will recognize its real heroes . . . One day the South will know that when these disinherited children of God sat down at lunch counters, they were in reality standing up for the best in the American dream and the most sacred values in our Judeo-Christian heritage, and thusly, carrying our whole nation back to those great wells of democracy which were dug deep by the founding fathers."

One thing is certain, King and Maxey wouldn't have been strolling alone. They would have been with a hefty security entourage, including an FBI detail. The Klan had vowed that King would not make it out of Mississippi alive. In one White House conversation tape-recorded just before King's visit, Attorney General Robert F. Kennedy told President Lyndon B. Johnson, "It's a ticklish problem, because if he gets killed, it creates all kinds of problems." Of King's Mississippi visit, Carmichael recalled in his autobiography, "I had heard that his people hadn't wanted him to come. SNCC can't protect you, they argued. SNCC will git you killed. So I took it as my personal responsibility to protect him in the Delta . . . We stayed real close whenever he was out and moving around. They would have had to kill a lot of us to get to him . . . Dr. King was cool. He talked about the need to build the party and left without incident. Not a peep out of the Klan. That's something I take pride in."

When Maxey and the other two lawyers, Samuel Fancher and Thomas Lynch, returned to Spokane, they gave a talk at the Unitarian Church. Maxey told those gathered that his lasting impression of Mississippi was its "complete lack of law and order" as far as the rights of blacks were concerned. Lynch said he was impressed by the young civil rights volunteers who are "in real danger, all the time." But then he told the audience that the state's black people are "locked in by a vicious system . . . that has them permanently cast in the role of something less than human." He said that he "was overwhelmed by the sickness of the white people I saw there. The situation in Mississippi cries out to heaven for justice." Fancher recounted how he heard one judge refer to a group of blacks as "a bunch of niggers." He also pointed out that all three of the Spokane men had stayed in a black hotel, since no white hotel would accept Maxey.

A decade later, when reflecting on the trip, Maxey told the *Spokesman-Review* that all three had been "threatened and abused as interlopers and outside agitators all over that whole damn country"—though no more than any other attorneys down there. "But it was one of the finest summers I've ever had," he added. "And I feel it was a reflection of America. It was the first time both black and white worked hand-in-hand in a humanitarian concern—the right to vote and the right to live."

Even so, right after the trip Maxey seemed more depressed than exhilarated. Freedom Summer, which had begun with such optimism, resulted in 1,000 arrests, 80 beatings, 35 burned churches, and 6 murders. At the Unitarian Church, Maxey summed up his disgust for Mississippi by calling it the "tail end of America." Four days after Maxey uttered those words, Mississippi authorities excavated an earthen dam in Neshoba County. There they found the murdered bodies of Schwerner, Goodman, and Chaney. They had pulled no publicity stunt.

I O

"THE SICKNESS OF OUR NATION"

On the same day in 1964 that the FBI was exhuming the graves of civil rights workers James Chaney, Michael Schwerner, and Andrew Goodman in Neshoba County, Mississippi, President Johnson convened the National Security Council to discuss commando attacks against U.S. ships off the coast of North Vietnam— an event that, indirectly, would have an enormous effect on Maxey's politics and law practice. The attacks came to be called the Gulf of Tonkin incident, which spurred the Tonkin Gulf Resolution, which led to massive U.S. involvement in the Vietnam War. Before the decade was out, Maxey would be handling hundreds of war-protest, draft-evasion, and conscientious-objector cases.

The first of these turned into one of the most shocking. The case began routinely enough when twenty-three-year-old Robert H. Greiff of Deer Park, Washington, a small town just north of Spokane, refused to report for induction after being drafted in September of 1963. Greiff had claimed conscientious-objector status in 1961, but the draft board turned him down and classified him 1–A. When he didn't show up for induction, he was arrested by the FBI and charged with violating the draft laws. Frank R. Freeman, the U.S. attorney, told reporters it was the first draft-evasion case to reach federal court in Spokane that decade (little did he know it was the beginning of an avalanche).

Maxey, who saw Greiff's case as a free speech and civil liberties issue, took on his defense. During the nonjury trial in the spring of

1964, Greiff testified that he had refused on grounds of conscience, not on strictly religious grounds. He said he did not believe in a supreme being, nor did he belong to any religious organization. He told the jury he refused to report "because of personal feelings against military service" and that these feelings would furthermore prevent him from doing battle even if a person attacked his mother, sister, father, or personal property. A draft board official testified that Selective Service requirements generally required a man to believe in a supreme being to be classified a conscientious objector. In any case, Greiff had never bothered to appeal his 1–A classification, which meant he had in essence forfeited his rights. Maxey based his defense on the argument that Greiff did not even know he had the right to an appeal.

Federal judge Charles L. Powell ruled, in essence, that ignorance was no excuse. Greiff was "not entitled to claim ignorance of the appeal process." He found Greiff guilty and in sentencing made it clear that he had no patience with a normal, healthy, high-school graduate who would willfully abandon his duty to serve his country. "I owe an obligation not only to this boy, but to the many other boys who took his place in the military service when he did not go—some of whom might be serving in Vietnam," Powell said. He sentenced Greiff to one year and a day in federal prison,

Maxey and fellow lawyer Riner E. Daglow appealed, but the appeal was turned down in July of 1965, at which time Greiff was hauled off to McNeil Island Federal Penitentiary in Puget Sound. And that's where the story would have ended, except for the package that Freeman, the attorney who put Greiff away, received at home on October 30, 1965. Freeman was alone in his home when the package arrived, and he began to carefully unwrap the large box, which seemed to have some kind of spring pushing up on the lid from inside. "I thought it was some type of jack-in-the-box gag for my birthday and I kept my hand on the box while I was unwrapping it," Freeman told the *Spokesman-Review*. That action saved his life. When he peeked inside, he saw that the box was filled with blasting caps and dynamite, easily enough to kill a man. Because Freeman kept his hand on the top and didn't open the lid all the way, the detonator didn't work. A horrified Freeman called authorities, and demolition experts from Spokane's Fairchild Air Force Base dismantled the bomb.

Then another bombshell arrived: U.S. marshals descended on the Greiff farm in Deer Park and arrested Greiff's fifty-nine-year-old German-born father, William Hugo Greiff, for mailing that potentially lethal package. Federal authorities said that the handwriting on the label matched the elder Greiff's handwriting. "Wearing a faded gray shirt, overalls and a heavy set of work shoes, the wiry brown-haired Greiff was brought to the [Spokane] County Jail to be fingerprinted and photographed," wrote reporter Bob Hill of the *Spokane Daily Chronicle*. "There, he immediately asked for an attorney and within a matter of minutes was in conference with Carl Maxey."

The case against the elder Greiff was strong, yet the trial, when it was finally conducted two years later, showed off Maxey's increasingly savvy legal skills. In 1966, Maxey filed a motion requesting that the federal court split the trial into two separate parts, the first to determine whether Greiff had actually mailed the bomb, the second to determine whether Greiff had been "legally competent"—in other words, sane—when he committed the offense. The *Spokesman-Review* noted that this was "an unusual procedure," yet a federal judge granted the motion for a two-part trial.

Maxey must have known that the first part of the trial would be an uphill battle. He called a handwriting analyst to challenge the prosecution's contention that the writing on the label was Greiff's. But Maxey's expert could only say was it was "inconclusive." More damaging was the testimony of a postal clerk who remembered the package. He remembered a man coming into the post office and weighing the package. Then he pointed out Greiff as the man who had brought it in. In closing arguments, Maxey could only say that the handwriting match had not been proven beyond a reasonable doubt, and that "there has been no testimony that Greiff had the ability to construct an explosive device like that sent to Freeman's home." The jury deliberated a little more than an hour before finding Greiff guilty. Round one was over, but it was by no means the conclusive round.

The second phase of the trial began the next day, with the same jury. This time, Maxey's hand was far stronger. He told the jurors in his opening statement that Greiff had been a good farmer and a hard worker until a major operation for ulcers in 1959 had slowed him down and triggered changes in his personality. Yet he didn't really begin to go downhill until his son's arrest and conviction for draft evasion. Maxey painted the Greiffs as a close-knit family, with shared antiwar values. He said that Greiff has fled Germany for Switzerland early in his life in order to avoid German military conscription and had then emigrated to the United States. His son, now out of McNeil Island prison, testified that his father had always taught him that "it's wrong to kill." He also said his father took his arrest and conviction so hard that, right before his incarceration, the younger Greiff was "more worried about him than I was about going to the penitentiary." He testified that his father would pace the floor at night, mumbling to himself, "They're all against us."

Neighbors testified that Greiff began "failing" in the fall of 1965 and that he developed suicidal tendencies. He told a neighbor he wanted to "take the car or truck and wreck it with himself in it." Maxey also called two psychiatrists who testified that Greiff was "mentally irresponsible" when the package was mailed. They said that Greiff had undergone a series of shock treatments over the last year. During Maxey's statements to the jurors, Greiff broke down and wept, according to the *Chronicle*.

The jurors deliberated a little more than two hours before coming in with a verdict: innocent by reason of temporary insanity. Both Greiff and his son broke into tears when the verdict was read. Maxey was naturally pleased that he had spared the elder Greiff from jail, but in later writings he was most proud that this was the first use in the state of "bifurcating the guilt and insanity phases of a trial."

Meanwhile, a subtle shift in Maxey's politics and approach became apparent after his searing 1964 Mississippi experience. At age forty, his idealism was giving way to the realization that the struggle would be long and hard, with no end in sight. He responded by throwing himself even more fiercely into problems right in his hometown, like housing and social-club discrimination, where he could make a direct impact.

The Elks, the Eagles, the Masons, the Moose, the Athletic Roundtable, and the Spokane Club—these were the institutions that defined Spokane's social scene in the 1960s. They were almost exclusively white. One local Eagles lodge had the words "Caucasian only" printed on its application form as late as 1971. When challenged on this, the lodge's manager claimed it was an old form, a relic from the past. Yet that past wasn't so distant. In 1967, a statewide furor erupted when two black members of the Renton Education Association were asked to leave the group's dinner dance at an Eagles hall in a Seattle suburb. Their fellow teachers walked out in protest. When Maxey caught wind of this, he indignantly demanded a hearing before the Washington State Board Against Discrimination. Then he attacked the clubs with a legal strategy that cut right to the heart of their profits and culture. He threatened to take away their liquor.

Social clubs had argued for years that because they were private they had a perfect right to decide whom they would admit as members. Maxey agreed with them—to a point. Yes, he said, they could "discriminate any way they please," but only as long as they didn't apply for a public right. One of those public rights was the right to sell and serve liquor. Maxey, somewhat disingenuously, argued that they could discriminate all they wanted as long as they gave up liquor. Along with Seattle attorney Kenneth MacDonald, Maxey filed a federal suit in 1968 against the Washington State Liquor Control Board, demanding that the board cease issuing liquor licenses to clubs that discriminate. "We believe that both the liquor board and the clubs have had a trouble-free sojourn for long enough," he told reporters. "They are working in a partnership agreement."

The *Spokesman-Review*'s editorial board, a reliable gauge of local establishment attitudes, worried that it was the clubs who were being mistreated: "Members of private clubs and fraternal organizations which now provide for the sale of alcoholic beverages would actually be the subjects of discrimination if they were forced by a federal court order to be deprived of a privilege long recognized under state law."

The federal lawsuit ultimately "fizzled out," as MacDonald put it, because it became too complicated and expensive. Maxey said lawyers in a case in 1972 in Pennsylvania "took our work product to the U.S. Supreme Court on an identical issue" and lost. Yet the lawsuit did win in the court of public opinion. In the lead were the Spokane Elks, who petitioned the national Elks organization to remove the word "white" from its membership bylaws just a few months after Maxey filed his 1968 suit. The effort failed, but the Spokane NAACP went on record applauding the local club's "gallant and unsuccessful endeavor."

Embarrassed by the publicity and under increasing pressure from members, many clubs opened up their membership bylaws to minorities and women over the next decade. Yet even then, changed bylaws didn't mean the restrictive atmosphere was much different. To Maxey, true change in Spokane came excruciatingly slowly. In 1978, he told the *Chronicle* with evident bitterness, "This is a very clubby town. Yet there is not one black member of the Elks Club and no others I know of in fraternities and social clubs." Maxey himself could have joined the Elks or the Spokane Club (the old City Club) after the bylaws were changed, but it was not in his nature. "I suppose I could have been more the comfortable Negro—I could have joined the clubs," he said in a 1988 interview. "Perhaps. I could have been less strident. But I doubt that I would have been as effective if I had tried to adopt any of those disguises."

As the mid-1960s arrived, Maxey turned his attention increasingly to Spokane's housing situation. With such a small black population, Spokane scarcely resembled the country's bigger, more segregated cities. "I remember taking my kids to Seattle and as we came across the Lake Washington bridge and came in and touched on Twenty-third and Madison [a black section of Seattle], they were overwhelmed! Scared!" recalled Maxey with a laugh. "My son said, 'Dad, are there any white people that live in Seattle?'"

In Spokane, the Maxeys had been accepted (if sometimes grudgingly) in their suburban-like neighborhood on F Street. Their experience had been smooth compared to that of some other black homebuyers of this era. Frank Hopkins, who owned the Ebony Café, bought a house on Spokane's North Side in 1961 and was almost ready to move in when someone broke out all twenty-eight windows in one night. Hopkins got the message and canceled the purchase. "I just had to let it go," he told reporters. The Reverend J. C. Brooks of the Bethel African Methodist Episcopal Church told the *Spokesman-Review* that same year that real-estate agents routinely steered black homebuyers to the unofficial "area for Negroes," a low-income part of town now called East Central, bordered by Division Street on the west, Altamont Street on the east, Ninth Avenue on the south, and Sprague Avenue on the north.

This kind of redlining, as the practice was known, was especially ironic in Spokane. The city had been settled in its early years with a western pioneer openness. "The funny thing is, the original three hundred [the city's black pioneers], they lived all over Spokane," said Maxey when he looked back on this issue years later. "The dominant number lived in the East Side area [East Central], but, by far, it couldn't be said it was just one area." He cited as an example the widow he lived with during his high-school years, at W. 917 Shannon, in the mostly white North Side.

But introducing new black families into established white neighborhoods—that was a thornier issue altogether. Generally, this de facto segregation was enforced by what longtime black resident Alfonse Hill called "a gentleman's agreement type of thing." Hill said that "there were a lot of places the Realtors wouldn't take you. As far as the South Hill? Forget it." The redlining often went beyond a gentleman's agreement. Sometimes the policy was written in black and white. A 1940s-era Spokane Valley code of ethics for real-estate agents, adapted from the national code, read, "A Realtor should never be instrumental in introducing into a neighborhood . . . any race or nationality or any persons whose presence will be detrimental to property values in that neighborhood." Redlining was not only encouraged, it was considered the ethical thing to do.

Meanwhile, deeds for homes routinely included restrictive covenants specifying which races could or could not buy homes. Historian Quintard Taylor cited a typical 1938 Seattle property deed that said, "The purchaser must be of the white or Caucasian race." The *Chronicle* ran a list of ten Spokane developments in 1968 whose covenants had been declared illegal following the Civil Rights Act of 1968, which focused on discrimination in housing, and subsequent Supreme Court decisions—an indication of how widespread these covenants were in the city. Maxey later said that Supreme Court rulings in the late 1960s "gave us a foothold to blast their legal foundations out from under them."

Maxey had become the region's point man in the struggle for fair housing. When Frank Burgess, a black Gonzaga University basketball star and law student, lost a lease on a house in 1965 because of "complaints by neighbors," Maxey stepped in and took the owner and real-estate agent to court. Burgess and his wife testified that they went to look at a house at 3009 W. Eloika, in a middle-class area on Spokane's North Side. They liked it and put down a month's rent, $80, intending to sign the lease and move in. A few days later, the agent called Burgess and told him that the neighbors had complained and that he was returning the check. In court, the agent said that the owner, who had moved to Billings, Montana, had simply worked out a trade for the house with a Billings resident who was moving to Spokane.

Maxey told the judge, Ralph E. Foley (the same man who had sent those Spokane Children's Home officials to the Walla Walla pen three decades earlier) that the refusal was clearly because of race. Yet Maxey's main legal argument was not about race; he simply argued that the $80 payment constituted a binding contract. Judge Foley agreed and ruled in favor of Burgess and Maxey. Foley did not rule on the racial question, except to acknowledge that it had been more difficult for a black person to find an acceptable house on short notice after the lease deal fell through. It had taken the Burgesses months to find a new house. Frank Burgess was later awarded $250 in monetary damages.

Evidently, many Spokane residents saw the incident in racial terms, because a group named Citizens for Reconciliation purchased an ad in the *Spokesman-Review* two weeks later which read in part, "WE ARE ASHAMED . . . that we have participated so long in a community attitude of racial discrimination in regard to housing, as was indicated in the case of Burgess vs. Griepp. WE DEPLORE . . . the fact that community pressure can be exerted [to deprive the rights of] one member of our community, because of his race, to live where he would choose." Fourteen prominent community members, including a minister and several doctors, signed the ad.

Mainline Spokane, however, actively resisted any push toward open housing. Samuel J. Smith, an influential black state legislator from Seattle, recalled that in 1967 it was the Spokane delegation that most fiercely resisted Smith's groundbreaking open-housing legislation. "I don't know why they were so much against it," Smith said in "Samuel J. Smith: An Oral History." "I figure [it was] because of the community from which they sprouted out." Maxey, as chairman of the Washington State Advisory Committee to the U.S. Commission on Civil Rights, later engaged in what he called "tremendous arguments" with James S. Black, owner of a Spokane agency and the president of the Washington Association of Realtors.

One of those arguments came during a noon meeting of the West Spokane Kiwanis Club in 1968. At issue was that proposed open-housing law, which specified that homeowners who wished to discriminate would no longer be allowed to use a licensed real-estate agent. Black opposed that law, and he outlined the argument as an issue of "basic property rights . . . the cornerstone of the American society and the American heritage." Maxey turned right around with his own appeal to basic American values. "Unless racial discrimination—concerning housing, employment and education—is eliminated, democracy as we know it in the United States is doomed," he told the Kiwanians. "Americans must pay a small price to gain the peace and dignity of our communities. Elimination of discrimination is surely worth the small inconvenience requested of some property owners." In another talk that year, Maxey added that the realtor's association was playing on the "prejudice of many white citizens." The realtors were trying to create a climate of fear in overwhelmingly white Spokane by, absurdly, "exciting them [white residents] into believing that there will be a Negro in every block."

By this time, it had been more than a decade since Maxey had been president of the Spokane NAACP. Yet because of his legal clout and standing in the black community, he remained a close advisor to the organization and an acknowledged mentor to its newer leaders. "Carl was always there on the scene to handle complicated situations with no cost to the branch," said Billy V. Morris, a past Spokane NAACP president, in an article he wrote for the *Spokane African-American Voice*. "I remember one time years ago, when some members were threatening to take an action that the then-president was against. The president stated, 'If you attempt to do that, I will tell Carl Maxey on you.'" That was enough to make people shape up.

Maxey also became deeply involved in another cause between 1964 and 1966, which sounds almost trivial in retrospect: the right for stores to stay open on Sundays. Spokane County, like many other counties at the time, had a law that prohibited sales of major items such as appliances and furniture on Sundays. In fact, Washington still had a 1909 "blue law" on the books prohibiting all trade and industry on Sundays. Most retailers were in favor of Sunday closure—they got the day off. As long as every other store complied, nobody lost business to competitors. But when a brash new retail chain, Valu-Mart, came to Spokane in 1964, it saw a lucrative opening. It started selling furniture on a Sunday and was promptly fined $250 plus costs. Valu-Mart hired Maxey, who appealed the fine on the basis of discrimination.

Maxey lost a superior court appeal and then took the case all the way up to the state supreme court. In his arguments in Olympia, Maxey pointed out that the ordinance was absurdly arbitrary; it allowed the sale of radios, for instance, but not televisions. Meanwhile, the state's blue law was hopelessly vague. It could even be strictly interpreted to ban Sunday baseball games and the sale of gasoline. "Because the general statue is so broad, any enforcement of a local ordinance must have a reasonable relationship with the general welfare," Maxey argued before the state justices. "To pick one isolated type of merchandising and not others is discrimination." He clearly thought the Sunday-closure laws were ridiculous and outmoded. So did the general public: they repealed the state's blue law by voter initiative in November of 1966. A few days later, the state supreme court ruled in favor of Valu-

Mart and Maxey, striking down the county ordinance by a 5–4 vote. Sunday closure went the way of the horse-drawn wagon. Maxey did not consider this a civil rights triumph, but he included it among his achievements for another reason. The kid from an orphanage wasn't merely practicing law—he had *changed* the law.

During this time, the massive escalation in the Vietnam War beginning in 1965 was having a profound effect on Maxey's politics. He became an early and outspoken opponent of the war, partly because of the inordinate participation of black soldiers. The same man who felt cheated out of combat in World War II had come to believe that black soldiers were being used as cannon fodder. Yet that was by no means the only reason he opposed the war. He had serious foreign policy, economic, and humanitarian objections as well. He was especially infuriated that the war was funneling money away from programs to fight poverty. He did not mince words in his public speeches. "And then there is Vietnam, where a mammoth modern war has been taken to a little people 7,000 miles from the United States," he thundered in one speech. "And while Congress argues about people [flag-burners] who are burning a bit of bunting, we have scorched lands, blown up houses and burned thousands of people to death. That, more than anything else, makes the [American] flag distrusted and feared."

His strident opposition led to disillusionment with the Democratic Party, since it was LBJ who, by 1968, had sent nearly five hundred thousand American troops to Southeast Asia. Maxey's relationship with the Democratic Party was already complicated. On the one hand, it was the Democrat LBJ who had pushed through the Civil Rights Bill of 1964. On the other hand, it was the powerful southern wing of the party that had so virulently opposed integration in any form. Senator Eastland of Mississippi, for example, was a Democrat. "There was an ongoing split in the Democratic Party in those days," said Ninon. "We were at odds with the Democratic Party a lot, because they were the old, settled union organizers, who didn't want to be on the cutting edge of civil rights and other issues. We were always over there as somewhat of a splinter group, trying to take over caucuses and all of the other things that people do."

When the presidential election campaigns of 1968 began, Maxey and Ninon joined forces with what she said was "quite a large group of people who were liberal Democrats." They all shared a dislike of LBJ and of the war, and they felt they had found the solution to both problems in Senator Eugene McCarthy of Minnesota, who had emerged as an attractive antiwar Democratic candidate. In January, Maxey was named one of three people to head the state steering committee for the Washington McCarthy for President Committee. Their plan seemed simple enough: to elect pro-McCarthy delegates to the county, state, and national Democratic conventions.

They had no way of foreseeing that nothing would be simple in politics in 1968, one of the most tumultuous political years in American history. It began when the North Vietnamese and Viet Cong launched the bloody Tet Offensive on January 30, shocking Americans who had come to believe that the war was almost won. LBJ's approval ratings plummeted. McCarthy, still considered a dark horse, went on to finish a close second to LBJ in the New Hampshire primaries in March, 49 percent to 42 percent. The next week, Robert F. Kennedy entered the Democratic race, sensing LBJ's vulnerability. On March 31, with McCarthy leading LBJ by a huge margin in Wisconsin, LBJ pulled a stunner. The sitting president announced, almost mournfully, that he was withdrawing from the race. From that point on, McCarthy's opponents for the nomination would be Kennedy and Vice President Hubert Humphrey, who was waiting on the sidelines.

Then, on April 4 came the stunning news out of Memphis: Martin Luther King Jr. had been killed by an assassin's bullet. Maxey was driving his car when he heard the news. "It was like a thunderous blow to one's midsection," he later told the *Chronicle*. "It just took the life and breath out of you. I had to pull over. There was surprise, of course, but everyone knew the likelihood because it had been such a bloody season." When the *Spokesman-Review* asked Maxey for a quote that night, his words were packed tightly with anger: "It's a tragic thing. It bespeaks of the sickness of our nation, and particularly the white community. It makes you wonder how many other martyrs black America will have to offer up . . . Racism is just a part of the American epic."

Riots erupted in at least sixty U.S. cities; fourteen people were dead by the next day. Stokely Carmichael, who had earlier supported King's nonviolent tactics, was widely blamed for a particularly destructive uprising in Washington, DC after he publicly predicted a violent struggle in which black people would "stand up on their feet and die like men." Angry crowds in Seattle set fire to four local businesses. Even in Spokane, officials waited nervously for trouble. No real trouble occurred, which might have had something to do with the attitude of the city's black leaders.

Maxey's remarks to the *Chronicle* the next day were filled with a bitter sadness, but he was certainly not following Carmichael's incendiary lead. "The white citizens interested in racial problems ask what they can do," said Maxey. "They can turn the martyrdom of Martin Luther King into an actual shrine for good, by insisting that fellow whites pass the necessary legislation, appropriate the necessary money and stop playing hanky-panky with Negro rights. Make this an article of faith and do something about it, for otherwise there will continue to be betrayals, riots and assassinations. Dr. King was filled with the Christian principle. The real tragedy to America is that the loss is greater to the white community, because we may not get as his replacement a person with those same Christian principles." Maxey's bitterness never fully faded after King's assassination. It marked a turning point in Maxey's public tone. For the next three decades, the themes of outrage, anger, and betrayal became far more common in his public utterances.

Hard on the news of this tragedy came another blow: the assassination of Robert F. Kennedy in June. The Democratic nomination was now a two-person race between McCarthy and Humphrey, a man Maxey regarded as no better than an LBJ stand-in. However, Humphrey had been busy locking up support among more conservative Democrats, including those of eastern Washington's Fifth Congressional District. When the district's caucus was held on June 30, it elected a straight ticket of Humphrey delegates. Maxey, a McCarthy delegate, was defeated.

Maxey still went to the state convention as the leader of Washington's McCarthy faction. Spokane County's McCarthy supporters announced that they would nominate Maxey as a delegate at-large. But the convention, held on July 13 in Tacoma, turned into a debacle for Maxey and the other McCarthyites. They were thoroughly routed, losing every single contested issue. All twenty-three of the at-large and "automatic" delegate slots (automatically given to sitting U.S. senators and representatives, for instance) went to Humphrey, even though Humphrey had won the district caucuses by only a slight margin. In the end, Washington sent forty-seven delegates to the Democratic National Convention; only seventeen were McCarthy delegates. Maxey was not one of them.

Angered by what he felt was blatant manipulation by the Humphrey forces, Maxey fought back in two ways. First, he and six other plaintiffs filed a federal lawsuit charging that the state party's delegate selection rules had deprived them of their constitutional rights. Maxey believed that, in light of recent Supreme Court rulings, the one-man, one-vote rule should be followed in selecting delegates to political conventions. Among other things, the suit charged that McCarthy voters were systematically excluded from precinct caucuses in several key counties. The second way he fought back was to book a flight to the Democratic convention in Chicago to challenge the state's Humphrey delegation before the convention's Credentials Committee. He told the *Chronicle*, just before leaving on August 16, "It is our contention that the will of the people was ignored by the Democratic Party in this state . . . The Humphrey-Johnson forces are denying McCarthy the opportunity to be heard or represented."

Maxey was hardly alone in making a challenge. Challenges were also mounted against delegations from fourteen other states before the hundred-member Credentials Committee. However, Humphrey had already virtually sewn up the nomination beforehand, and the committee was in no mood to accept any challenges from McCarthy supporters. According to Jules Witcover's history of the Democrats, *Party of the People*, two civil rights–related challenges from southern states were approved—one led by Mississippi civil rights leader Charles Evers and another challenging Alabama's pro–George Wallace delegation.

But all thirteen of the McCarthy challenges were rejected. In the end, Humphrey handily won the party's nomination on the first ballot.

That federal lawsuit resulted in an important triumph for Maxey two years down the road. When the case was finally decided in 1970, U.S. District Court judge Alfred T. Goodwin sided with Maxey and the other plaintiffs and ordered the Washington State Democratic Party to adopt new rules complying "with the spirit of the one-man, one-vote principle." This victory set a legal precedent and resulted in fairer delegate-selection rules not only in Washington, but also in several other states. This case was actually argued by cocounsel Kenneth MacDonald, Maxey having, as we shall see, his hands full in 1970.

In 1968, though, Maxey tasted only defeat and discouragement in Chicago. Even more discouraging was what he witnessed outside the convention hall and outside his hotel. Chicago mayor Richard Daley opened the convention by saying, "As long as I am mayor of Chicago, there will be law and order in Chicago." He was soon proven wrong. After an antiwar plank was voted down by Humphrey delegates, thousands of antiwar protesters "moved into Grant Park and were charged by police wielding nightsticks, clubbed to the ground and thrown into waiting paddy wagons," wrote Witcover. Delegates inside the hall were soon watching televised scenes of the chaos outside. Outrage began to build, especially among the antiwar delegates. Senator Abraham Ribicoff of Connecticut took to the podium to nominate Senator George McGovern and said, "With George McGovern as president . . . we wouldn't have to have Gestapo tactics in the streets of Chicago." Daley leapt up in front of the podium, shook his fists and shouted obscenities at Ribicoff, who stood his ground. Then, on the convention's last day, police and national guardsmen raided a farewell party for young McCarthy volunteers on the fifteenth floor of the Conrad Hilton. "The authorities clubbed them with nightsticks and dragged them into the hotel lobby," wrote Witcover. "McCarthy, notified by a volunteer, . . . demanded that the prisoners be released. The scene was a sorry coda to a convention that left the Democratic Party in shreds."

Maxey did not get swept into any of the chaos in Chicago's streets, but he later said he witnessed scenes of brutality that he would never forget. The entire dispiriting scene embittered him even more toward Humphrey and the Democratic establishment. Back home, he immediately helped launch a new statewide organization of disenchanted Democrats: the Washington Democratic Council. He became its chairman, and in a speech at the founding convention in Seattle in September, he asked rhetorically, "Why would anyone under 45 vote for Hubert Humphrey?" He picked that number for good reason. He was forty-four at the time. "I can't support Hubert Humphrey today and I can't support him at the end of this campaign," Maxey said in his keynote speech. "The patriotism that says my country right or wrong is the patriotism of a bygone era." Then, in a wry slap at two different targets, he added, "Richard Daley has about as much chance of understanding youth as I have of joining the Washington Athletic Club"—referring to Seattle's version of the exclusionary Spokane Club.

Back in Spokane, less than a month away from the election, Maxey addressed a standing-room crowd of three hundred at Gonzaga's student union as part of the university's Black Man in America lecture series. He delivered a public scourging to all three presidential candidates, including the Democratic one. He said he could not condone Humphrey's part in "planning the Vietnam War," saying that "Hubert Humphrey supped the delights of Lyndon Johnson's table and I cannot support him." The *Spokesman-Review* noted that this remark brought "strong applause from the noticeably sympathetic audience." Maxey also blasted Richard Nixon's notion of justice as being "equated with arrests, filling the jails with demonstrators and giving federal aid to Southern segregated schools." He saved one last zinger for third-party segregationist candidate George Wallace: "The best thing you can say for Wallace is that he's the worst of the three."

Most of Maxey's speech centered on the theme of "law and order versus justice." His comments were a measure of how disillusioned he had become about racial justice in the United States. He said that the kind of law and order preached by the candidates was a mere "euphemism for racial oppression." He said law and order had come to mean the "legal execution of Negroes and the poor." Jesus Christ, he said, was killed in the name of law and order. "Where was law and order when four little girls were blown up in a church in Mississippi [he meant Alabama] where they were worshiping?" Maxey fulminated. "Where was law and order when they burned our churches, bombed our homes and killed our leaders—who called for law and order then?" This was a searing speech, even by the incendiary standards of 1968 politics. He told the students he hoped his words would be a "call to arms." He told them he hoped they would not "leave these hallowed halls and go out in the world and be 'chicken.'"

One Gonzaga student certainly chose not to be "chicken" that October. The occasion was the campaign visit to Spokane of Governor Spiro T. Agnew of Maryland, Nixon's running mate. Spokane, which now had a city population of about 188,500 and a metro area of about 276,000, was never blasé about the visit of any national candidate. And since conservative Spokane tended to lean Republican, Agnew's speech became a downtown-clogging event, drawing a crowd estimated at 2,000 to the Parkade Plaza, a brick-paved courtyard lined with stores and balconies. Agnew paraded into the city with a small motorcade and was ushered to a platform set up near the plaza's fountain. Hundreds of balloons soared into the blue sky. Reporters were told that he would deliver one of his standard campaign policy speeches, about natural resources. Yet circumstances soon pointed Agnew in a different direction. As Agnew launched into his speech, a group of Gonzaga students carrying Humphrey signs began chanting, "We want Humphrey! We want Humphrey!"

Agnew, well seasoned in dealing with disruptions, smoothly switched to the topic of dissent in democracies: "Dissent is proper in this democracy. But when dissent prohibits others from being heard it is not the type of dissent we need. This type of dissent which is evident here does nothing but lead to anarchy and frustration." Warming to this new theme, Agnew said he believed in voting rights for eighteen-year-olds (the limit was twenty-one at the time), and he advocated an "intern system" in government so that youth could learn how government really worked. "Many young people, however, say they cannot participate in government and in politics," Agnew continued. "I say to you, they can if they just go to work within the framework of the two major political parties. The Republican Party welcomes them if they just quit crying and start working. This will accomplish more than just carrying obscene signs down the street."

This kind of talk played well with the crowd. The *Chronicle* reported that the hecklers "failed to disturb his aplomb." Agnew then contrasted the protesters with a young group of his supporters in the audience, described by veteran *Chronicle* political writer John J. Lemon as "a group of smartly clad young women in white blouses, skimmer hats and Nixon-Agnew ribbons." Agnew proclaimed that "despite voices of dissent from a few, this generation has produced the finest group of young people we have ever had in this country."

After that he switched to an attack on the third-party platform of George Wallace and Curtis LeMay, which he said "bristles with increased iron-jawed defiance of good judgment." He accused them of irresponsible talk about the use of nuclear arms. "The United States has never been a saber-rattling nation," said Agnew. "I want to remind you that, [when the United States had] the only nuclear capacity in the world, we could have conquered the world, and for those who called us imperialists, look at our conduct." At this point, a voice from a balcony above the platform shouted clearly, "Warmonger!" Agnew stopped his speech and looked around. "Who said that?" A young man described by Lemon as a "dark, longhaired youth" grasped the balcony railing and shouted, "I said it." Then he flashed the V-for-peace symbol and said, "What the hell do you think this means?"

Some people in the crowd shouted, "Get him!" Others began to boo as two bystanders attempted to yank the young man forcibly from the railing. A Spokane police officer, already on the balcony, grabbed him and pulled him away. The officer told the young man he was under arrest and began to hustle him off the balcony. Agnew looked up at the commotion, which had lasted less than fifteen seconds, and said, "Well, it's really tragic to think that somewhere, somebody in that young man's life has failed him." The crowd responded with applause and boos.

That young man was Peter Jerome McDonough, a twenty-year-old Gonzaga University senior from Sacramento, California. As the officer led him away, Secret Service agents converged and led him into an office next to the plaza. They searched and questioned him. Then they drove him to the police station and booked him for disorderly conduct, with bail set at twenty-five dollars. Fellow Gonzaga students threw some money together and bailed McDonough out right away. Maxey was right there, offering his services pro bono. To Maxey, the arrest was a clear violation of free-speech rights. He told reporters, "We do not believe this young man should be arrested or incarcerated because of a simple exercise of free speech."

At his municipal court hearing a few days later, McDonough told Justice of the Peace Ellsworth Gump, "I didn't go there to embarrass or insult the candidate. I didn't agree with him and thought it was my place to say something, so I did. I am concerned about the country and our involvement in Vietnam. I think it is wrong to be there." A group of Gonzaga students were in the courtroom to support him. Film footage of the incident was shown, and when Agnew was shown saying "somewhere, somebody in that young man's life has failed him," the students began loudly laughing and clapping. Gump ordered the courtroom cleared, declaring that if people were allowed to express approval or disapproval in a courtroom, any court would descend into "complete chaos," a remark that would come to bear on another Maxey case two years later. Gump relented soon afterward and allowed the students back in.

In McDonough's defense, Maxey argued that the student had simply exercised his right of free speech in a public forum and had not been "riotous" or unduly disruptive. Maxey also presented a petition from 465 Gonzaga students and faculty members attesting to McDonough's good character. Maxey then moved for dismissal. Gump was not swayed. He denied Maxey's motion and found McDonough guilty. "The peace and good order of the community has been offended by your words and actions," ruled Gump. "The way things are going, we are in a tough position as to what can be done to keep order. We all have the right to speech and dissent, but there is an orderly way to do it or we will end up in shambles. Perhaps the $100 fine is sufficient to deter others from doing the same."

Less than a week later, Maxey filed an appeal to the superior court, which was heard in January of 1969, right after Agnew was sworn in as the new vice president. At this second nonjury trial, McDonough delivered what the *Chronicle* called "an intense recital of his views against what he called 'an immoral war.'" He also said he believed that shouting a protest at politically rally "is as American as anything." Judge Ross R. Rakow was not inclined to rule on how "American" it was. He said at the beginning that he had narrowed the issue strictly to whether McDonough was in fact guilty of disorderly conduct by interrupting the speaker. So Maxey's strategy was to assert that it was already a raucous event, with dozens of Humphrey backers jeering throughout the speech. None of them were arrested for disorderly conduct; McDonough shouldn't have been either.

It didn't work. Rakow ruled that "no man may exercise his rights at an unreasonable expense to others" and upheld the conviction and hundred-dollar fine. Maxey immediately announced he would appeal the case to the state supreme court. It took more than a year for the case to make it into the court's docket. By then, May 1970, the arguments of Maxey and his law partner Gordon Bovey were three-pronged: (1) The city's disorderly conduct ordinance was unconstitutionally vague, (2) McDonough's free-speech rights were abridged, and (3) shouting one word was hardly being "disorderly."

As it turned out, only the last argument was necessary. On May 26, 1971, the justices ruled in favor of Maxey and McDonough and reversed the conviction. Justice Hugh J. Rosellini (no direct relationship to the former governor) noted in his majority opinion that the "political rally was a noisy and partisan event . . . Shouting the word 'warmonger' but once—without more to indicate a further purpose or intention of breaking up the meeting, or to deprive the speaker of his audience, or to interfere with the rights of others to hear, or the speaker to speak—did not amount to a disturbance of the peace, in fact or in law." Three other judges joined the five-judge majority, but they wrote a separate opinion stating that the city's law was constitutional.

McDonough was far out of earshot when the ruling was announced. He was in the middle of a two-year stint as a teacher at the Mpima Seminary in Kabwe, Zambia. He had lost his student draft deferment upon graduating from Gonzaga, and as he explained in a December of 1969 letter to Maxey from Zambia, the draft board gave him two choices: "They told me I could either go to Africa as a II-A [deferred because of occupation] or stay at home as a C.O. [conscientious objector] . . . So I figured that teaching school would be a bigger help than dumping bedpans in some hospital." Maxey wrote back, gave him an update on his appeal, and also gave him an update on Agnew. "The more we see and read of Agnew, the more your comment becomes appropriate," wrote Maxey in late 1969. "Isn't it idiotic that you should be arrested for calling a warmonger a warmonger? Agnew should have been in jail four or five times over."

As it turned out, Agnew avoided jail, but just barely. In 1973, he reached a plea agreement with the U.S. Justice Department on charges of income tax evasion and money laundering. He resigned the vice-presidency and pleaded nolo contendere (no contest) to a single charge of tax evasion. He was fined ten thousand dollars and sentenced to three years of probation. Agnew's political career ended in disgrace.

Perhaps somewhere, somebody in Agnew's life had failed him.

11

A RIGHT HOOK TO SCOOP JACKSON

Maxey's passionate hatred for the Vietnam War led him to revive his ambitions for elected office, which had lain dormant after being soundly trounced by Kathryn Mautz, now a Spokane County District Court judge. This time he chose a far bigger target. He waded fist-first into a political showdown with one of the most famous Vietnam hawks in the country: Senator Henry "Scoop" Jackson.

In January of 1970, Maxey announced that he was seeking Jackson's U.S. Senate seat and would run against him in the September Democratic primary. This was an audacious move: the Senate had only one black member at the time, Edward W. Brooke of Massachusetts, and before him there had been none since Reconstruction. Yet under any circumstances, this was a frankly quixotic fight, since Jackson was a firmly established political institution in *both* Washingtons—the state and the nation's capital. By 1970 Jackson had already been a U.S. senator for eighteen years. He was the chairman of the Interior Committee and a senior member of the powerful Senate Armed Services Committee. In 1960, John F. Kennedy had come within a hair of naming him his running mate. In 1968, another president had offered him the post of secretary of defense. That president was Richard Nixon, a Republican. Scoop turned it down, mainly because he was a lifelong, loyal, unwavering Democrat. But Maxey believed that Jackson was the wrong kind of Democrat, a prowar Democrat, leading his party in exactly the wrong direction. Maxey was, to put it bluntly, infuriated with what Jackson had become.

Maxey admitted that he had once been a "great supporter" of Jackson, who was mostly liberal on social issues and had been an early champion of civil rights. Maxey had worked enthusiastically on Jackson's Senate campaigns through 1964. "I kind of like the guy," Maxey had said earlier. In 1970, though, Maxey saw him merely as one of the main apologists for—and architects of—Nixon's bellicose Vietnam War strategy. "Jackson, viewed in one dimension, votes liberal; viewed in another, he is the most conservative senator in the United States," Maxey said in announcing his candidacy. "His espousal of liberal programs is completely negated by his voting for military expenditures which sap the money and vitality of the country."

Going after Jackson made no practical sense. Jackson had mountains of campaign money at his disposal and was overwhelmingly popular in the state among practically every voting bloc except the McCarthy antiwar faction. One potential Republican challenger famously quipped that running against Jackson "would be like trying to climb Mount Rainer barefoot." Yet Maxey, never one to back away from a cause, decided that someone had to make at least an effort toward taking back both the Democratic Party and the country. He did not entertain any illusions about his chances. "No, he never thought he could pull it off," said Lou Maxey. "Not even close. Never. He did it just to give people a voice." He told the AP right after entering the race that "the victory is in the running." In a classic Maxey phrase, he said that "even a cat can look at a king, and this black cat has looked at King Henry Jackson and seen a political schizophrenic." A popular antiwar sign at the time offered another diagnosis: "Henry Jackson suffers from a military-industrial complex." Nor did Maxey believe that Jackson could heal the nation's racial wounds. "I submit that someone must try to end the racial strife, the nearly open warfare in our cities during the summer, the specter of blacks fighting construction unions," said Maxey.

By some measures, the notion of a Maxey versus Jackson duel was not so one-sided. Maxey had a statewide reputation as a man of principle and was by now one of the acknowledged leaders of the state's increasingly powerful antiwar movement. Robert G. Kaufman summed up the standing of both candidates in his 2000 biography, *Henry M. Jackson: A Life in Politics*: "Few men in American politics could match Henry Jackson for integrity. Carl Maxey came close." "Integrity" was probably not the word Jackson supporters would have used to describe Maxey's subsequent campaign rhetoric, which sometimes bordered on vitriolic. In one of Maxey's milder jabs, he called Jackson "a short, fat white Republican masquerading as a Democrat."

"Our destiny is in the hands of fat-cat contractors, bellicose generals and a Napoleonic little senator who can juggle bombs and ballots, conservation and nerve gas on a platform of the continued draft that kills your sons and brothers of your city," Maxey said in an April speech. He accused Jackson of being in an "unholy alliance" with Nixon. He proposed an "ABM-Jackson-watch" (referring to the anti-ballistic missile program that Jackson supported) and suggested that "when the hands reach the midnight hour, it explodes." He implied that Jackson's "fall from grace is much like Humpty Dumpty's and I don't believe either Henry or Humpty can be repaired." The Washington State Democratic Party's entrenched leaders were appalled by this attack from within. Karen Marchioro, an up and coming young party district chair, said the old guard was "infuriated and bewildered" by the mere fact that Maxey was running.

The political mood of the country was tense and angry on the heels of the May tragedy at Kent State University in Ohio, where National Guard troops killed four students at an antiwar rally. During an emotional "day of mourning" for the Kent State victims, Maxey stood before a crowd of ten thousand in front of the King County Courthouse and urged the impeachment of both Nixon and Jackson.

Jackson's strategy was to ignore Maxey completely. He made a point of never making any kind of joint appearance with Maxey, nor did he respond to Maxey's criticisms, even when he attacked the institution to which Jackson belonged, saying, "Almost everything I know about Congress is immoral." Still, Kaufman wrote that "Maxey's attacks genuinely bothered him, despite his outward composure." Jacksonbashing was only part of Maxey's strategy. Maxey certainly made his own positions clear—probably too clear if he truly wanted to be elected. Among the issues he publicly endorsed: immediate withdrawal of all U.S. troops from Vietnam; amnesty for draft resisters; a volunteer army; a reduction of the armed forces from 3.5 million to 1 million men; an end to ABM and MIRV missile construction; a guaranteed national annual income; legal abortions; and a redirection of national priorities toward poverty and unemployment.

Race was an issue in the campaign as well, if only because of the color of the candidates. The AP felt obliged to note in its initial story that Maxey was "the only Negro attorney in Spokane." Nor did Maxey shy away from discussing race, especially when he wanted to assign responsibility for America's current political and social crises. "It is the middle-class whites who are the villains," he said in a May press conference at the Spokane Press Club. "They are the ones who are insensitive and they are the ones who must be educated." In an earlier interview with Jack Mayne of the AP, Maxey said that the white middle class must be turned away from its preoccupation with war, space travel, and excess corporate profits and toward issues that show they have "compassion for their fellow men": pollution, poverty, racism, and unemployment. Maxey scoffed at the suggestion that being black (by now he rarely used the word Negro) would help him in his campaign. "The fact that I'm black hasn't helped me in the past and has made me feel the sting of racism," he said.

Maxey's son Bill, on summer vacation from the University of Oregon, campaigned for his father and quickly discovered what a black candidate was up against. "We went door to door for him up in Hillyard," said Bill, referring to a lower-income area of Spokane. "I was with a friend I had gone to high school with. This lady came to the door and we were telling her what we were doing. Her husband came to the door and pulled her away and said, 'I ain't voting for that nigger.' She was very apologetic."

Maxey was also at a serious disadvantage in funding. In August he told reporters that he had spent about $24,000, much of it his own money. "That should prove that you don't have to be rich to run for office," said Maxey, trying to put the best face on it. "I'll offer to open my books to anyone and I wish Jackson would do the same." The funding gap was so lopsided that Maxey's entire war chest was a quarter of what Jackson had received from Republicans alone. That's right, the Republicans had pledged $100,000 to the campaign of a Democratic senator. Maxey made hay out of this revelation, saying that it only proved what he had been saying all along: "The incumbent is more of a Republican than a Democrat." The Republican donors said the money was for use in the Democratic primary only, to ensure that Jackson was renominated. It went without saying that they viewed the prospect of Senator Carl Maxey with horror. In any case, Jackson never used most of the Republican money and returned it to its donors.

As for Maxey, it didn't help his finances much that he had pledged to give half of what he raised to college students to spend on any antiwar candidate of their choice. When reporters asked if he could run a Senate campaign on such a shoestring, he replied, "Most of us do not have Boeing Co. money." This was yet another dig at Jackson, who had long been saddled with the moniker, "The Senator from Boeing." Yet despite his funding shortfall, Maxey still managed to campaign all over the state, nearly nonstop. "He hired a private plane," said Lou Maxey. "He would speak in any little town to any group. And when he'd talk to a labor group, they were hard-line traditional Democrats. But they would always leave just blown away. He knew all about farm policy and labor policy, and he spoke directly to the people specifically."

Lou, who was working for a Spokane ad agency, created a Maxey campaign ad that spoofed Jackson's ads, which depicted him as a committed environmentalist, walking through the woods. The Maxey ad showed a silhouette of a soldier marching into battle, with the words, "No Deposit, No Return. Is Vietnam Henry Jackson's idea of conservation? Vote for Carl Maxey." The ad ran in the sports sections of both Seattle papers. She later heard the Jackson campaign was furious over the ad, which they thought was a low blow.

For a few stunning weeks, it began to look as if Maxey could pull off a coup. Maxey rolled into Seattle's King County Democratic convention—the biggest county in the state—with a well-organized group of supporters. It was, according to Marchioro, the only county in the state in which Jackson did not control the party apparatus. Many of Maxey's supporters were young; most were unconnected with the "traditional" state Democratic machine; all were fervently antiwar. One week after the Kent State shootings, emotions were boiling over. During the vote on who to endorse for Senate—Jackson or Maxey— the Maxey delegates filled the hall with the chant, "Peace! Now! Peace! Now!" One old-line delegate pleaded with the crowd: "If you reject Sen. Jackson, you will throw out 18 years of seniority in the U.S. Senate. It will make us, not him, look like a jackass." The crowd was unmoved. When the votes were counted, the King County Democratic convention had thrown its endorsement to Maxey by a vote of 508–485. The result "really tore the sheet within the party," said Marchioro. A jubilant Maxey called it "a good right hook to Jackson's belly." That wasn't the only pugilistic metaphor that Maxey delivered. "It was a slap in the face of a man who has served eighteen years in the Senate," said Maxey. "It was a well-deserved slap in the face, however."

Jackson pretended not to care. He said the "real convention will be held in November and I have no doubt about the outcome." He said the King County results had been rigged. But they were not rigged at all, according to William W. Prochnau and Richard W. Larsen, veteran *Seattle Times* political correspondents who witnessed these events. In their 1972 book *A Certain Democrat: Senator Henry M. Jackson*, they said that the antiwar Democrats and the Washington Democratic Council (the leadership of which Maxey had resigned in order to run for Senate) had "moved aggressively into precinct caucuses," seized control in several counties, and had caught the old-line Democrats by surprise. Prochnau and Larsen said the Democratic generation gap was easy to see on the floor of the hall. When it became clear that Maxey had won, two middle-aged women "flounced" out of the hall, snapping, "Ridiculous. Just absolutely ridiculous." Yet just behind them stood a teenage delegate, flashing the peace sign and a "great grin of triumph to a half-dozen long-haired friends watching from the gallery."

The King County convention went beyond endorsing Maxey. It

adopted a platform that Jackson could not conceivably embrace: legalized marijuana, legalized abortion, legal safeguards for the Black Panthers, withdrawing all troops from Southeast Asia, and ending all weapons sales to Israel and any other Middle Eastern country. The *Seattle Post-Intelligencer* reported that the platform's supporters called it "an extremely relevant social document" while its detractors said it came "directly from Moscow and Hanoi."

This victory gave Maxey a wave of momentum rolling into the Washington State Democratic Convention on July 10 and 11. It was held on Maxey's own turf in the Spokane Coliseum. Once again, his antiwar legions arrived in force. Prochnau and Larsen, who were there, noted that the antiwar forces had made surprisingly large inroads into many of the thirty-nine county delegations. "In better years, [Jackson] might have gone down onto the floor, milled among his friends, the delegates," they wrote. "But this year there were too many strange faces down there, waving the two-fingered peace sign, some so hostile they might lower one finger."

The state's Democratic leadership had done a head count and decided it would be prudent not to hold an endorsement vote for the Senate primary. Jackson might have won, but only by an embarrassingly slim margin. Or he might not have won at all. They also decided to juggle the convention agenda so that Jackson would not share the stage with Maxey. Maxey was given a brief slot on Friday, and the state's two Democratic powerhouses, Senators Warren Magnuson and Jackson, appeared together on Saturday for Magnuson's keynote address.

When Maxey strode onto the stage, it was clear that he felt he was being shoved to the back of the bus. "Where is Henry Jackson? Henry, wherever you are, let's debate the issues. But oh, no!" shouted Maxey. "We have all been advised that he won't show today. In the true spirit of the Washington State Democratic Party, under its present leadership, the rules have been changed to accommodate him, but not anyone else. I would not even have accepted this invitation to appear had I not expected him to be on the same platform. Or is the United States Senator too proud to appear on the platform with a black brother from Spokane and debate the issues?" Maxey complained about having been allowed only "a full ten minutes" to discuss the "crises of our time," railing that "as we play out the charade of this political convention system, one can truly appreciate the remarks of George Bernard Shaw: 'A democracy is a device that insures the people that they will be governed no better than they deserve.'"

Maxey expressed his support for Magnuson and recited a litany of the ways in which Jackson compared unfavorably with the state's senior senator: "Maggie" had voted against the ABM missiles, had taken a stand against nerve gas, had never accepted money from Republicans, and had never been offered a cabinet job by Nixon. Then Maxey launched into the meat of his speech, a platform on behalf of "the young, the old, the black, the poor and those who will form a coalition of conscience." He advocated turning the Democratic Party into a party:

"For ending the war—NOW!!

"For granting amnesty—NOW!!

"For a just and human society for all—NOW!!

"For an end to racism in labor unions, in schools, in housing, in work—NOW!!

"For a guaranteed annual income—NOW!!"

By this time, Maxey's gallery supporters were joining in on each chorus of "NOW!!"

Maxey continued on with several more emphatic demands—a volunteer army, an elective abortion bill, equal rights for "our Indian and Chicano brothers," and an end to political conspiracy trials. The choruses of "NOW!!" reverberated through the massive, barnlike coliseum. In one last blast against Jackson, Maxey urged the passage of a resolution nicknamed the "Elks Club Resolution," banning elected officials from belonging to a lodge or club that practiced discrimination. Jackson was, rather famously, an Elk. Maxey concluded by saying, "To turn these priorities around is the reason I have chosen to run. It is with this faith and determination that the Democratic Party can get its rebirth, and it is with this faith and determination that I campaign."

Subsequent events at the next day's session gave Maxey even more faith. Jackson's appearance on Saturday hardly resembled a Jackson love-fest. Prochnau and Larsen described the scene vividly: "Jackson, a tense smile frozen on his broad Norwegian face, moved to the front of the stage, followed by Magnuson and their two wives. Below, the floor of the Coliseum convulsed. The peace delegates were marching now, intermingling with Jackson's people, jostling occasionally, shoving their placards up and down among the Jackson placards. The din grew, 'We Want Jackson!' clashing with a unified chant of 'Peace! Now!' . . . "

"Then the crowd pushed onto the stage itself. The senator was amid the demonstrators, friends, foes, and they moved their conflicting standards up and down, piston-like, in his face . . . A delegate elbowed his way to the microphone and, capturing his strategic target, amplified the peace chant. Briefly the sound of the Jackson Establishment was overwhelmed by the thunder of the dissidents—a cadenced 'Peace! Now!' . . . For a moment, Jackson was lost from view in the crowd of bodies. Then the hierarchy cut the microphone's power . . . gradually the roar subsided; the demonstrators left the stage and settled back into their seats."

Jackson's job was merely to introduce Magnuson, and his brief remarks were received neutrally. The convention roared when Magnuson finally got around to endorsing Jackson, yet later in the day it became clear that the anti-Jackson New Left platforms were winning the day. The convention approved planks calling for a Vietnam troop pullout and amnesty for draft dodgers. They even approved the Elks Club Resolution. "The senator's lieutenants lost every skirmish," wrote Prochnau and Larsen. The new head of the Washington Democratic Council went to the microphone and declared "a great victory." Maxey later claimed, with only moderate exaggeration, that he had "won the state Democratic Convention endorsement." If he had added the words "in effect," it would have been true.

Yet, like the King County victory, it was symbolic rather than practical. Jackson considered it another insult and it merely strengthened his resolve, according to Prochnau and Larsen, to make his primary victory even more crushing. Jackson still owned the vast middle of the electorate, and most Washington residents had become accustomed to senators with clout. If Maxey had ever really entertained thoughts of winning or at least forcing Jackson to surrender—"Remember what happened to Lyndon Johnson," Maxey once said—those thoughts began to fade through August. Mount Rainier is an extremely tall mountain to climb without shoes.

Just five days before the primary election on September 15, Maxey recruited an old political ally, Senator Eugene McCarthy, to give him one last uphill push. McCarthy arrived in Seattle for two last-minute Maxey rallies. McCarthy may have had his own motives for the appearances—he took this opportunity to tell the *Los Angeles Times* that he was available to run for president again in 1972. Still, McCarthy, no friend of Jackson's, delivered a speech that attacked him one more time for never seeing a defense-spending bill he didn't like: "Henry Jackson and some others in the Senate would only feel safe if the sky was black with strategic bombers, if there were so many nuclear submarines they were running into each other . . . They would still say they were not enough."

Then McCarthy got the audience laughing by speculating that the United States had other weapons gaps to worry about: The Amazon Indians have more poisoned darts than we do, he said. We're also short of catapults and crossbows! He said he hesitated to mention these things, because Jackson might offer them as an amendment to a military spending bill. But it was no longer 1968, and McCarthy had nowhere near the stature he held in those days. About twenty-five hundred people showed up to hear McCarthy and Maxey in Seattle that day, respectable but not near enough to indicate that Maxey was building momentum toward an upset. As for Jackson, he was unfazed by McCarthy's criticism. He told the *Washington Post* that McCarthy had "absolutely no standing in the Senate." Jackson slipped in a zinger when said he was "very proud of the fact that, during my term in the Senate, I opposed both McCarthys, Eugene and Joe."

In AP interviews right before the vote, Maxey tried to cast the election as "a referendum for or against the war in Indochina," saying that "if reluctant liberals who manifest distress about this condition get out and vote, I think we can win. If they stay home, we'll lose."

The *Spokesman-Review*'s editorial board expressed anxiety about an opposite problem: a low turnout that might aid Maxey and lead to a outcome beyond contemplation. "When a small vote occurs, the chances of freakish results are enhanced," said a September 15, 1970, editorial.

The paper needn't have worried. Maxey had too many strikes against him: his relative lack of experience and clout; his lack of big-time funding; his advocacy of eyebrow-raising programs such as a guaranteed annual income; and, of course, his color. By the time Election Day rolled around, he was lowering expectations by saying publicly that he expected about 10 percent of the vote, while privately he was hoping for 15 percent. When the results were in, Maxey ended up with about 13 percent, compared to 87 percent for Jackson. The final tally: about 497,000 for Jackson, about 79,000 for Maxey. It was, in fact, the crushing defeat that Jackson had wanted.

Maxey put the best possible spin on the outcome, saying that he was pleased to be over the 10 percent mark. He also blamed Washington's blanket primary system for the size of his defeat, claiming that "there was a deliberate pattern of Republican crossover voting" in the Democratic contest. Then he capped off a hostile campaign by refusing to endorse Jackson over his Republican opponent, a state legislator named Charles W. Elicker, in the general election. Maxey said he wanted his supporters to "do their own thing." Jackson hardly needed Maxey's endorsement. Jackson went on to defeat Elicker by a margin of 82 percent to 16 percent. This lopsided victory put Maxey's loss in at least a slightly more positive light. The black cat from Spokane had nearly outpolled the Republican candidate.

12

THE SEATTLE SEVEN CIRCUS

While Maxey was swinging away at Scoop Jackson, an anti-war protest in downtown Seattle was turning violent. This event would lead, nearly a year later, to what Maxey described as a "riotous, disgraceful courtroom event"—caused by his own clients. The Seattle Liberation Front, a loose collection of activists including ex-members of Students for a Democratic Society (SDS) and Weatherman, had organized a TDA (the day after) demonstration in front of Seattle's federal courthouse. The plan called for demonstrations to erupt all over the country on the day after the Chicago Seven defendants were hauled into jail. When "the day after" arrived on February 17, 1970, the Seattle Liberation Front issued a call for protesters to converge on the federal courthouse to "shut it down."

The protesters did more than that. A crowd estimated at about two thousand gathered at the courthouse doors waving red and black flags and carrying signs saying, "We Want This Courthouse" and "Stop the Courts." Seattle's acting police chief, Frank Moore, claimed that many of the protesters were bristling with more dangerous items than signs. "They were armed with paint bombs, tear gas, rocks, clubs, iron pipes," said Moore. "This was a declaration of war."

The Front had urged the mayor and governor to allow them to enter the courthouse without interference from police so they could express their "dissent from the present murderous policies of the government." This was a request that neither mayor nor governor had the power, much less the inclination, to grant. Police with loudspeakers ordered the angry crowd to disperse as they pressed in toward the courthouse and the nearby Federal Office Building. Some people in the crowd began throwing rocks, shattering the glass doors of the courthouse. Tear gas grenades were then touched off at the entrance, sending both demonstrators and police stumbling away from the doors. "I can't breathe, I can't breathe," the Associated Press quoted one police officer as saying as he fumbled for his gas mask. According to one report, tear gas wafted through the shattered doors, into the courthouse, and into an open elevator containing a federal prosecutor.

The demonstrators regrouped outside and hurled more rocks, breaking windows and splattering the exterior with orange and blue paint bombs. Then police decided they had seen enough. "Police squads, swinging riot sticks freely, rushed from the city's main library across the street from the rear of the courthouse and broke the crowd into smaller groups," reported the AP. "Officers half-carried and half-dragged one youth, whose face was bloodied, through the courthouse lobby. He was clubbed and kicked by officers who rushed him to a waiting elevator."

The crowd began chanting "Downtown! Downtown!" Some of the protesters took off running through Seattle's downtown streets. The police did not follow them right away; the riot squad was still busy with the crowd at the courthouse. Many of the protesters went on a rampage through the commercial center of Seattle, hurling rocks and iron pipes through storefront windows. "The officers played a game of catch-up with the demonstrators, chasing them from one location to another," said Police Chief Moore. The ensuing skirmishes left traffic snarled and dozens of store windows smashed through a ten-block downtown area. Finally, after two hours, it was all over. About seventy-nine protesters were arrested on various charges, including federal trespass, property damage, resisting arrest, and assaulting police officers. About twenty injuries were reported, but amazingly, none serious.

A Seattle public defender, John Darrah, called for an investigation into police brutality, but even he conceded that the authorities had been provoked. "The events may fairly be termed a violent assault upon the federal courthouse and an intentional confrontation with police," said Darrah. The American Civil Liberties Union condemned the violence, saying "irresponsible acts of violent demonstrators may jeopardize the rights of more responsible people to demonstrate peacefully." Even the Seattle Liberation Front delivered a kind of semi-apology, saying it regretted "the violence that occurred at our antiwar, antirepression rally." That didn't prevent eight people connected with the group from being indicted, on April 16, for conspiracy to riot and destroy public property. The press instantly dubbed them the Seattle Eight. When one of them, Michael Justesen, disappeared and went underground, they became the Seattle Seven—Chip Marshall (Charles Clark Marshall III), Michael Lerner, Jeff Dowd, Joe Kelly, Michael Abeles, Roger Lippman, and Susan Stern—the ringleaders of a raucous legal circus that lasted all the way through 1970.

Maxey ended up right in the middle of that circus. The group hired him to be one of their four attorneys because, as firebrand Stern wrote in *With the Weathermen*, her 1975 autobiography, "he was the most respected lawyer in the state of Washington, and he was black." He was also particularly prominent at the time, because he was in the middle of the Scoop Jackson race. "He was older [than the other defendants and lawyers], which made him venerable in the judge's eyes," wrote Stern. "He also had a good rapport with judges and since he was admittedly liberal and a staunch Democrat, he would offset the youthful enthusiasm of Jeff and Lee."

"Jeff and Lee" were two of the other lawyers, Jeff Steinborn and Lee Holley. The fourth lawyer was Michael Tigar, a hotshot young UCLA law professor who had worked on the Chicago Seven trial. The lawyers shared the entire group's defense, but for the record each defendant had one counsel; Maxey's official clients were Stern and Abeles. The group's two most articulate leaders, Chip Marshall and UW philosophy professor Michael Lerner, proceeded pro se—meaning they represented themselves—which "gave us more latitude to express the political issues at hand," as Lippman later explained.

"They were a bunch of really bright kids," said Lou Maxey. "But I can say this without fear of contradiction: Carl was the only attorney there who was really serious about winning the case." Steinborn, who went on to have a prominent Seattle practice, said that "Carl was the one guy who lent a practical hand to the team. He is the one who showed at the meetings and did the trial preparations. I was right out of law school and didn't know what the hell was going on." Maxey believed from the beginning that the case was winnable, despite the fact that at least one of the Seattle Seven defendants unquestionably had joined enthusiastically in the TDA violence. Stern had been one of those armed with iron pipes. "I ran for several blocks smashing windows, feeling that elation once again as the glass gave beneath my blows," she wrote in her book. "In one glorious instant, I saw [a fellow rioter] throw a pipe right through the windshield of a lone pig car; the windshield shattered and the car careened crazily." Others, including Lerner, the organizer of the Seattle Liberation Front, had been committed to a peaceful demonstration, much to Stern's disgust. "They would describe it as educational and peaceful," she wrote. "They would discourage any idea of violence. Abeles and I were in complete agreement; destroy the Federal Courthouse, off the pigs."

U.S. attorney Stan Pitkin faced a more difficult question entirely in proving that the defendants were truly guilty of conspiracy to incite a riot. The Seattle Liberation Front was a loosely affiliated and in many ways dysfunctional group. The core of the group—Marshall, Dowd (invariably called "The Dude"), Abeles, and Kelly—were brand new to Seattle. They were known variously as the Sundance Collective, after their favorite outlaw, or the Ithaca Boys, because they had just arrived from Cornell. Many people came to the Front's meetings and crashed at their houses—some were violence-prone ex-Weathermen like Stern and some were more partial to Lerner and Marshall's focus on education and organization. At planning meetings, everybody had a chance to say their piece—rarely was any consensus reached. They "organized" the TDA by issuing manifestos, announcing when and where to gather, and by handing out flyers at high schools and on the Ave (the main drag) in the University District. Yet whether they were capable of willing a crowd of two thousand, including many anarchists and Weathermen, to do their bidding—that was harder to swallow.

Some of the "conspirators" were not even present at the Seattle TDA protest. Lippman had moved to San Francisco a month earlier and was at the Berkeley protest. Kelly had been waylaid in Chicago by legal troubles from previous incidents and didn't show up in Seattle until after the demonstration. "Several of [us] didn't even know each other," wrote Lippman in a 1990 account. "I didn't meet Abeles until after the indictment. Susan Stern, who had been an activist for several years, had differences with most of the defendants, as did I. Mike Lerner was visiting professor of philosophy at the University of Washington. As far as I could tell, none of the other defendants got along with him." Stern echoed these sentiments: "I detested Roger Lippman, I detested Mike Lerner," she wrote later. "I detested Mike Tigar and Lee Holley."

With this kind of antipathy and dysfunction, planning a legal strategy was a challenge for Maxey and the other lawyers. "Nobody agreed on anything," wrote Stern. "Everybody had their own idea about everything. According to communistic principles everybody had to be heard. You couldn't order someone to shut the fuck up and slug him, like I wanted to do with Lerner and Lippman just about every meeting." Maxey, however, managed to command their respect. "From my standpoint, he was the only adult in the trial except for me," said Lerner thirty-six years later. "And I wasn't much of an adult." Kelly said in a later interview that "Maxey was the father, uncle and brother figure to all of us, particularly Stern and the four of us from Ithaca. He was with us, in that he thought we were being prosecuted unfairly and persecuted by the government to quash antiwar activity. But he was always trying to be a calming influence on us. He didn't try to jerk the reins in on us real hard. He just told us, look, we can win in front of the jury."

As for Stern, she said that Maxey treated her "like a lovable but unruly daughter." Unruly, yes. Lovable? Well . . . Stern, never the most stable of personalities, was particularly out of control that summer between her arrest and the trial. She says in her autobiography that she and her friend Anne Anderson called themselves the Macho Mamas. "We drugged. We drank. We roared. We swaggered. We were crude and vulgar. We fucked everything we could get our hands on. We took a hit of acid and THC every day . . . My rallying cry was, 'Sex, dope and violence.' Everywhere I went the people loved me." Maxey later wrote, "It was the most difficult case that I have tried, because of the personalities of the defendants." Matters were not helped by the fact that some of them were often stoned. Various kinds of dope were ever-present; Stern was a serious user of barbiturates, along with acid and THC. "We would go to their house in the University District and we didn't have to say a word to each other: don't smoke the joints," said Lou. "No shit. They [the defendants] thought they were so tough. But after we would leave their house, we would go out to after-hours clubs in the Central District that they could never have imagined."

One of the major points of dispute was whether to turn the trial into Chicago Seven–style political theater or whether to simply try to win the case. There was no question about where Maxey stood. "Carl Maxey disagreed with all of the defendants about trial tactics," wrote Stern. "The lawyers were afraid of a circus, like the Chicago 7 trial; the defendants wanted to go down with a bang and not a whimper." The pretrial maneuvering presaged what was in store. The trial venue had been moved to the federal courthouse in Tacoma, so in October the Seattle Seven issued a list of demands for the Tacoma mayor. For one thing, they wanted food, housing, and medical care provided for the masses of demonstrators expected outside the courthouse every day. Lerner also issued a demand that there be "day-to-day coverage of the trial" by newspapers and TV. This ultimatum turned out to be hardly necessary. Tigar appeared on the *Dick Cavett Show* before the trial even started. As the case progressed, it continued to make head-lines all over the country.

In November, Chip Marshall demanded that Judge George Boldt disqualify himself because he belonged to the Tacoma Club and the Shriners and thus could not conduct an impartial trial. Boldt found "no basis in fact or in law" for the motion. Lerner declared that the entire "federal judiciary had dirty hands" concerning its failure to stop the war. So he requested that a judge from a "neutral nation"—possibly Sweden, a third-world country, or the United Nations—hear the case. This, too, was denied. Judge Boldt did approve a more urgent motion—a last-minute postponement of the trial. Stern had discovered just days before that she was pregnant. She wanted to have an abortion and then have time to recover.

Maxey tried to talk her out of the abortion, according to Stern. "Listen, Susan," she quoted Maxey as telling her in a fatherly manner, "if we postponed the trial now for you to have an abortion, then the judge might sequester the jury over Christmas vacation and those people are going to be pretty damn mad at you defendants if they can't be home for Christmas . . . It will look good in the courtroom to have you come in, glowing and pregnant, maybe with some knitting." Stern wanted none of it. Eventually, the lawyers worked out a deal with Boldt to postpone the trial for two weeks while Stern had her abortion. The trial began on November 23, and the three-week delay was a "godsend," according to Stern, since they had been totally unprepared for the original trial date. She said they all prepared for the trial with a "new seriousness"—although for this group "serious" was relative. They continued to party hard most nights.

Two days before the trial opened, prosecutor Pitkin promised that there would be no Chicago Seven–style uproar. Lerner agreed, telling United Press International (UPI) that the defendants had no intention of turning the case into a media spectacle. "We are very different from the Chicago Seven," said Lerner, who went on to explain that the Seattle Seven were "serious organizers" as opposed to "media stars." However, the UPI noted with considerable foresight that if the defendants continued to insist that the Vietnam War—and the federal court's complicity in it—were the real issues of the trial, it "could result in conflict with Judge Boldt."

In its opening statements, the government painted the Seattle Seven as having encouraged violence during planning meetings and speeches. Then the defendants carefully organized a two-pronged plan of attack at the courthouse that day. The prosecutor said one group converged with the other, by design, and started attacking the courthouse. The actual event was far more chaotic and disorganized than this and failed to take into account that at least two of the conspirators, Lippman and Kelly, weren't even present.

Maxey, along with Lerner and Marshall, delivered the opening statements for the defense. Marshall said "there was no conspiracy because there was no need for one." People were rioting all over the country of their own volition. Maxey began his remarks by making a joke to the jury about the outmoded federal courthouse in Tacoma. "The next time I run for political office I am going to offer a better and newer courthouse to the people in Tacoma," he said, drawing a laugh. Maxey then quickly established the theme of his argument, saying, "The evidence will show that this was a demonstration called by the people of the United States," not any group of seven. He asserted that one of the real reasons for the prosecution was "to crush youth and put them on notice that no one can exercise these very things that they talk about—peace and freedom." Maxey told the jury that the true rhetoric of incitement was not coming from his defendants, but from the Nixon administration, which had characterized protesters as "peace snobs" and "long-haired rascals," and he asked, "Well, how many inciting speeches has Spiro Agnew made, anyway?" Mostly, Maxey hammered away on the idea that a "conspiracy" between the defendants was strictly imaginary.

The trial continued routinely enough in its first several days. Yet it was already clear that this was not a trial marked by decorum. Some defendants had a habit of shouting out remarks and comments—Dowd once accused the judge of being "deaf, dumb and blind," for example. Boldt repeatedly admonished the defendants for making "contumacious" remarks. Boldt also spent a lot of time attempting to steer Lerner's and Marshall's remarks away from Vietnam and back to the facts of the case. The judge lectured the defendants repeatedly about getting to the courtroom on time in the morning and eventually gave them a 9:00 A.M. deadline. Forebodingly, some touchy confrontations took place over how to handle the Seattle Seven's large contingent of supporters, bused in from Seattle. They clogged the gallery, laughing, jeering, and applauding. After a while, Boldt ordered their numbers restricted; they had to wait outside in the rain. The Seattle Seven vociferously demanded, to no avail, that their supporters be allowed inside the courthouse.

Occasional moments of comedy punctuated the proceedings. Stern said she kept "nibbling the ear" of young lawyer Steinborn at the defense table because she was "terribly sexually attracted to him." Maxey didn't think that played well with the jury. "Maxey and Tigar and Lerner complained to both of us repeatedly, but we never stopped," she said. She also said that the defendants routinely got stoned in the defense room. "Maxey tried to restrain us, Tigar protested, but we ignored them; after all, it was our trial," wrote Stern. "Carl wasn't really very happy at all," said Lou. "I mean, they were smoking dope in the defense room!" At one point, Stern delivered a lengthy lecture protesting the prosecutor's use of the word "gal." She told the judge it was the same as "calling a black man a nigger." At another point, Dowd presented a pair of binoculars to Judge Boldt because of his repeated difficulties in telling the defendants apart. One defendant accused the judge of being like "a good German," to which Boldt blandly replied that he was actually of Danish descent. "Well, then something's rotten in Denmark," retorted Stern.

But the comedy ended abruptly when prosecutor Pitkin announced he had a surprise star witness, an undercover FBI informant who had infiltrated the Weathermen, the SDS, and the Seattle Liberation Front. "The few minutes while we were waiting for the witness to make his appearance were awful; who of our friends, lovers, acquaintances, was an informer, a pig?" wrote Stern. The witness was Horace "Red" Parker, a young "activist" and acquaintance of both Stern and Lippman. Lippman later wrote that Parker had not been particularly trusted, but "nevertheless there was shock in the courtroom that day when we learned he had become a paid FBI informer."

Parker was on the stand for two days, detailing a sordid story of drugs, explosives, guns, Marxism, armed struggle, and attempts by the Weathermen to incite high-school kids to riot. He quoted Abeles as passing out TDA armbands and saying, "If the pigs try and stop us—kill them." At this, according to Stern, the prosecutor turned and smiled at the jury. They did not seem amused. "I tried to see us from their point of view, absorbing that list of incitement and violence," wrote Stern. "I could see that we must look pretty horrendous to these staunch middle-class Tacomans."

The defendants and lawyers met far into the night to work out a strategy to discredit Parker's damaging—to say the least—testimony. Maxey took the lead in the cross-examination. He lambasted the serious discrepancies between Parker's testimony and his written report. For instance, in his report Parker had credited someone else, not Abeles, with the line, "If the pigs try and stop us—kill them." Stern recounted that Maxey went about "expertly building his questions, [and] he made it clear that Red Parker was not always so reliable in his reporting." Maxey also showed that much of Parker's testimony had nothing to do with the TDA planning and protest and that he had been involved mainly with people who were not even defendants in the case. Maxey actually managed to elicit a critical admission from Parker. Parker had been intent on painting the entire group with the Weatherman brush and he claimed to have intimate knowledge of all of the defendants. Yet Maxey finally got Parker to admit that he actually knew only Lippman and Stern (both former Weathermen) and that he barely knew Lerner and the Ithaca Boys—the core of the Seattle Liberation Front—at all.

It was up to Marshall, acting as his own attorney, to administer the coup de grâce in cross-examination. First he got Parker to admit that he was taking so many drugs during his time with the Weathermen that he himself had been concerned about being addicted to both codeine and speed. Then he made Parker admit that he had encouraged people, as part of his cover, to violate laws—and that the FBI had directed him to do so. Parker admitted he brought a gun to one of the houses and taught people to shoot. Finally, Marshall elicited the following exchange, recorded in the trial transcript:

Marshall: It's very important that people like us be brought to justice, isn't that correct? I mean, you feel very strongly that we are bad people and should be brought to justice?

Parker: That's one way of putting it.

Marshall: All right. So I mean, you would go to almost, not any length, obviously not killing somebody, but almost any length of trickery to bring us to justice?

Parker: Yes, any length.

Marshall: Any length—and for months and months you took people who thought perhaps that you were their friend, and you were willing to lie to them in order to get us, isn't that correct?

Parker: That is absolutely correct.

. . .

Marshall: You are willing to go, as you say, to any length to get us?

Parker: That's correct.

Marshall: Do you still feel that way?

Parker: Yes.

Marshall: You were willing to lie to get us?

Parker: Yes.

Marshall: [Turning to look at jury] That's what he said.

The prosecutor, according to Stern, just put his head in his hands. The defendants' supporters in the gallery applauded and shrieked. It was the sound of Parker's credibility being sucked right out through the courtroom doors. The prosecution appeared to be in disarray after that, and the trial was delayed when the prosecution was not ready to present its next witness. "Once Parker was discredited, that was the end of the prosecution's case," said Kelly years later. "But we weren't smart enough to sit down and keep our mouths shut. We were just young and impetuous."

Just when victory seemed assured, the Seattle Seven managed to touch off a procedural stick of dynamite over a side issue: those precious demonstrators outside the courthouse. On December 10, two days after Parker left the stand, the defendants arrived at the courthouse to find their supporters standing outside in the cold rain. The federal marshal refused to let them into the vestibule of the courthouse. A heated argument ensued between the six "boys" (Stern was absent that day because of illness) and the marshal. Dowd, The Dude, ran into the courthouse and up to the judge's chambers to demand a hearing. He began pounding away so hard on the judge's door that, according to Boldt, "it could be heard in the courtroom and it almost broke the door." Boldt opened the door only long enough to see Dowd standing there, and then he turned around and went back to his chamber. A bailiff later ushered the angry Dowd and Holley into Boldt's chamber, where the judge promptly cited Dowd for contempt.

Dowd and the other defendants, still seething, retreated to the defense room and resolved not to budge until Boldt agreed to a hearing about the spectators. So when the judge arrived at the courtroom to open the morning's proceedings, there was only one man sitting at the defense table: Carl Maxey. "I have been here since 9 o'clock," Maxey told the court. "As a matter of fact, I have been the only guy that's been here except the reporter." Why wasn't he in the defense room, showing solidarity with his clients? "It wasn't a matter of disagreement with us," said Lippman in a later interview. "He was there because that was his role as he saw it: to represent us in the courtroom and play the role of what you might call the establishment lawyer. Everybody was caught up in something quite beyond our control and nobody knew what to make of it. Everybody went with their own instincts, and that was his."

Boldt called the jury into the courtroom and ordered the bailiff to fetch the defendants. The bailiff came back empty-handed. Tigar and the other lawyers showed up and asked that Dowd be granted a hearing. Boldt refused and once again sent the bailiff down to the defense room. The bailiff came back and told the judge the defendants had locked themselves in. Boldt, with rising ire, then stomped to the defense room, his robes flying behind him, followed by a retinue of lawyers. Just then, the defendants opened the door. A wave of marijuana smoke ("an unction for the frenetic Dude," wrote Stern) rolled out and hit Boldt right in the nostrils. "Shouts from the hallway could be heard in the courtroom," reported Jack Wilkins and Robert Boxberger of the *Tacoma News Tribune*. "Loud and boisterous epithets and obscenities were repeatedly shouted," said Boldt later.

Boldt ordered the defendants into the courtroom and Chip Marshall obeyed all too enthusiastically. Marshall galloped past Boldt, down the hall, and entered the courtroom first. Boldt "walked rapidly," in his words, to his chambers and then arrived, panting, at the bench. He was greeted by the sight of Marshall, leaning against the jury box, explaining that the whole thing was the court's fault.

"We would like to explain to the jury why we refused to come in at the beginning of this trial," Marshall told the jury.

"Be silent, Mr. Marshall," boomed Boldt.

"The judge ordered him, Jeff Dowd, for contempt and we should have a hearing—," continued Marshall.

"Mr. Marshall, please be silent!"

Finally, Boldt, at the end of his rope, dismissed the jury, declared a mistrial, and charged every defendant with contempt of court (except the absent Stern). "It is clear, and who could doubt, it is the purpose and intent of the defendants to totally disobey the admonishments of the court," said Boldt. He also said he had "grave doubts that the jury could continue unbiased" after the defendants' shenanigans. Boldt summed up by declaring the entire debacle to be the "most degrading and outrageous contempt of court I have ever seen." But he didn't know what would happen four days later.

On Monday, December 14, Boldt called the defendants back into court to sentence them for contempt. The defendants were defiant, convinced that the entire "misunderstanding" had merely been the government's way of salvaging a case it had clearly lost. "A trap was set and we walked into it," said Lippman in his published account. After Boldt read their contempt citations aloud, each of the defendants, except Lerner, ripped their citations into pieces and flung them in the air.

"That's what we think of it," said Kelly, tossing his confetti.

"Pick up the garbage, judge," said Marshall.

Lerner contented himself with claiming that Boldt had gone "berserk." Dowd unveiled a Nazi flag and said it should replace the U.S. flag, which "was born in revolution." Dowd handed the Nazi flag to Abeles who walked up and threw it at the judge. Boldt said testily, "Stay back of the bar, see that the defendants stay back of the counsel table." He had marshals whisk the swastika flag out of the courtroom.

Maxey, in his statement, was clearly disheartened and deeply conflicted by the entire mess. He told the judge he certainly did not approve of a man "sitting with his feet on the counsel table or using vulgarity in the hallways or courtroom." He did not agree with his defendants' overarching concern over having their boisterous supporters in the courtroom. He said they needed them "like a hole in the head." But he tried to put the best face on it for his clients. "Mr. Tigar says that we are watching a new society being born," said Maxey. "I guess we are. The beginning of the society is certainly a tumultuous experience . . . But I think, in the main, most of it was not just spurious vulgarity. It was the sincere, very sincere attempts on the part of these young people to communicate to you." He asked the court to take into account their youth and inexperience and to show some compassion in their sentencing. They would learn a valuable moral lesson. "Maybe the new generation of revolutionaries will rise up and [discover] some compassion and understanding of other people," he said. Maxey ended by saying he doubted that he would be on the defense team when the case was retried.

Then it was Stern's turn. Stern was in the awkward position of being the only one of the seven not cited for contempt. This, she felt, would not do—not do at all. "It's not that I wanted to go to jail; it's just that I wanted the judge to know that I was just as contemptuous of him as the boys were, that women could hate just as much, could be just as disruptive and deaf to authority," she wrote. "I was caught up in the drama of it all. To be a defendant in a famous conspiracy trial and not go to jail—what a farcical anti-climax." So, as described by the UPI, when all of the boys and the lawyers finished making their statements, "Mrs. Stern strode up to the podium, took a wad of gum out of her mouth and said: 'Let me state for the record I am in contempt of this court.'" The judge told her to sit down and be silent. She would not. He told her to sit down again. She would not. Then he told her that there would be penalties if she defied his order, but if she wanted to speak in defiance of his order, to go ahead.

She launched into a twenty-minute speech, which began with her thanking Maxey for defending her as best he could. "Although Carl Maxey and I have divergent views upon what kind of order should exist in a court, that I don't recognize personally, I respect his opinions as to those views," said Stern. "I respect him as a man. I'm still glad he was my attorney, I still believe in his desire to make sure that myself and my co-defendants do not end up in jail." But, she said, only she personally could express her feelings and ideals so that the jury could understand.

Then she proceeded to blame America and its legal system—and by extension, the judge—for all of the Vietnamese people who are "dead, napalmed by the system you purport to keep in order." She went on, "I say it is you burning those children, men and women . . . Give them back to me, give all the Vietnamese men, women and children who have been killed back to me and let them sit in this courtroom and let's ask them what they think." She told Boldt that the onus of the My Lai massacre was on his shoulders. She then compared him to Pontius Pilate, having "washed his hands" of Vietnam and the American ghettos. She said that after the revolution there would be a different kind of humanity and "it won't include people like you."

Finally, Boldt ordered her to stop, saying she had "consumed more time than any other speaker." She attempted to conclude by talking "about the mistrial at which I was not present." Boldt informed her that she "knew nothing about it" and ordered her to conclude. She would not. He ordered her three more times to conclude.

"She will if you will shut up for a few minutes," shouted Abeles.

"You have been in contempt continually throughout this diatribe," Boldt finally told her. "I now hereby find you in contempt."

"You are in contempt of the Vietnamese people!" shouted Dowd.

Stern announced that she wanted to continue and that "they will have to drag me off to stop me." The judge replied, "If that is necessary—"

Dowd, overwrought, shouted at the judge, "Come on, let's see it, man! Let's see them drag her off. I want to see the sight of those killers dragging off a woman who has just got out of the hospital two days ago. And you, you old killer! You're so bloody it's unbelievable!" By now most of the defendants were shouting. Marshall announced that he was "walking out of the courtroom" and was ordered by the judge to stay put. Abeles said, "You're a judge of justice? My ass, you're a justice."

Boldt then ordered twenty federal marshals into the room; they had been waiting in a room next door. They grabbed Stern from behind and started to drag her out of the courtroom. Most of the defendants and some of the lawyers—but not Maxey—rushed forward and began struggling with the marshals, trying to get them off Stern. Tigar caught a shot of mace right in the face. Pandemonium broke loose. Abeles jumped on a marshal's back. Dowd was jumping up and down, shouting, "Kill the kid! Kill the kid! Kill the kid! Kill the kid! Kill the kid! Kill the kid!"

"I was swinging with my arms," wrote Stern. "Steinborn later told me I broke a pig's nose. I saw a hulking marshal grab Joe by the balls and drag him across the courtroom. I saw another slug Abeles and drag him away." Some of the supporters in the gallery also joined in the fight and were forcibly evicted. The marshals wrestled several of the defendants to the floor and handcuffed them. The judge left the bench shortly after the fight started but later said that "more than a half-hour of riotous conduct" continued in the courtroom and that he could hear it from his chambers.

What did Maxey do in the middle of all of this? Maxey always found it hard to stay aloof from a fight, but in this case, he managed. "I think he just stood here in amazement, as did I," said Lerner, the only defendant who did not join in the fight. "We couldn't believe what we were seeing." One thing is clear from the judge's later remarks: Maxey did what he could to restrain his clients. Maxey knew no good would come from slugging a federal marshal, and he was right about that. About an hour later, Boldt had the handcuffed defendants brought back into the courtroom for the reading of a new set of contempt citations, these stemming from the brawl. The defendants made further outraged statements; Dowd called the judge "a lying dog."

By this time, Boldt certainly had no interest in teaching lessons about compassion to revolutionaries. He handed down new six-month contempt sentences to all of the defendants except Lerner, who apparently had never left his chair. Boldt, clearly shaken by the events of the day, said the jail time would do them good. They could "reflect upon their past misconduct and what it has brought them." He continued, "I believe Divine Providence may have given this court, and others, guidance to an effective solution of disruptive trials. I pray it may be so."

Then Boldt ordered that their sentences be served right away, before a new trial on the original conspiracy charges would begin. Five of the defendants now faced yearlong jail terms on two contempt charges each; Lerner and Stern faced six-month terms on one charge each.

Boldt also administered what one reporter called a "verbal slap" at lawyers Tigar, Holley, and Steinborn. Boldt said they had repeatedly refused to restrain their clients from misconduct. The judge had good words for only one man on the defense team: Carl Maxey. "Mr. Maxey at no time was seen or heard to conduct himself other than within proper professional conduct," said Boldt in one of his contempt certificates. "The judge finds that in the particular circumstances in which he was situated, Mr. Maxey did everything he reasonably could to prevent or restrain his clients and other defendants from misconduct and to assist the judge's efforts toward a fair, orderly and expeditious trial."

All seven defendants were taken immediately to the Tacoma City Jail. The next day, Boldt denied bail, despite pleas from Maxey. Boldt ruled that the defendants were likely to go underground if released; besides, he said he had information that they had threatened Boldt and the court with violence. Within days, the defendants were scattered around federal prisons throughout the West. "Jeff [Dowd] and I received a hero's welcome from the prisoners at McNeil Island," wrote Lippman. "They had been following the trial on TV news and newspapers . . . More than one person who had been sentenced to 25 years by Judge Boldt said, 'I wish I'd done that!'" The Seattle Seven had become a cause célèbre in liberal circles. *The Nation* magazine ran a story about the trial titled, "The Orderly Perversion of Justice." The *New York Review of Books* printed a letter soliciting donations to the defense fund.

The seven were in jail about a month before Maxey and the other lawyers finally convinced the U.S. Ninth Circuit Court of Appeals to grant bail of twenty-five thousand dollars each. By February of 1971, the seven were all out on bail and they had filed an appeal of the contempt sentences. In March, Maxey invited all of the defendants to Spokane to discuss strategy—and to watch the most famous draft evader in America, Muhammad Ali. "Carl bought tickets to the Ali/ Frazier fight on the big screen in Spokane and called us a week ahead and said, 'Come on over, we're having dinner at my house and then we'll watch the fight,'" said Kelly later. "We just jumped at the chance."

In November of 1971, the court of appeals overruled the contempt charges on the grounds that Boldt had not been specific enough in his contempt citations. The *Spokane Daily Chronicle* editorialized that Boldt "must have paused and gasped in disbelief" when he heard about the reversal. The government decided to renew the contempt charges, this time with a judge less emotionally involved. In February of 1972, the case was sent to U.S. District Court judge Russell Smith of Missoula, Montana. "Carl said, 'Well, you've got yourself your goddamn third-world country,'" recalled Lou with a laugh.

The defendants decided to go with only one lawyer this time: Maxey. Despite his earlier vow to be done with the case, he agreed to take it on. The defendants finally realized that what they needed most was experience and competence. "He was a very established figure with a very solid reputation in the bar," said Lippman in a later interview. "He was someone who could relate to the court and who the court could relate to." That was key, because the defendants decided that they wanted to cut a deal. No Montana trial ever materialized; Maxey arranged a plea-bargain solution in Seattle with the judge and prosecutors. "The political situation at the time did not support another political trial, and it would have ended up the way the first one did, given our personalities," said Lippman. "So we agreed to plead no contest and the prosecution agreed not to make a case."

Seattle journalist Walt Crowley was there and described the scene in his 1995 book, *Rites of Passage: A Memoir of the Sixties in Seattle*: "There was no cheering crowd, no restless masses waiting outside the courthouse, not even any unusual degree of security. Just seven very nervous young people who had decided that the legal limbo of their lives was a worse prison than anything the Feds had." Stern wrote in her journal that day, "We are the picture of obedience. We are deplorable. It's a disgrace, but we grit our teeth and get on with the farce."

Judge Smith gave them reduced sentences, ranging from one month to five months. Lerner didn't even have to return to jail because credit was given for time already served. In 1973, when all had finally completed their terms, the government announced that it would not refile the original conspiracy charges. The Seattle Seven case was closed. They never served a lick of time for the Seattle antiwar riot; they served time only on the contempt charges stemming from the courtroom brawl.

Marshall went on to work in real-estate development. Dowd became a Hollywood producer and the inspiration for "The Dude" in the film, *The Big Lebowski*. Lerner became a rabbi and well-known author on liberal Judaism and the religious Left. Lippman did energy-conservation research in Seattle. Kelly became a federal employee—a fisheries biologist for the Bureau of Land Management near Wenatchee, Washington. He remained close to Maxey until Maxey's death. "I kept in touch with Carl and regularly had dinner, drinks, and watched old fight tapes with him over the next twenty-five years," said Kelly. "Carl never failed to remind me, every time I saw him, that if we'd have listened to him we probably wouldn't have gone to jail and we probably would have had a victory in the courtroom."

Stern wrote her sensational memoir, *With the Weathermen*, in 1975 and sent a copy to Carl and Lou Maxey with the following inscription: "Thank you, Carl especially, for being there when I needed you so many times, so many unthanked times, now finally in ink, thank you. I love you both." A year later, in 1976, Stern died of an "apparent heart seizure" during an extended session in a Seattle sauna. She was thirty-three.

When the government finally slammed the case file closed, Maxey publicly summed up his feelings: "I am pleased to see that the government had determined not to re-prosecute. But there are two matters of grave personal concern to me: The defendants' intemperate conduct and the government's bringing this case of dubious merit in the first place. I'm glad it's over."

13

THE MAXEY TEMPER

Maxey remained totally committed all of his life to non-violence as a way of fomenting social change, yet on a personal level the ex-boxer had a strong fighting streak—which made his forbearance in the Seattle Seven melee all the more remarkable. He had what his colleagues called the Maxey temper. "My dad was a pretty fiery person," said Bevan. "Very loving, very giving, fun to be around. But I mean, he was very committed and he had a short fuse. Anybody who talks honestly about him will tell you about that." Pat Stiley agreed: "The effects of racism were always simmering not too far under the surface for Carl. The pent-up anger was so well pent-up, but it had to go out someplace, sometime, somehow. And it did, in a variety of ways."

Spokane attorney Martin L. Salina could certainly testify to that. Once, Maxey and Salina were arguing on the phone. Maxey's anger kept ratcheting higher. "We had a lot of custody disputes and he would often end up yelling at me and hanging up," said Salina. "This time, he uttered an unkind expletive, and I said something like, 'Back at you, big fella.'" Maxey, livid, offered to come over and kick Salina's ass. Salina said fine. Maxey jumped in his car, drove to the attorney's office and stood fuming in the reception area. One of Salina's partners, Joe Delay, tried to mediate. But Maxey lost control. "By gosh, he crossed the room and threw a punch and it grazed my cheek," said Salina. "Joe collared him and ushered him out."

"Thank God he didn't file charges," said Bevan later. "Oh, God no," said Salina, when asked if he ever considered it. "Absolutely not. I did not take it personally. It blew over rather rapidly." About ten years after this event, Salina wrote Maxey a letter in which he said that even though they had "had their ups and downs over the years . . . you have been a role model for me in many areas." Many years later, Salina said, "Carl was a complicated guy. A real complicated guy. He was a tremendous mentor. But I was starting to challenge him in the courtroom and he saw it coming and didn't want another competitor. But once we had our little visit, that ended. I ended up being a huge, respectful member of his fan club."

Not everyone was so forgiving. Maxey's many detractors saw his belligerence as a sign of his hypocrisy. In public, he wore a virtuous mantle of King-like pacifism; in private, he could be mean, aggressive, and downright bullying. The truth is, he had struggled since childhood with these two opposing parts of his personality. There was the Carl who despised the orphanage bullies and then there was the Carl who knew how to pound opponents into submission. Understanding Maxey means understanding how he constantly attempted to reconcile these two impulses. For instance, when he was a champion boxer he discovered he could dominate almost every opponent. But what did he take the most pride in? The fact that he had the discipline not to "addle somebody's brains." When the Seattle Seven melee broke out, he almost certainly understood the brash anger behind it. Yet he had the discipline—and the respect for the courtroom—to stay put. The tension between these two parts of his personality may even help us understand his deep respect for King's nonviolent principles. For the weak and submissive, nonviolence might come naturally. But for the strong and aggressive, it takes discipline. It is indeed, as King wrote, "not a method for cowards."

So when Maxey aimed that punch at Salina's nose, it wasn't a sign of hypocrisy. It was a sign that sometimes Maxey's discipline failed him. The most surprising thing is that it didn't fail more often. He needed to constantly work off his aggressive tension; even his colleagues in his law office understood that. That's why, right after the punching incident, the secretaries bought Maxey a new piece of office décor: a punching bag. It was installed in a corner of his office and he often used it to channel his anger. "I'd be in there taking dictation and he'd get more mad and more mad and he'd really start going on that punching bag," remembered Marsha Dornquast. "There was an almost childlike quality about Carl," said Stiley. "Quick temper, quick forgiveness, his emotions written all over him at all times. Which I think had to do with his upbringing, being an orphan."

Bevan said Maxey was famous at the law firm for throwing prospective clients out of his office if they "came in with a bad attitude or wanted to hire him for all the wrong reasons or be disrespectful." Bevan remarked, "He'd toss 'em out. I don't mean he'd grab them by the neck, but he'd say, 'Get out.' Sure, it was embarrassing to us and we were like, 'What has dad done now?' But I can't think of an occasion when he wasn't right." Maxey also had a habit of dictating angry letters when he was riled—letters to newspapers, clients, other lawyers. His secretary followed an office rule: she was instructed to hold those letters for twenty-four hours until she could stick them under his nose and say, "Did you really want to say this?" Usually, the answer was no—although, when he reached his sixties and seventies, the answer more often became, "You're goddamn right."

Maxey's office at his law firm became notorious for intimidating décor in addition to the punching bag: historic weapons, including spears, firearms, and a cudgel with a spiked iron ball on a chain. He also made no secret of the fact that he kept guns at home and he loved going out to the range to fire them. This made him feel at least slightly less vulnerable when the racial threats arrived. Dornquast said that when he got a new gun, he used to come out to their place in the boondocks and fire off the whole magazine in practically one deafening burst.

Bevan said he believed that his father's righteous anger was a fundamental part of what made him a success. He could never have struggled up from nowhere without it. "That anger, if he didn't have it, people would have walked right over the top of him," said Bevan. Maxey usually managed to channel that anger into a weapon just as potent—humor. Judge John Schultheis once related a discussion he and Maxey had in chambers after Maxey learned his client would get a particularly stiff sentence:

Maxey: What am I supposed to tell my client?

Schultheis: Tell him the judge is a stupid S.O.B.

Maxey: I already told him that.

As Bevan later said, "My dad was the only one who could call you a son of a bitch, and you'd *like* it."

Stiley said that in his earlier years with Carl—the late 1960s and early 1970s—he was astonished by how well Maxey kept his anger in check, at least publicly. Maxey remained, in some ways, the little boy who had smiled when the rake was broken over his head. "People were lucky they didn't get their blocks knocked off for some of the racist things they would say in his presence," said Stiley. "But he wouldn't react. But in the evening, he'd say, 'Did you hear what that S.O.B. said? Goddamn, Pat, you want to throttle the guy.' . . . Sometimes, he'd be almost in tears."

In the early 1970s, Maxey's stress level shot even higher than usual because of profound changes in his personal life. Merrie Lou Douglas had accompanied him to those Seattle Seven meetings not because she worked for Maxey—she worked in an advertising agency—but because they had become a couple. The relationship began way back in 1964, just months after they met. Lou, as Carl began calling her, was on exactly the same wavelength as Carl when it came to politics and activism. Her father, Louis H. Douglas, was a professor of political science at Kansas State University in Manhattan and her mother was a teacher at Manhattan High School. This white family was extremely outspoken on the subject of racial equality and integration. In fact, the local Klan or its sympathizers burned crosses on their front lawn more than once. Her father told the *Manhattan Mercury* that he believed the cross burnings were because "of my whole family's friendliness and association with minority races, and in particular, my daughter's association with them."

"This was the early 1960s in Kansas, and it was inhuman," said Lou. "These were some bad, bad days. I remember [white] soldiers from Fort Riley chasing me in a car because they knew I was from the

Douglas family." She said that she was harassed so unrelentingly that she left high school early and enrolled in Kansas State as a sixteen-year-old. Then, after one year, she was advised to leave the university for the same reasons. "They said, 'It would be better if you left,'" said Lou. "So my mother put me in a car and drove me across the West, trying to find a school that would take me, because I had college credits but I still didn't have a high-school diploma. We went through Colorado and all of those little schools in California. And then we went to Pullman, and, bingo! I was enrolled."

Washington State University agreed to take her Kansas State credits and apply them to high school, which meant that they considered her a high-school graduate. She entered as a freshman and quickly became involved in the YWCA as the head of its race relations committee. "I liked to think of it as the most radical group on campus," said Lou. "And it was, I'm not kidding. They sponsored the voter-registration project I went on in Nashville during the summer of 1963." She spent eight weeks in Tennessee registering black voters and when she returned she told the *Lewiston (ID) Tribune* that she wanted to remain active in social causes for the rest of her life. "Once you get committed, there really is no way out," she was quoted as saying. "Besides, I don't want to get out."

She met Maxey in Pullman when her group invited him to speak in 1963. Then, in 1964, when he was booked for another speech, he called her in advance and asked her to dinner. "We went out to dinner and, frankly, I fell in love with him," she said. "He started asking me to write speeches for him, right off the bat. From that minute, done, we were together." And then, as she put it with a laugh, "we were married eleven short years later." They saw each other regularly during those years. She was younger than Carl by twenty years, committed to liberal causes, and an absolute knockout.

While Maxey's marriage to Ninon still appeared strong, there is no doubt that he was completely smitten with Lou. He wrote impassioned letters to her as early as 1964. And Lou nearly idolized him: she thought he was brilliant, possessed of the "best character judgment" of anyone she had ever known, and, by the way, he was beautiful. "He was really a gorgeous guy," she said. "A brown-eyed handsome man."

Lou moved up to Spokane when she graduated in 1966, only twenty years old, with a degree in sociology and a minor in political science. She went to work in a Spokane advertising agency, a job she kept for the next fifteen years. By 1970, she was accompanying Maxey on his campaign and on his trips to Seattle, sometimes identified as an assistant. He was gone from home quite often. "Carl and his circle of male friends in those days were hell-raisers," said Lou. "I think Ninon was used to him being gone a lot." This was the era of Frank Sinatra's Rat Pack—and Maxey ran with his own local Rat Pack, comprised mostly of fellow lawyers. "He had his faults," said Bevan. "He liked the ladies too much, that's for sure. Way too much, maybe."

Maxey played hard, but he was working even harder. "We were always so busy. Carl was constantly engaged," said Lou. "At one time, he was running against Henry Jackson, trying the Seattle Seven case, handling two first-degree murder cases, plus the three hundred ongoing domestic files [divorce cases]. I mean it was the kind of ongoing stuff that most people couldn't handle one part of. Bevan always said, 'How did he do it?' He just did it. He said, 'I could do that standing on my head.' And in the middle of this there was, like, oh yeah: me and him." By this time, Ninon knew all about Lou and Carl. Various helpful acquaintances had made sure of that. "People had certainly told me about that [his dalliances]," Ninon later recalled. "It wasn't news to me. I knew something was going on for a long time."

Meanwhile, Ninon began her own new romance. In the early 1970s, she enrolled in Eastern Washington University to pursue a master's degree. She met a handsome, accomplished professor there, Raymond Schults, who happened to be a friend of Carl's. He soon became a much closer friend of Ninon's. Once, during a party at the Maxey house, a friend took Carl aside, pointed at Schults and whispered the news to him: that man is having an affair with your wife. Of course, Maxey was hardly blameless; he had Lou. But that didn't stop the Maxey temper from exploding. Maxey followed Schults outside, confronted him, and punches began to fly. Carl proceeded to "drop him like a sack of potatoes," according to Bevan. Schults later said he took a hard punch, all right, but denied crumpling like a burlap bag. He said he got right back up and held his own. Schults had been an amateur boxer too.

No permanent injuries resulted, but the marriage was damaged beyond saving. In fact, it was Ninon who ended up asking for a divorce. She was tired of Carl's unfaithfulness, tired of hearing about Lou. Both Bill and Bevan were insulated from this; neither had any idea anything was wrong. One day in 1972, Carl told Bevan, then fifteen and in possession of a learner's permit, that he wanted to take him out for driving lesson. "He kind of insisted," said Bevan. "And then later he said, 'Let's go have a Coke.' And that's when he told me they were going to get a divorce. And when we got home, my mom was waiting for me there, to tell me the same thing." Bevan remembered it as surprising, but not necessarily traumatic. Bill was twenty-three at the time and he said it would have been much more traumatic if not for the civilized way both parents handled it.

"Really, I had tremendous respect for both of them," said Bill. "Whatever they were doing, we were sheltered from it to a certain extent. It just seemed like, all of the sudden, this is what was going to happen. It didn't seem like there were a lot of fights and things going on, like some people go through for years. No, this was something that had apparently developed or happened, but by the same token, they had been able to maintain a sense of civility and respect to one another. I wasn't judgmental about who was wrong or who was right."

As an experienced divorce lawyer, Maxey knew the pitfalls to avoid. He and Ninon worked out the split amicably. She would move out (and go on to marry Schults before long), while Carl would keep the house on F Street. And Bevan would remain with Carl. "I loved my mom to death and she was a wonderful mother, but I think even she realized that I had a kind of unique bond with my dad," said Bevan. "I stayed with him and there was no fight about that. She moved into an apartment in [nearby] Browne's Addition. I'd go over there every Sunday for dinner, and we stayed close."

When the divorce became final in 1972, Lou at first maintained her own home in Spokane's East Central neighborhood. Bevan remembered that one day, not long after the divorce, his dad told him they were going to dinner at a friend's house. Bevan assumed they would be visiting one of his dad's old friends. "I'm thinking, 'An older black woman,'" said Bevan. "So we go to the door and knock-knock and who comes to the door but this striking, beautiful lady with long dark hair, almost down to her butt. She's pretty tall, about five eight, and a nice figure. And I'm going, 'Ohhh. OK, I get it. All right, I get it now.' I was young, but I wasn't stupid."

That was Bevan's first look at Lou. Maxey had waited a long time before introducing them. "I think he wanted to see how I got along with those kids," said Lou. "It was very important to him." Before long, she was helping out around the house. "I was working an 8:00 to 5:00 job and living on the east side and I'd get up at 5:30 A.M. or 6:00 A.M. and go over and cook breakfast for Bevan and then go back home to get ready and go to work," said Lou. "When Carl thought it was appropriate, I can't remember how long it took, I was staying there overnight. It took a while. He was a traditional guy in a lot of ways."

Lou was worried about how she would get along with Bevan, since he was in the emotional teen years and she was only eleven years older. Yet they hit it off "really easily," she said. "Like any teenager with a stepmother coming in, there were going to be times when you're going to be defiant," said Bevan. "But generally speaking, we got along very well. We obviously spent a lot of time together. I was very close with my dad and they were inseparable, so we went on trips together and did all kinds of things."

Early in 1974, Carl took Lou and Bevan on a vacation to Africa, including Morocco, the Ivory Coast, Senegal, and Kenya, the longest vacation they ever took. Bevan said the trip "was a very, very special thing" for his father, a way of exploring his roots, even though the details of those roots would have to remain a matter of conjecture. Bevan had fond memories as well. He remembered playing in a local basketball game in the Ivory Coast and showing off his skills as a varsity player. "At that point in time, I had a very large red Afro," said Bevan. "When they see an American guy rolling in, and playing hoops, that was a big challenge. I kind of went out of my way to give them what they were expecting. I dribbled through my legs and behind my back." He also remembered going to a nightclub with Carl and Lou. Bevan had inherited from his father a taste for snappy clothes. He was dressed in his most stylish '70s American outfit: a bright canary-yellow *Superfly* suit with bell-bottoms and platform shoes. "There were so many girls around me, it wasn't even funny," said Bevan. "My dad was saying, 'You have to be careful, now. I don't want anything happening to you. Because your football coach will kill me if there's anything wrong with you.' He was talking about venereal disease!"

When they returned home that summer, marriage still did not seem to be in the offing. "People would say, 'When are you and Carl going to get married?'" said Lou. "And I would say, 'Whenever he's bachelor of the month in *Jet* magazine.' I thought, 'What an insane question.'" Not so insane after all. One day in the summer of 1974, while the two of them were in bed, he asked her to marry him. "It was one of the biggest surprises in my life," she said. "I just started laughing. And the next day I remember we looked at the Lewis and Clark High School football schedule and picked a date, right after the Shadle Park [High School] game. It's true. Bevan was on the team and that was a huge part of our lives, too."

Only about a month elapsed between the proposal and the marriage. The marriage was *right* after the football game, on the evening of September 27, 1974. The plan was to go to the game and then to the home of their friend and fellow attorney, Mark Vovos, and tie the knot. "I remember sitting at the game, going, 'Bevan, please, just have a good game.' I can't remember whether he made two or three touchdowns," said Lou. "And there was this whole spread in the paper the next day, with pictures of Bevan Maxey. And he said, 'That was my present to you.' What a sweet thing."

The Vovos' home was decorated for the event in black and white for obvious reasons. The flowers were black and white, the cake was black and white, the groom and bride were black and white. Bill Williams, now a superior court judge, pronounced them man and wife. They went to Sam's Pit, Spokane's foremost—actually, only—barbecue, soul food, and after-hours liquor-and-gambling emporium. The proprietor, Sam Willis, was one of the couple's closest friends. "And the place promptly got raided," said Lou. "I thought, 'This is the story of our lives.' But it didn't really get raided. They [the police] came in and said, 'What's going on?' and we told them it was a wedding party. Then they didn't do anything."

Carl and Lou's true intimates attended the Sam's Pit party. The couple threw a fancier party the next night for the hundreds of people in their wider social, legal, and political circles at the posh Davenport Hotel. "I designed these really nice invitations and he gave me this list that had all of these big names on it, like the Foleys [Judge Ralph Foley and his son Tom Foley, the district's Democratic congressman]," said Lou. "Everybody showed up. People came from Seattle and all over. I said, 'Carl, it's because they love you. They don't care if I'm Dick the Devil.' They were just happy that he was happy." Some of Carl's friends weren't entirely happy. At first, his law partner Bob Bell "wouldn't walk down the street with me," said Lou. She thought he considered her "the interloper." But he eventually came around.

Meanwhile, Maxey had become the city's unofficial lawyer for all things countercultural. By one published report, he carried a caseload of fifteen hundred conscientious objector petitions before local draft boards. In fact, in the late 1960s he had hired long-haired Gonzaga University School of Law student and activist Pat Stiley as a clerk to help out on draft cases. Stiley had shown up in Maxey's office one day to get help for his roommate, who had been indicted for refusing to step forward for induction. "I worked on that case through law school and Carl tried it," said Stiley. "He won in front of a hostile judge, a hard-ass who had never acquitted anybody [in a draft case]. The judge made it clear that he didn't have any sympathy for someone who wouldn't serve his country. And I watched him try that case, and I thought, 'That's what a trial lawyer should be.'"

Stiley and Maxey hit it off almost like father and son. When Stiley graduated from law school, Carl hired him to be the firm's draft specialist. In one of Stiley's early cases, a judge refused to let him in his courtroom because he had a ponytail. "I went back to the office and said, 'What am I supposed to do? I've got a client over there,'" said Stiley. "And Carl went through the roof. He got on the phone to the judge and said, 'You what? You . . . [growl-growl],' and the judge reversed himself."

Maxey may have been a countercultural lawyer, but he had an inordinate amount of clout with the establishment judges. One client's irate husband, feeling wronged in a divorce action, expressed it like this: "That judge did everything Carl Maxey asked him to." Not quite, but Maxey did have plenty of persuasive power with many members of the bench. Stiley believed that was for three main reasons. First, Maxey had been a "respected son of the community" even before he went into law. "You'd be surprised at how goddamned excited many powerful members of the community get about Gonzaga sports," said Stiley. Second, lower-court judges knew that Maxey was very well connected with higher-court judges like Bill Williams, who was on his way to the state supreme court. Third, Maxey was an uncommonly eloquent and dynamic speaker, a dominant force in the courtroom.

"I think it was part of his boxing background, to be aggressive from the get-go and by God, if someone takes a swing at you, swing back twice as hard and twice as fast," said Stiley. "That applied to his method of argument and presentation as well. You didn't take him on verbally unless you knew what you were doing, or he would just stomp your butt. By the time I got together with him in the late '60s, he had established himself as the powerhouse of domestic law, no doubt about it, and the guy to go to for criminal defense. He was a tiger."

Maxey was also the lawyer of choice when counterculture newspapers and rock concert organizers needed legal help. In 1968, the *Spokane Natural* alleged that a certain city official was a slumlord. Spokane mayor David H. Rodgers went on the attack in an angry press release. He called the *Spokane Natural* a "hippie paper, which can best be described as a gutter publication dedicated to the spreading of deliberate obscenities and creation of unrest and chaos and degrading the morals of our young people." Maxey, the paper's attorney, regretted that the mayor "wasted so much time vilifying the *Natural*" and so little addressing the issue. "A good many citizens are condemning young people for not taking part in democratic processes," said Maxey. "In this case, they should be complimented for their disclosures."

Then, in 1971, Maxey went to bat for the Universal Life Church, a loosely organized institution even more nondogmatic than the Unitarians—and far more free-spirited. The Universal Life Church sponsored a "picnic" at Farragut State Park, a serene spread of pine forest and grassy meadows on the shores of Lake Pend Oreille in the northern Idaho panhandle. This was no ordinary church picnic: a crowd of at least 15,000 young people, or 30,000 by organizers' estimates, showed up to listen to music, bask in the sun, and, according to sheriff's reports, take drugs. The Kootenai county sheriff, Stanley C. Johnson, said that drug use was "open and widespread" and that cocaine and marijuana were openly advertised at the picnic. The Kootenai County prosecutor vowed that the county would ban these kinds of festivals in the future.

Maxey, in rebuttal, told the press that the prosecutor had no idea what he was talking about—the prosecutor wasn't there, of course— and that he had no way of supporting charges of widespread drug use. He noted that the sheriff made only eight arrests all weekend. "There were more people at this picnic than the total population of Coeur d'Alene, Idaho, and there was less crime," Maxey said. "There wasn't even a reported incident of a fist fight. The merchants, who were originally hostile, have clearly become some of the most avid supporters. They have exclaimed, over and over again, how well-mannered the young people were." He said that park officials, too, commented favorably on how the attendees kept the park free of litter and free of conflict.

"As to nudity," said Maxey, "the main complaint seems to be that some people went swimming in the buff, but, really, who hasn't on occasion swam nude, at least in their youth? The obscenity, if any occurred, was from the middle-class citizens who own the property up there, lining the banks of the swimming hole with their expensive boats, armed with binoculars, trying to get a peek. All in all, the only complaint that could be made against the picnic comes from those persons who are entirely anti-youth, who simply cannot understand that young people have chosen a method of expression that is not consistent with theirs. In general, it was communing with nature and listening to music, much better than the average adult picnic that is overly supplied with booze."

About this time, Spokane was immersed in planning its own party, the biggest in the city's history: Expo '74, the Spokane World's Fair. Maxey was not actually opposed to the Expo, but he served as a gadfly. During a meeting of the Concerned Black Citizens in 1971, he recommended that the minority community take a "hard look" at the referendum to approve the event. His issue, characteristically, was funding priorities. "I am not recommending you vote against it," he told the group. "All of us are for river beautification [part of the Expo plan], and it is nice to know that it can be done with federal funding. But it is amazing that when 14 percent or more of Spokane's housing is substandard, we can't have federal funding to improve housing conditions . . . [It is] amazing that the promoters of Expo '74 have not made any bona fide attempt to involve either the poor or the minority people in the fundamental planning."

Spokane was the smallest city ever to attempt a World's Fair, but Expo '74 went on to be a huge boost in morale and prominence for Spokane. Over five million people attended. When it was all over, an ugly railroad yard had been converted into Riverfront Park, one of the city's enduring attractions. The city also had a new opera house and convention center. Yet after it was over, Maxey represented a local group that demanded an accounting of the fair's funding and finances. "Expo and city officials have said it was a success," said Maxey in a 1975 *Spokesman-Review* interview. "With success like that, who needs failures? . . . They [Spokane city council members] should all resign."

Expo '74 did finish with a small deficit, but quickly paid it off through donations. Nothing ever came of Maxey's charges. But Maxey was in no mood to be kind to the Spokane City Council, because that same year he became involved in one of the longest and most complicated cases of his career: a lawsuit against the city for dumping raw sewage into Long Lake, a dammed-up section of the Spokane River downstream from the city. During a three-day stretch in October of 1975, about 160 million gallons of sewage accidentally bypassed the city's sewage treatment plant while it was being modernized. This brown, lumpy sludge poured directly into the river and was washed downstream into the lake. Residents reported that a "foamy, brown gooey mass" floated atop the water and that their beachfronts were lined with odiferous hunks of sewage. The lake subsequently erupted in massive blooms of toxic algae, and lakefront residents proceeded to raise their own legal stink.

About twenty-two of them hired Maxey to handle their damage claims, worth a total of $5.2 million. The case dragged its way slowly through the courts, punctuated, as Maxey cases often were, by eruptions of public controversy. One came in 1977 when Maxey filed a motion in superior court asking that acting city manager Glen A. Yake—the man who actually ran the city under Spokane's form of government at the time—be held in contempt for criticizing superior court judge Harold D. Clarke, who had ruled that the city was partly liable for the damages. The city manager had issued a press release saying that no damage had been done by the bypass and that the "judge's opinion misinterprets the law."

Maxey wasn't just defending the judge's honor, he was also defending his case against a prejudiced jury pool. The city manager had also said that "the city does not have insurance that would pay for the award." The city "does not manufacture money," said Yake. "Every dime we spend comes from the citizens. An award of damages in the amount the property owners are seeking would necessitate a major increase in sewer rates for the citizens of Spokane." Maxey saw this as a blatant scare tactic. "Continually, we are told that the taxpayers are going to have to bear the burden," he said . "All of these are less-than-thinly-veiled efforts to create a partial attitude among potential jurors." Maxey eventually withdrew the contempt motion, saying that his point had been made, and Judge Clarke chided city officials for expressing "rather pointed views" through the media instead of through legal channels.

Clarke eventually ruled that the city and the state Department of

Ecology shared the blame for the sewage overflow. In 1980, he awarded damages of $386,596 to the homeowners, which included a fee of $88,500 for Maxey's work on the case over four years. The affidavits filed on the issue of Maxey's attorney fees revealed how his fellow members of the bar thought of him circa 1980. "It seems almost incredulous to me that someone of Carl Maxey's ability and talent could devote four years to a case like this and be awarded a fee less than $500,000," wrote Michael Hemovich, president of the state bar association. "I believe there are few attorneys or firms in this community possessing the necessary experience and skill . . . to conduct a case of this magnitude," said Spokane attorney Jack Dean. All Maxey said was, "It is not my practice to conduct five years of litigation on a voluntary basis."

Maxey also continued to handle antiwar protest cases, some routine, others that would shatter lives. One such case was that of Joe Schock, an ex-Marine from Lewiston, Idaho, who returned from Vietnam in 1969 with four medals, an honorable discharge, and profound doubts about the war. He soon hooked up with antiwar groups at the University of Idaho in Moscow and at Washington State University in Pullman, right across the border. On the night when the nation was rocked by news of the Kent State shootings in 1970, one protester took what antiwar groups euphemistically referred to as "direct action." He tossed a gasoline firebomb over the fence at the National Guard armory in Lewiston. Jeeps and trucks exploded into flame. Firefighters arrived to a nightmare scene in which dozens of vehicles were engulfed in orange fireballs. In all, twenty-nine military vehicles were destroyed, worth $250,000. Schock was arrested at a police roadblock near the armory. Police said his clothes reeked of gasoline. He was tossed into the Nez Perce County Jail on a fifty-thousand-dollar bond and was charged with destroying federal property. Antiwar groups on both campuses took up a collection and hired Maxey to defend him.

In a hearing before U.S. District Court judge Ray McNichols—described by local officials as "packed with peaceniks" and "hippy types"—the first thing Maxey did was request that Schock's bail be reduced to ten thousand dollars. "Joe's credentials and his war record were so impeccable," Maxey later told reporter Ted Cilwick of the *Moscow Idahonian* and *Pullman Daily News.* "The judge could at least understand his motivation . . . He at least had a reason for hating the war." The judge was so sympathetic that he released Schock on his own recognizance—no bail required at all. As it turned out, the judge may have been *too* sympathetic. Two months later, Maxey informed the court that Schock had not responded to Maxey's phone calls or letters for weeks. "The danger signals are up," Maxey told the court. Schock had fled and the judge issued an arrest warrant the next day.

Schock went to Canada, the West Indies, and Algeria, and finally surfaced in French Martinique in early 1971. The French government refused to extradite him to the United States, and he was granted political asylum and he moved to a town outside Paris in 1972. When Cilwick contacted him in Paris in 1990, Schock said, "If I'd have stayed in the States, they would have crushed me like a worm." Maxey didn't blame him. He told Cilwick that Schock should never expect "any sympathy from George Bush." Schock declared he had no intention of ever returning home and never did.

Meanwhile, Maxey's political ambitions had cooled since the Scoop Jackson race. Yet his sense of political indignation remained more fierce than ever. Nothing stirred that indignation more thoroughly than the continued revelations about President Richard Nixon's role in the Watergate scandal. As early as April of 1973, when news was just emerging about involvement by White House staff, Maxey was blasting away at Nixon. "President Nixon and his administration are totally hostile, arrogant and contemptuous of the American people," Maxey told students at North Idaho Junior College in Coeur d'Alene. "The best that can be said for the president's conduct is that he should have known these were his men doing his bidding in a manner not uncommon to him. The most that can be said is that he directed it with full knowledge."

By October of 1973, Maxey was standing in the plaza of the Spokane Federal Building, thundering for Nixon's immediate impeachment. "If Richard Nixon is above the law, by God, I am above the law and so are you," Maxey told a crowd of two hundred gathered for an impeachment rally sponsored by the Washington Democratic Council. "We are all equal in the eyes of the law and that's what this is all about. It's a loss of confidence we've been experiencing. Nixon is saying in effect that he can manipulate the Congress and compromise the courts and thus can do what he wants to the American people because they are too dumb to understand."

Special Watergate prosecutor Archibald Cox had just been fired on Nixon's orders, and Maxey told the crowd that anybody surprised by that was either "naïve or a fool." He said that Nixon was the first man in history to "build his own wall to butt his head against." Maxey continued, "The issue is not between the young and old, the rich and poor, the liberal and the conservative. We all must unite and bring this administration down. Somewhere, Nixon must tell the American people the truth. His hands are sullied by arrogance and indifference. So get up and do your duty." Almost a year later, facing impeachment proceedings, Nixon resigned.

Maxey's political ambitions may have peaked in 1970, but that didn't prevent him from running for another office in 1976: vice president of the United States. This wasn't as ambitious as it sounds. He had a spot on Washington's 1976 presidential ballot as Eugene McCarthy's presidential running mate, but it was an entirely symbolic position. McCarthy had decided to run on a third-party ticket because of what he considered an unpleasant choice between incumbent Gerald Ford and Jimmy Carter. Maxey had once again agreed to become McCarthy's state campaign chair. Because McCarthy wasn't planning to name a running mate until October, he had to designate a "stand-in" running mate in several states to meet the ballot deadline. Washington was one of those states.

So Maxey became McCarthy's stand-in vice presidential candidate on the Washington ballot. When asked if he had any ambitions toward becoming McCarthy's real running mate, Maxey told the *Spokesman-Review* it would be "presumptuous" of him to speculate. As it turned out, McCarthy chose no running mate and left the local names, including Maxey's, on each state's ballot. So Maxey's name has gone down in history as the recipient of thirty-nine thousand votes for the second-highest office in the land. That was a miserable vote total: McCarthy's luster had clearly dimmed considerably since 1968. The McCarthy-Maxey team scrounged up only about 2 percent of votes cast, or about half of what Maxey himself had received in his Scoop Jackson race. McCarthy did even worse nationally, failing to top even 1 percent.

That entire campaign was discouraging for Maxey, but he was vastly cheered around that time by the athletic accomplishments of Bevan. Maxey had always been proud of his boys' athletic achievements. Both had been all-city athletes in high school, and Bill probably would have received a college basketball scholarship if he hadn't been injured his senior year. Bevan was a three-sport all-city athlete—basketball, football, and baseball—and was awarded a football scholarship to Washington State University in Pullman (WSU).

During Bevan's freshman year, WSU coach Jim Sweeney called Bevan at home one Friday night and told him to be ready for the next day's UCLA game being played in Spokane's Albi Stadium. That was surprise enough, since Bevan didn't even think he would be allowed to suit up. The next day, to his surprise, Sweeney actually ordered him into the game. Carl and Lou were in the stadium watching and celebrating their first anniversary. Bevan took up his wide receiver's position. The WSU quarterback lofted a pass in his direction. "I caught it and just took off, running for my life, thirty-four yards," said Bevan. His father practically levitated clear above the grandstand. It was Bevan's first-ever collegiate pass, and Bevan raced in for a touchdown. "He was floating," said Bevan. "I don't think he touched the ground all night, he was so happy. It sent him sky-high."

By the mid-1970s, there were about forty-three black attorneys in the state, but only one other in Spokane: Tolmon "Toby" Gibson, who graduated from Gonzaga University School of Law about twenty years after Maxey. In 1975, Gibson told the *Spokesman-Review*, "Spokane is a conservative yet fair town. There is a little reluctance to welcome something new with open arms, but [if you are] willing to take time, you can gain acceptance and respect—and maybe even some affection." Maxey was growing too cynical to believe that any more. In the same article he charged that Spokane's racial attitudes had not changed for the better and neither had the nation's. "It's like a bad movie," Maxey complained. "You know what's going to happen but there's not a thing you can do to stop it."

Maxey continued taking criminal cases of all kinds, but the core of his practice remained divorce law. This was a source of some chagrin to Maxey, if only because of the legal pecking order. A family law practice was considered a lesser kind of law practice. "You were a guttersnipe if you did family law," said Marsha Dornquast. "You were at the bottom of the totem pole." Yet a man who grew up with no parents and no family was acutely aware of how important family law could be. "Carl knew that everything flowed from there, from the family, in terms of what happens in society," said Lou. "All of the violence flowed from there. If you can heal people at that point in their lives, that's what he tried to do. He tried to get people back together. He'd rather have people reconcile their marriage than to have a good case."

His family law practice was remarkable if only because of its sheer volume. Bill Maxey, who had gone into his father's practice right out of law school in 1975, said that at one time his father had 300–400 active divorce files, "which required constant monitoring." Maxey showed up at work at 7:00 A.M. and worked late into the evening. The bulk of his days were spent at the Spokane County Courthouse. "I don't think any young lawyers from today [can understand] how many divorce cases and criminal cases he litigated," said Bevan, who also joined his father and brother in the practice after graduating from Gonzaga University School of Law in 1983. "It was inconceivable. We have what we call the family law calendar or docket, and there were days when he would have fifteen cases on the docket. You might have lawyers going over there today and, on an extraordinary day, having five cases. But fifteen?" Lou added, "He'd come over to court and say [to one of his legal assistants], 'Now, show me who my client is?' There were so many. But he'd still kick ass."

With this many cases, money was no problem even with all of the pro bono work the firm did. A 1981 *Spokesman-Review* article asked prominent local people about their salaries. Maxey said he didn't want to give an exact number. "I'll put it this way," he said. "It's in the $100,000 area. I've paid more income tax than the last three presidents—but I don't have any write-offs." Other lawyers contacted for that story said they wouldn't be surprised if Maxey's true number was closer to $200,000. "One of his favorite lines was, 'We're not doing too bad for three spooks in a small town,'" said Bevan.

Pat Stiley was also a partner by the latter part of the '70s, and the Carl-and-Pat team seemed to be an inseparable combination. Stiley did a lot of Carl's legal research. "We were a perfect match," said Stiley. "He had all the verbal skills but he hated research. But if you gave [the research] to him, nobody had a chance against him. He could read it and grasp it and turn it into—I'd hear him the next day arguing in court, and it was dynamic." Stiley and Maxey were inseparable outside the courtroom too. "My relationship with Carl from about 1968 to late 1981 was like a son in a lot of ways," said Stiley. "There was hardly ever a dinner I wasn't with him. Hardly ever a lunch, hardly ever a working hour. I spent as much time with him as Lou or Ninon did. I had him all day and evening, they had him all night."

Maxey needed all the help he could get, because divorce cases were the "toughest area of practice of all," Maxey told the *Spokane Daily Chronicle* in a 1981 interview. "There's nothing that brings out hostility more than any run-of-the-mill divorce," he said. "I've had death threats night after night in divorce cases. It's a war; it's not a game. People have been killed in my office over a divorce case." That was, unfortunately, true. In 1977, Marilyn Wineinger, age forty, had retained Maxey for her divorce. On March 16, Maxey invited her and her husband, Donald R. Wineinger, age forty-three, a minister for the Worldwide Church of God (made famous by radio evangelist Garner Ted Armstrong), to meet at Maxey's office in the Rookery Building. During that meeting, Mrs. Wineinger told her husband she was filing for a divorce. Maxey explained the process to both of them. The meeting was not particularly volatile; the couple agreed on a joint petition for dissolution. Maxey ended the meeting by giving them paperwork to fill out. He also scheduled another meeting later in the week. The couple walked out into the hall on the second floor and continued to talk.

Bill Maxey had joined his father's practice by this time and was returning from lunch at the Ridpath Hotel's Silver Grill restaurant. "This couple was still standing right in the foyer and we walked by them and they were talking," said Bill. "So we went back in and got kind of settled in . . . and I'm on the phone with another attorney and I hear a couple of metallic sounds. I thought somebody had closed a filing cabinet. Then a few moments later, I hear the scampering and scurrying of feet. I said, 'Mike, hold on a minute, I've got to check on something. Something's happened here, I don't know what.' I walked out of my office, went to the back door, and there was this couple. They were laying on top of each other. The husband had shot the wife and then shot himself." Onlookers gathered and ambulances came screaming up to the Rookery Building. The wife was pronounced dead at the scene with two gunshot wounds to the head. The husband died a half hour later; he had put one bullet in his temple.

Sometimes, the volatile emotions in a divorce case were aimed more directly at the lawyer. One Spokane husband, still bitter and broken twenty years after his divorce, put it this way: "My ex-wife ruined my life. She and her attorney, Carl Maxey." Maxey's former boxing coach, Joey August, wryly alluded to this kind of antipathy in his speech inducting Maxey into Gonzaga University's athletic hall of fame. "A lot of you guys don't like him," August told the gathered crowd. "A lot of you divorced guys *really* don't like him. But your ex-wives do." Wives were, in fact, more prone than husbands to hire Maxey, a pattern that Bevan attributed to his father having remained an outsider to Spokane's white, clubby establishment. "The men were from the establishment and tended to go with the white lawyers, because that's where the money was," said Bevan. "The women were the ones, traditionally, who needed the protection the most." So the wives tended to seek out a bulldog, and in Spokane Maxey was clearly the biggest, baddest bulldog on the block.

Most divorce cases were routine, but some turned into highly publicized soap operas, as in the Sharon and Mohammad Marashi divorce case. A federal judge later compared the whole sordid affair to TV's *Dallas*. It had everything except the "who shot J. R." cliffhanger. Episode one of the soap opera began when Sharon Marashi walked into Maxey's office in 1984 and handed him $5,000 to represent her in her divorce suit against the well-known local pediatrician Dr. Marashi. That $5,000 had come from a generous benefactor: Steve Danzig, the husband of Sherry Danzig, Dr. Marashi's newest girlfriend. The spurned spouses had teamed up to get revenge on the doctor.

The second episode came when Dr. Marashi yanked $103,000 from his bank account and gave it to his father, he said, as repayment for medical school. Judge John A. Schultheis, presiding over the case, was livid about this for two reasons: first, he had previously ordered that the bank account be frozen until the divorce was resolved, and second, he discovered that the money had not gone directly to the doctor's father, but to a secret Swiss bank account. The money was untraceable from that point on. Maxey declared that the truth was obvious: the doctor spirited the money away to keep his wife from getting her due. An irate Schultheis ordered Dr. Marashi to return the money. When the doctor said he couldn't, because his father had already used it to pay off creditors in his native Iran, the judge tossed the doctor into jail for thirty days for contempt of court. The judge also warned the doctor that if that money wasn't back in thirty days, he'd slap him in jail for another five months.

Meanwhile, Dr. Marashi's wife told the court that she had not received "a single penny" of the $2,370 monthly child support her husband had been ordered to pay. So the judge ordered the doctor's Mercedes to be sold for $50,000 and the money placed in the trust account that Maxey was holding to pay Sharon's bills. These financial details were especially titillating to the people of Spokane, considering that Dr. Marashi had been Spokane County's top public health officer four years earlier and had complained that he wasn't paid sufficiently. The county commissioners had given him a $22,000 raise to $46,000 a year, which made him the highest paid person on the county payroll—and the job was only part-time. He still had his private pediatrics practice. The titillation was heightened by the doctor's allegations that his wife was "mentally unstable." Sharon's mother came to her defense in court, saying that Dr. Marashi had never seen Sharon's "true self." Her mother claimed that "he has dominated her their entire married life and treated her as a Persian wife instead of an American woman. I feel he is upset because for the first time during their marriage Sharon is standing up to him."

In the drama's third episode, a month later, the judge made good on his word and slapped the doctor with another five months of jail time on the contempt charges. Dr. Marashi told the judge that there was no way to get the money back from Iran. Meanwhile, no bank would loan him the money because he was a jailed physician whose patients were "bailing out," as his attorney put it. The judge was unmoved. "If this isn't contemptuous attitude or conduct, I don't know what in God's name is," he said. "You can apologize, but you did it," Maxey lectured the doctor in court, twisting the knife a little harder. "[This was] an act that can't be undone."

The doctor had been allowed out on work release during the first month, but now he was ordered into the Spokane County Jail without work release. Two months later, the judge finally relented and let Dr. Marashi out of jail. The money was still missing, but the judge finally concluded it was "irretrievable." The cash had gone through Iranian black market moneychangers who would be "put in front of a firing squad," if they admitted they had handled the money, said the doctor's attorney. "Marashi, looking frail, wept when Schultheis said he could go free," wrote Richard Wagoner in the *Spokesman-Review*.

Yet that didn't save Dr. Marashi from enduring the soap opera's final episode: his federal trial three years later on five counts of tax evasion. This trial was a direct result of that nasty divorce case, because the star witness against him was his ex-wife Sharon. She was granted immunity from prosecution in exchange for giving details about his tax-cheating schemes. She gave details, all right, some of which were not obtained through, well, proper channels. As it turned out, she and Danzig had teamed up on another mission in the middle of the divorce proceedings. They had hired a private investigator to break into the garage at the doctor's condo and to go through his records. Later, while the doctor was dallying with Danzig's wife in Europe, they snuck into the doctor's office and hired a locksmith to open his desk. They were looking for proof of his affairs, not his tax records. But when the husband wished aloud that "there was something that would really hurt" the doctor, Sharon suggested that they go to the IRS with their suspicions of his tax fraud. "I was vindictive, yes," admitted Sharon, during the tax trial.

She and Maxey met with IRS investigators, who told her that she would get "the innocent wife treatment" if she told all, even though the tax returns were joint returns. Dr. Marashi was convicted in 1988 on three counts of tax evasion and sentenced to six months of work release and three years of probation. His medical license was suspended, and he quit his practice and filed for bankruptcy. He had lost, he later said, everything. In 2004, he told the state clemency board that he still owed the government $285,000. He was living on Social Security in Bellevue, Washington, and suffered from congestive heart failure. Divorce, in this case, was indeed a war, not a game.

Cases like this took up the bulk of Maxey's time, though he still thought of himself as, first and foremost, a civil rights lawyer. Yet as the '70s dragged on, the nature of the civil rights movement was changing. Maxey was increasingly dismayed by what he saw as a nearly complete lack of progress. During the nation's bicentennial celebration in 1976, he found little reason to join in the festivities. "Why should we celebrate, when the black unemployment rate is twice as high as the white, when blacks are occupying 50 percent of all prison cells, when blacks have half the opportunity to attend schools as whites, and when blacks have to march and fight to get unfair treatment in the judicial system?" he said in a speech at the Ridpath Hotel. The occasion was Spokane's Black Bicentennial Reunion, a gathering of black Spokane natives from all over the country. For them, the "old days" evoked mixed emotions.

"But when we gather and reminisce about the 'old days' in Spokane, the talk is of the Harlem Club and Chester's Chicken Inn—not of the Davenport Hotel or other spots where we were not allowed," said Maxey. "And if the Spokane Club is mentioned, it is because some of us knew it well—from the kitchen or behind the bar—but never as members. So, to those of you who chose to leave Spokane and make your home elsewhere, I say you are no more fortunate nor unfortunate than those of us who remained here. Because, to paraphrase our great poet, Langston Hughes, what we all suffer is what America is."

In 1977, Maxey took the drastic step of resigning from his post as chairman of the state advisory committee to the U.S. Commission on Civil Rights. President John F. Kennedy had originally appointed him to the post in 1963, and he was subsequently reappointed by presidents Johnson, Nixon, and Ford. He was the senior state chairman in the nation. But under President Jimmy Carter, he was fed up. He blamed Carter, a Democrat, for a "total failure to address himself to the priorities he promised before the election." In a resignation letter to Carter, he wrote, "More and more people are becoming unemployed. More people are suffering from poverty and racism than ever before. And the priorities that you promised the people of feeding them, providing employment and health insurance are not being met." When asked by reporters if he thought there was a threat of renewed urban rioting, as in the 1960s, he answered, "I absolutely predict it."

On a more practical plane, Maxey's reasons for quitting were because of the Carter administration's decision to regionalize the commission, a move Maxey called "foolish" and one that would "totally destroy what effectiveness we did have." In retrospect, Maxey's decision seems rash, since soon afterward the commission would effectively champion tough new provisions in the federal fair housing laws. However, even if Maxey had kept his seat he might have quit in a far more indignant huff in the 1980s over President Ronald Reagan's attempt to stack the commission with conservatives.

In Spokane, Maxey was heartened by one development in the area of racial equality. James Chase, Maxey's longtime ally in the local NAACP chapter, had been elected to the Spokane City Council in 1975. In 1979, an interviewer asked Maxey if he had any further political ambitions. "No, not at all," said Maxey. "We have [a] very excellent black man in the midst of our municipal politics. He's a source of satisfaction to everyone. He doesn't need my help." In 1981, Chase ran for mayor of Spokane. This overwhelmingly white city, with a black population of around 1.6 percent, gave Chase 82 percent of the vote.

He became one of Spokane's most popular mayors and today the city's newest middle school is named after him.

Maxey's civil rights work increasingly involved such dispiriting cases as the Craig S. Jordan shooting in 1975. The seventeen-year-old Jordan was shot to death by a Spokane police officer at the scene of a house burglary. The officer said he believed that Jordan was armed and preparing to turn and shoot him, so the officer fired in self-defense. The boy was indeed a burglar; he had been arrested several times before and had admitted to seventy-five house burglaries. But, as it turned out, he was an unarmed burglar, and an autopsy revealed that Jordan had been shot in the middle of the back. The shooting shocked Spokane's black community and sparked a thirty-person protest at the police station the next day. Another fifty people showed up at the Spokane City Council meeting to call for an independent investigation into the incident.

Maxey, retained by the boy's mother, Carrie M. Jordan, said he wanted a coroner's inquest because "you can't allow the police to investigate themselves." Maxey asked for a coroner's inquest that would include a jury with "minority representatives" and presided over by a district court or superior court judge, not a coroner. County prosecutor Donald C. Brockett finally agreed to hold a coroner's inquest— but not of the kind that Maxey wanted. A deputy coroner presided and the jury was all white. Maxey later called Brockett's jury selection process "incredibly naïve." A smoldering Maxey told reporters that "Brockett equates all-white with all right. Everyone involved in this entire episode was white except the deceased, a 17–year-old, unarmed black man."

Maxey, in fact, refused to sit at the counsel table at the inquest because he had been told that he could not ask any questions and had no say in which witnesses would be called. The jury ruled unanimously that the officer shot in self-defense. Brockett announced he would not file any charges. "It's just a whitewash," said a grim Maxey. "It's apparent from this travesty that there must be a viable method for getting a full and complete investigation when a death is caused by a policeman. At present, a citizen has no protection against the police." Brockett tried to ease the racial tension by saying, "Whatever be our race, creed or color, we can attempt to improve our concerns for the other." Maxey replied, "While I certainly agree with his final comments, non-whites cannot trust him [Brockett] to be sole guardian of their rights."

This was the first of many skirmishes with Brockett, who would become Maxey's nemesis for the rest of Maxey's career. Brockett would later accuse Maxey of turning every issue into a racial one, a criticism that was shared by plenty of people in the law enforcement and legal communities. As one prosecutor said, only half jokingly: "We'll have a white victim, a white defendant, a white judge and a white prosecutor. And Maxey will still stand up and say, 'Race!'" Maybe this assessment contained the smallest kernel of truth. Maxey was not averse to making race the center of a debate, since in many cases it clearly *was* the center of the debate.

"Carl obviously did not have a bigoted goddamn bone in his body," said Stiley. "And I say that realizing that there were times in Carl's career where people effectively accused him of reverse racism . . . But he felt racism strongly and there was never a moment when he didn't feel it. And he was aware of what it had taken to overcome it." Lou recalled that "people would say to Carl, 'I don't think of you as being black.' That's supposed to be a compliment? He'd say, 'Well, you white son of a bitch, you'd better.'" Stiley did notice, however, that in Maxey's later years he began more often to "lash out and play the race card, so to speak." This was part of a pattern of increasing bitterness that gained momentum in the 1980s. In fact, in 1981, some of those closest to Maxey began to notice that he was becoming discouraged nearly to the point of self-pity—or even to the point of serious depression.

"I'd say, 'Carl, what the hell are you depressed about? You have a beautiful family, an outstanding law practice, you're a hero to so many goddamn people, you can weather any kind of criticism and you can just sit back,'" said Stiley. "He'd say, 'I'm fifty-seven years old, what have I done? I haven't done anything. I haven't made the mark on society that I was capable of doing.'" Stiley was so concerned about Maxey's state of mind that he and Lou got together behind his back and planned a huge surprise party at the Ridpath Hotel to celebrate his thirtieth anniversary as a lawyer. "We got the priest from his childhood [Father Byrne], we had childhood friends flown in from all over, we had hundreds of people there," said Stiley. "We went through his old newspaper clippings and had them blown up and put on boards all down the hallway. I think all of that love and affection and respect did a lot for him. He was up half the night talking with Father Byrne and everybody. I didn't hear a depressed word out of him for five years after that." But his depression had not vanished for good.

14

RUTH COE'S GREEK TRAGEDY

In 1981, Spokane was making national news for a particularly lurid civic trauma: the arrest and trial of the notorious South Hill rapist. The South Hill rapist had been terrorizing the city's upper-middle-class neighborhoods for years, stalking and raping as many as thirty-seven women, often as they jogged along the city's scenic High Drive or walked from their bus stops. By 1980, the attacks were increasing in frequency and brutality. In some cases, the rapist jammed his fist, covered with an oven mitt or a thick leather glove, down the victims' throats to keep them from screaming. The rapist often told the women he knew where they lived and he would come back and kill them if they told anybody.

The police quietly formed a task force. Then in January 1981, the *Spokesman-Review* published a map showing the rape locations and their correlation with the bus routes, along with a story titled "How the South Hill Rapists Work." By this time, the city was in a full-blown state of alarm. The *Spokesman-Review* pointed out that rapes in the city had skyrocketed from 49 in 1978 to 127 in 1980. The only voice of calm seemed to come from the *Spokane Daily Chronicle*, whose managing editor wrote in an editorial, "It is hoped that every man out jogging is not hounded off the streets because some rape reports have said the attacker wore jogging clothes." That managing editor's name was Gordon Coe. Imagine the uproar when police announced in March that they had finally arrested the South Hill rapist: Frederick "Kevin"

Coe, the son of that same *Chronicle* managing editor. No wonder some people called the region the Ingrown Empire.

The arrest and subsequent trial made news all over the country, including, of course, at the *Chronicle*, where Gordon Coe had taken a leave of absence. The evidence against Coe was voluminous, if mostly circumstantial, and it included a number of positive identifications by the rape victims. Coe's defense, widely believed to be orchestrated by Kevin himself, was one of flat denial. Both of Coe's parents, Gordon and Ruth, took the stand on his behalf and produced various alibis. Ruth, age sixty, was a well-dressed, flamboyant woman who wore a jet-black wig. She testified that she and "Son" as she called him, had attempted a kind of citizen's arrest of the South Hill rapist. The two of them, she said, had actually gone out several times on their own surveillance excursions. "Son would jog, and I would follow in the car at a very slow place," she testified. "[We were] very unsuccessful, so we did give up."

That would explain, she implied, why he and his car had been seen so often near the bus routes and near the scenes of the crimes. Fred (who had changed his name to "Kevin" for reasons known only to him) also took the stand on his own behalf. In between telling virtually his entire life story—large segments of which were absurdly exaggerated—he adamantly denied ever owning gloves, ever owning oven mitts, ever owning a stocking cap and, of course, ever raping anyone. "His mother, seated in the back of the tiny courtroom, smiled and nodded as he made his points and occasionally emitted a loud sigh or muffled comment when the prosecutor [Don Brockett] registered objections," wrote Jack Olsen in his bestselling 1984 book about the case, *Son: A Psychopath and His Victims.*

The jury bought none of it. On July 29, 1981, Kevin Coe was convicted of four counts of first-degree rape. Coe's parents were angry and defiant. Ruth told *Spokesman-Review* columnist Chris Peck that she believed that Judge George Shields had not played fair. She said that, in hindsight, she would "never try to play fair again, because the law doesn't play fair." At this point, Kevin and his parents were terrified that he would be sent to the state prison at Walla Walla, where they were convinced the other inmates would declare open season on the famous "rapo." Prosecutor Brockett had raised an even more alarming sentencing option: he pointed out that state law still allowed convicted rapists to be castrated. So the Coes grasped at one final straw—that Judge Shields would sentence Kevin as a sexual psychopath, meaning he would be sent to a state mental hospital, not a prison.

That's where Maxey entered the picture. He and Gordon Coe had become "fast friends" after "we had combated for years over his editorial policies," Maxey later said. Maxey had heard the judge raise the possibility of sexual psychopathy at one of the early sentencing hearings, and Maxey took it as an invitation. He contacted the Coes and told them that he thought he could maneuver Kevin into such a sentence. So the Coes hired Maxey for the sentencing phase of the trial, which would be held in a week or two. Maxey later said he was doing it all for the "glorious fee of one dollar." In *Son*, Olsen described Maxey's entry onto the stage: "Always controversial, he had built a flourishing practice specializing in divorce cases. Although resented by many local lawyers for a tendency, as one observer put it, 'to keep throwing his blackness up to the court for special treatment,' the talented Maxey was considered by other Spokanites as an earthly version of St. Jude, the patron saint of impossible causes. The Coe family handed him one: Keeping Fred from the penitentiary."

Maxey's strategy was a risky one. The judge had earlier said that he couldn't recommend the sexual psychopath option because Coe's flat-out denials indicated that he would not be amenable to treatment. So Maxey, in essence, talked Coe into confessing to one rape. Maxey arranged for Dr. Robert A. Wetzler, a well-known psychiatrist in the field of sexual psychopathy, to interview Coe one more time. This time Coe told Wetzler that he had committed one of the rapes and would be amenable to treatment for his sexual problems. Even then, Coe was coy about his admission. He told the psychiatrist he was "jealous of the South Hill rapist" and had committed a "copycat rape." In any case, when Maxey put Wetzler on the stand during the sentencing hearing, Wetzler dropped the bombshell: Coe had confessed and was begging for treatment. In his closing statement, Maxey took a potshot at

Brockett by saying "nobody had to be reminded . . . that somebody can be castrated." Then he asked the judge for a sentence that "sends you out better than you came in, a program you can survive." In other words, a sentence consisting of treatment and rehabilitation.

It didn't work. On August 17, 1981, in a proceeding broadcast on live TV, Judge Shields announced his sentence: a prison term of twenty years, a second term of twenty-five years, a third term of thirty years, and a fourth term of life, all to be served consecutively. Maxey was stunned. He clearly felt the judge had led him on with talk about the sexual psychopathy program. "We accepted his full-blown invitation and that invitation was never withdrawn," Maxey told reporters. "I got to work on it right away and gave the judge what he asked for. And then he turns around and gives the longest sentence ever handed down in the state of Washington."

Yet this "invitation," if there had really been one, had been premature. Shields had subsequently come to the conclusion that, by law, he could not place Coe in the sexual psychopath program unless the prosecution requested it. And Brockett had certainly requested no such thing. As Maxey later put it, the prosecution "had been literally out for blood." Within two months, Coe was sent to the corrections center at Shelton and then on to the state prison in Walla Walla. Coe later reasserted his innocence and said it had all just been a ruse. "As a strictly legal ploy, it makes good sense, but it didn't work," Coe told the *Seattle Times*. "The judge, in fact, tricked us."

Ruth Coe certainly didn't blame Maxey. She reserved all of her venom and scorn for Brockett and Shields. In a discussion with a stranger a few months later, Ruth went on the following rambling tirade: "The judge and the prosecutor just, you know, just lined up. But at any rate this filthy judge—20, 25, 30 and life—he was doing it just to make a big man of himself. Now, he also said that if my son would plead guilty to even one, they would suggest sexual psychopathy for him. Now, a very dear black attorney here in Spokane, whom we've known and dearly love, saw my husband and me and [told us] . . . 'I want to be on the sentencing part,' and he offered this for $1 and we shook hands . . . And Carl Maxey, the attorney, felt that the judge was honorable and would go with what he had said." The stranger then said, "But apparently he didn't," to which Ruth replied, "I want the prosecutor out and I want the judge out."

This conversation was captured on tape because the stranger was actually an undercover policeman. He was posing as a hit man after police had received a tip that Ruth wanted to take out a contract on Brockett and Shields. About two months earlier, not long after Kevin's conviction, Ruth had met by chance a former massage parlor operator named Violet Cooper, who had joked about having Mafia connections. Ruth pounced on this, asking breathlessly if Cooper really knew Mafia people, because she was in the market for a hit man. Cooper later told her lawyer, who called police. When the Spokane police confirmed the tip, they converted undercover cop Richard Jennings into an imaginary hit man named "Terry," who called Coe in November of 1981 and asked her if she was still in the market for a "job that you need to be performed very discreetly." She responded with an enthusiastic yes. A meeting in a parking lot was set up, with Jennings wired for sound. Here's how part of that conversation went:

Jennings: We are talking about the same thing; you want those people . . .

Coe: Gone.

Jennings: Dead?

Coe: Dead. Right. If I had my druthers, I'd have that prosecutor just made a complete vegetable so that he could never, ever be anything but a vegetable, so that they had to care for him forever, and he lived on and on that way. And the judge . . .

Jennings: Just tell me what you want.

Coe: Well, uh, and that judge, I'd like him gone—dead—and I'd like both of 'em dead, really, except that with Brockett, I felt that—he's a man about 46 or 47 and he has been so filthy, and my feeling for him is that I would love to see him just an addle-pated vegetable that had to be cared for—that his family had to take care of the rest of his life. I mean diapers and all the rest of it. He wanted 42 years of my son's life gone. I'd like to see him sit 42 years in . . . umm, as a baby. But, um, to have him gone would be great, too. I mean, you can never be sure, I suppose, how you clobber them, that could be the way it'd come out. So dead is great. But I do think he should suffer . . .

Ruth Coe was arrested the next day, November 20, when she handed Terry a five-hundred-dollar down payment. When the officers approached her in the parking lot and arrested her on charges of soliciting first-degree murder, she muttered disgustedly, "I thought so. I thought so. That's right, I really did think so." Ruth's arrest made national and international news; the *London Daily Mirror* ran the headline, "Sex Shame of Town's Top Family." The *Spokane Daily Chronicle*, whose managing editor had finally formally retired, put the story on the front page as well, with the headline, "Coe's Mother Faces Death Plot Counts."

There was never any doubt about which lawyer Ruth would hire. Maxey interviewed her in jail within three hours of the arrest. He described her to reporters as "not too rational." Maxey volunteered to represent her for a reduced fee, at least in part because he truly did feel sorry for her. "I think my father was just trying to help a really weak person and trying to take care of that person," said Bevan Maxey. "It was just a sad pathetic situation, where a lot of horrible things had happened as a result of her son. She loved her son and was weak and people knew it. Certain people, I think, tried to take advantage of that." Carl also believed he could make a strong case for entrapment and for diminished capacity—the inability to form a "specific intent" to commit a crime. He told *The American Lawyer* magazine, which did a major spread on the case in December 1982, that he chose to argue diminished capacity instead of insanity because if she were found insane, she would be committed to a mental institution. He said he never thought it was "a tryable case in the normal sense"—those tapes were too incendiary. But he was convinced that he could at least portray her as a tragic figure instead of as a criminal deserving of hard time.

The first thing he did was beg out of the Kevin Coe appeal, because "there's only so much of me to go around." He denied any personal conflicts with Kevin, who had been blaming his conviction on his lawyers, but it was clear from later statements that Maxey was sick and tired of Kevin's big mouth. The next thing Maxey did was attempt to knock Brockett and his entire staff off the case. Judge Shields had immediately bowed out, for the obvious reason that he was an intended victim. In fact, all ten of Spokane's superior court judges excused themselves from any dealings with the case, because Shields was their colleague and friend. Yet Brockett, amazingly enough, still wanted to try the case himself. "It would make me a better advocate if I had a personal interest in the case," Brockett told *The American Lawyer*. Common sense eventually prevailed, and Brockett handed the case over to a King County prosecutor. Meanwhile, Judge Robert Bibb, from Snohomish County, was chosen to preside over the trial.

Then Maxey pulled a maneuver that took the judge and prosecutor by surprise. He waived the right to a jury trial. As *The American Lawyer* pointed out, one of Maxey's strengths was his rapport with juries. "Maxey knows he is unique, and he doesn't hesitate to play on it—particularly before juries," the magazine said. But in this case, Maxey suspected that a judge with a keener knowledge of the nuances of diminished capacity would be more sympathetic than a jury—especially a jury that had just heard Ruth cooing on tape about turning Brockett into an addle-pated vegetable.

The trial began on May 17, 1982, and from the beginning it had all of the earmarks of great theater. "It was just like watching a play," said reporter Rick Bonino, who covered the trial for the *Spokesman-Review*. "It wasn't like any other trial—it was just like entertainment. There were all these unexpected twists and turns." For one thing, Maxey's defense was based on portraying Ruth as crazy (or at least "diminished"), which didn't prove difficult in the least. One psychiatrist testified that Ruth saw "horns growing out of the head" of Judge Shields when he pronounced sentence on Son. "She felt the devil was out to destroy the Coes," said the psychiatrist, who added that Ruth thought the "devil was out to make a mockery of the criminal justice system."

She also heard voices in her head—including Kevin's and another voice she thought might be God's—telling her to "do something, do something." She was acting on that demand when she hired the hit man, said another psychologist. Other doctors testified that she had been diagnosed with manic-depressive disorder for at least ten years. Her husband testified that she had for years abused a variety of prescription drugs—"an absolutely appalling jumble of chemicals"—and that after Kevin's verdict, suicide had seemed to "loom on the horizon." The prosecution's case in response was straightforward enough: forget about all the psychiatric mumbo-jumbo—Ruth was motivated strictly by old-fashioned revenge and hate.

The first dramatic moment arrived early when the hit-man tapes were played in court. For the first time, the world heard that Ruth Coe wanted Don Brockett in diapers. Ruth was not present during the playing of the tapes; Maxey had convinced the judge to let her leave the courtroom. But the drama's biggest twist came a few days later: the complete nervous breakdown of the defendant. It started when prosecutor Mary Kay Barbieri gave copies of the Ruth Coe hit-man tapes to local NBC affiliate KHQ. The tapes had already been played in open court and complete transcripts had been published two days earlier in the *Spokesman-Review*. Yet when the judge heard that KHQ had the tapes, he issued an order that they not be broadcast. Doctors had warned the judge that broadcasting them would "facilitate a full-scale psychotic breakdown" in the defendant.

KHQ promptly aired the tapes anyway, on both their radio and television stations, citing its First Amendment rights. Ruth and Maxey were walking back to the courthouse after a lunch break when she heard about the broadcast. She immediately "suffered a total fit of emotional prostration" and became hysterical, Maxey told Bonino. Maxey managed to get her to his office and immediately summoned psychologist Anna Kuhl, who had been testifying that morning. Kuhl found Ruth to be "over the edge and into the pit and [didn't] feel she [could] come out again." Maxey went into his front office and told *Seattle Post-Intelligencer* reporter Timothy Egan, "I've got a sick woman on my hands who collapsed back there and refuses to go on with the trial." When Maxey saw a KHQ reporter, he angrily barked, "Go in the back room and take a look at my client. You guys don't give a shit about humanity." Kuhl later said that the public airing of the tapes had "made them concrete" in Ruth's mind, a reality she couldn't tolerate in her manic-depressive state.

Judge Bibb reconvened the trial that afternoon and, clearly incensed, immediately cited KHQ for contempt of court (overturned two years later by the state supreme court). Maxey moved for a mistrial, saying in an affidavit that "my client refuses to allow me to present any evidence on her behalf." Barbieri publicly worried about "how this [was] going to play," and it played sensationally. "Suicidal Coe Hospitalized; Lawyers Asking for Mistrial," shouted *Spokesman-Review* headline. On a practical level, her breakdown meant that Ruth did not take the stand that afternoon as planned. Instead, she was placed on suicide watch in the psychiatric unit of Sacred Heart Medical Center. "I don't know if I can strongly enough relate to you the seriousness of the problem," Kuhl told the judge. "The potential for her to commit suicide . . . is extremely high." Kuhl said Ruth needed at least forty-eight hours of intensive therapy before doctors could even decide whether she could stand trial. Bibb recessed the trial for the weekend. He later admitted to Olsen that he was a bit skeptical about all of Ruth's histrionics, but "didn't want blood on my hands" if the psychologists turned out to be right.

When court reconvened on Monday—the mistrial motion denied—Ruth looked as if she had spent a restful weekend in the hospital. "To reporters, Mrs. Coe seemed more at ease than at any time since the since the trial had begun," wrote Olsen. However, the defense soon announced that Ruth would not be taking the stand after all, implying that this was Ruth's decision, not the lawyers'. The prosecution called another psychiatrist, who testified that the tapes showed a woman who was not psychotic at all, just "clearly preoccupied with her task." That witness also pointed out the obvious: Ruth Coe had a very, very "heavy" relationship with her son.

Barbieri, in her summation, hammered away at what Ruth had revealed on the tapes: "Anger, revenge and determination are what you hear . . . Her intention is stated over and over again. She intended that they be killed." Maxey then delivered what may have been the most fiery—and most over-the-top—closing argument of his career.

In its more prosaic passages, he summarized the main points of the defense, beginning with entrapment: nobody would ever know who first suggested the idea of a hit man when Ruth talked to Violet Cooper, and Ruth certainly never followed up with any hit-man ideas until an undercover cop called her two months later. As for her diminished capacity, the tapes themselves "show[ed] . . . amazing madness more than any other thing."

Then Maxey defended Ruth for believing passionately in her son's innocence: "I've got two sons and I'd go to the mat for them. But I'm not a manic-depressive." Clearly improvising, he then recited several lines of what he called a Carl Sandburg poem: "There were children in the ships, there were children in the towns. War is for everyone. War is for children, too." This is actually a paraphrase of the Robert Frost poem "The Bonfire," which Maxey had quoted from during the Scoop Jackson race and in antiwar speeches. In those contexts, the verses made sense. The poem's theme is that children suffer in wars too. Yet in this context, the connection was puzzling. Maxey said his client's condition had reminded him of these lines. Maybe he meant that Ruth, like a child caught in a war, was a victim of a larger tragedy. To rebut the prosecution's contention that Ruth's illness was not serious, he reached back for a line from *Romeo and Juliet*: "He jests at scars that never felt a wound."

Maxey began his crescendo by paraphrasing one of his favorite Martin Luther King Jr. speeches, the famous "Drum Major for Justice" speech: "Think of the good man who . . . said, 'Don't mention that I have won the Nobel Peace Prize or many others. Just say that I wanted to be able to have them say on that fateful day that they buried me— that I tried to feed the hungry . . . That I tried to clothe the naked. That I tried in all of my life to visit those who were in prison. That I tried to love and serve all of humanity. Yes sir, if you want to say it, say I was a drum major, a drum major for justice.' That's what Ruth Coe was all her life—until she became mortally wounded with a disease that prevented her from being able to form a specific intent!" Ruth Coe? A drum major for justice? "It didn't make any sense at all," said Bonino. "It was just Carl getting carried away."

At first, none of Maxey's arguments seemed to have worked. When Judge Bibb rendered his verdict two days later, he first said he had not bought the entrapment theory one bit: "The defendant approached Jennings' offer like a hungry trout snapping at a fly." Nor did he buy much of the defense testimony about Ruth's diminished capacity. He conceded that the defendant had "suffered a partially disabling, serious mental illness since 1971." He also acknowledged that at the time of the crime she was undergoing "severe stress caused by a series of highly emotional traumatic events." But these problems did not make her delusional, nor did they prevent her from being able to form a specific intent. "The case reads a bit like Greek tragedy by Euripides or Sophocles," said Bibb, as quoted by Olsen. "A symbiotic family relationship, catastrophe caused by man or the gods, avengement and the judging of the avenger again by the gods or fate or by men. And the human emotions described by the ancient Greek playwrights of anger, hate, the desire for revenge—human emotions that exist today—I must find to be the precipitating cause of the defendant's conduct, not a diminished mental capacity, whether with or without inducement from the police."

None of these statements boded well for Maxey's defendant. Olsen reported that Gordon Coe just shook his head. But Bibb wasn't finished. "This is certainly not to say that the defendant's mental condition and the tragedies that have befallen her should not or will not be considered by the court," he continued. "There has to be a place for mercy in any civilized system of justice, and in my view the facts of this case will justify a substantial degree of mercy being shown the defendant, absent any showing that she presently presents a danger to others. I conclude that the defendant was guilty as charged." Maxey couldn't have been too surprised by the verdict, but Bibb gave plenty of reason for optimism about the sentence. Barbieri, in her sentencing statement, asked the judge for a minimum of five and a maximum of twenty years in prison. Maxey simply asked for the maximum amount of sympathy for "one little 61–year-old lady who is a manic-depressive." He mentioned the immense suffering she had already endured and concluded with a quote attributed to Abraham Lincoln: "This, too, shall pass."

Then Ruth delivered her first and only lines upon the stage. She stood up, thanked the judge, and said, "I can't let this case end without making a public apology to Judge Shields—Judge George Shields and his family—and to Donald Brockett and his family." And with Maxey's arm enveloping Ruth's shoulders, Bibb began to read his sentencing ruling: "Mrs. Coe, the crime you have committed demands a prison sentence in every case almost without exception." But then he recited all of the mitigating circumstances in her case: her "emotional vulnerability," her lack of any criminal record, and of course, the family's series of unfortunate events. Then he pronounced sentence: twenty years in prison, suspended; one year in the county jail of her choosing; and ten years of probation.

Maybe Maxey's over-the-top oration *had* worked. The whole thing amounted to one year of easy time, with the possibility of work release. This was virtually the lightest possible sentence. "In essence, the judge bought the diminished capacity defense," a satisfied Maxey later told *The American Lawyer*. Assistant prosecutor Rebecca Roe was clearly shocked. "You don't just take a class-A felony and say she's a pathetic 61–year-old lady and forget about it," she fumed. Brockett was even more appalled. He said it was a perfect example of why sentencing guidelines had to be stiffened. "Judge Bibb said justice needs to be tempered with mercy," Brockett told reporter John Webster of the *Chronicle*. "As a person who's in the system, who now can sympathize much more with the victims, I think it might be well for judges to remember that mercy has to be tempered with justice." Brockett later called it "a sentence of the heart and not the head."

Meanwhile, in the prison at Walla Walla, Kevin Coe told the *Seattle Post-Intelligencer* that he couldn't understand why the defense hadn't used every weapon at its disposal, namely, himself. He bragged that he would have made an "excellent witness," saying, "I don't know why they didn't call me to testify. I helped prepare their case." When a reporter asked Maxey if Kevin had indeed helped prepare their case, Maxey shot back, "Like the shark helps the swimmer." Then he turned on his heel and walked away. "It was one of those classic Maxey comebacks, totally off the cuff," said Bonino.

A few weeks later, Ruth and Gordon made noises about appealing the verdict, but Maxey clearly wanted none of it. Olsen reported that Maxey had told a friend right after the sentence, "I would be crazy to appeal this one, wouldn't I?" In fact, when Ruth said she might appeal, Maxey said he would resign. "I just wish to end the odyssey," he said. Ruth eventually decided not to appeal. She spent part of her year at the Geiger Field Work Release Center in Spokane, where she was released on weekdays to attend interior-design classes. In February of 1982, she was transferred to a Seattle work-release facility to be closer to her daughter. As she left for Seattle, she vowed never to return to Spokane and never did. Maxey was there to see her off. He admitted to a reporter that he "smiled broadly as she drove off into the sunset."

Maxey wasn't quite finished with the Coe family saga yet. In 1984, the Washington State Supreme Court overturned all four of Kevin Coe's convictions on the grounds that a number of witnesses and victims had undergone hypnosis to "assist" them in recovering memories. A new trial was ordered in which Kevin's confession became a key issue. So Maxey landed in court, not as a defense lawyer, but as a witness. In an often-exasperated tone, Maxey testified that Kevin had been "grabbing at what he perceived to be an offer" by the judge and that Maxey had advised him that his confession could not be used against him in any other proceeding. On February 12, 1985, Kevin Coe was reconvicted on three of the rape counts and sentenced to life plus fifty-five years. As of 2008, he was still an inmate at the Walla Walla prison.

Eventually, even Judge Bibb came to believe that he had been too lenient with Ruth Coe. In 1988, six years after her conviction, Bibb wrote Maxey a letter, apparently in response to a request from Maxey that she be released from probation. By this time, Ruth had survived at least one drug overdose (two days after Kevin's reconviction) and was having health problems. She died in 1996. "Having now sat on the Superior Court bench for 14 years, I sometimes reflect back on various cases . . . and at times have second thoughts on my rulings," wrote Bibb to Maxey. "With respect to Mrs. Coe, my second thoughts have been that I should not have granted her probation, or at the very least, that I should not have granted her work release for the one-year county jail sentence. Under those circumstances, I must advise that I would decline to grant any motion on her behalf to release her from probation prior to its expiration in the ordinary course." Bibb also went out of his way to congratulate Maxey on the "excellent impression you made upon me" in handling the case.

That was quite a tribute to Maxey's rapport with judges. Yet it fell to Don Brockett to pronounce the ultimate—although clearly unintentional—tribute to Maxey for his role in this particular Greek tragedy. "She [Ruth] wanted me made into a *baby*," Brockett told *The American Lawyer*. "I don't know of anybody but Carl Maxey who could have convinced a judge to feel sorry for her and disregard what she had done."

15

"NO GODDAMNED AWARD"

Following the Ruth Coe case, Maxey resembled a unique Northwest cross between Martin Luther King Jr. and Johnny Cochran—although it's hard to imagine the flamboyant Cochran, of the O. J. Simpson trial, claiming his favorite book to be Dickens's *A Tale of Two Cities*. Maxey did, in a 1982 feature story about the favorite books of prominent Spokanites. "In my mind, it's probably the finest book ever written," said Maxey. "If I were isolated and could have only one book for company, that's the one I'd want."

This isn't a surprising choice. Not only did Maxey have a childhood right out of Dickens, he also shared the writer's concern for social justice. Maxey once wrote in an op-ed column that "one has only to read the first two pages" of *A Tale of Two Cities* to know that Washington's criminal sentences were too harsh. Slightly more surprising was Maxey's enduring affection, mentioned in the same article about favorite books, for the swashbuckling adventure stories he loved as a boy, *The Three Musketeers* and *The Count of Monte Cristo*. But overall, Maxey was proud of being well-read and loved to sprinkle quotes from Rudyard Kipling, Langston Hughes, and Winston Churchill into his speeches and summations. "In the practice of law, I've found that the people I perceive to be the most effective and the most efficient are always the people who are well-read," he told the paper. "You just can't keep a handle on modern events if you don't read."

Maxey remained in great demand as the go-to lawyer for people in trouble. His "one o'clock cattle-call" method of handling office appointments became legendary in the local legal community. Everybody who wanted to see him was told to show up at 1:00 P.M. They all gathered in the waiting room and, one by one, were summoned into his office. Maxey gave them as much time as necessary and then called in the next client. Sometimes, people would still be in the waiting room at dinnertime. For many people in trouble, the wait was worth it.

Still, as Maxey turned sixty, he had not particularly endeared himself to large swaths of the Spokane populace. He was no longer King Carl to the region's more conservative, establishment citizens, who long ago had been turned off by his liberal politics, strident tone, and unrelenting attacks on the status quo. Many considered him a combination scold, show-off, and shyster. *Spokesman-Review* sports columnist John Blanchette later recalled in print that "something in [Maxey's] method—or perhaps it was just his choice of clients—had made him a target of some scorn in our newsroom" in the early 1980s. "Fairness. Justice. No favorites," wrote Blanchette. "It's amazing how unpopular those causes can be." Although Maxey was active in the state bar association and had lots of friends on the bar and the bench, plenty of his fellow lawyers resented him as well. "I know I've been the subject of some wrath and criticism from my co-attorneys with the bar because I get so much publicity—so they say," he told the *Spokesman-Review* in 1979. "I think I also take cases that are difficult, conscience-striking cases, troubled cases and controversial ones."

Even Maxey's penchant for defending the most "under" of the underclass—"bikers and bad guys," in Blanchette's words—caused people to brand him with guilt by association. This is an occupational hazard of all criminal lawyers, who do not often have the luxury of representing unblemished angels. Yet Maxey was often the subject of particularly overheated rumors. Bevan Maxey remembered "a lot of wild things" attributed to his father, including that he "ran a string of whorehouses." Another time, a fellow lawyer sent Carl a copy of an affidavit from a witness in a drug case who asserted that Maxey was "the biggest marijuana dealer in the state." These kinds of rumors persisted all of his life, although none ever went past the whispering stage. In fact, he was too busy juggling his massive docket of cases to be a drug-and-whorehouse czar. And though Maxey was no puritan, his law license was as vital to him as oxygen. He was careful not to jeopardize it.

Maxey once landed in hot water with the state bar association, though the water was actually more like lukewarm. In 1983, Maxey had accepted a rifle and a shotgun from a down-at-the-heels client as security in a divorce case. He mounted the shotgun in his office and sold the rifle without the permission of the owner. In 1985, the bar association sent him a "letter of censure," the mildest form of lawyer discipline, for selling the rifle, although the letter specified that Maxey had a "good-faith belief" that he had been entitled to sell the property. Maxey bought back the rifle, returned it to the client, and never sought payment from her. The issue was closed.

Some of the rumors about Maxey no doubt came from the company he kept. He certainly wasn't afraid to make his affection known for one particular "saint-and-sinner-type dude": Sam Houston Willis, who ran the infamous Sam's Pit, site of Maxey's wedding party. Maxey later described Sam's Pit as a "freewheeling establishment that sold illegal booze and where people of the night met." In 1981, four years after Willis's death, Maxey told the *Spokane Daily Chronicle* that Willis "did sell whiskey, and sure, there were some prostitutes hanging around his place. But his was the only place to serve people of the night and the poor. Instead of committing burglaries, [they] could go up to his place and get something to eat." Willis had another side as well, one that "won praise even from the police," said the *Chronicle*. He fed poor people at the Pit for free every Sunday, and he held annual picnics in Liberty Park with free "soul food" for those with no money. "He probably bought a full suit of clothes for everybody on Skid Road at some time in his life," Maxey said. "He was veritable house of charity all on his own. He was without a doubt the toughest man I knew, physically. He was also the softest touch in town." Maxey initiated a public drive to have a statue of Willis erected in Liberty Park. It was a touching gesture, but with zero chance of success. Most Spokane residents had never met Sam Willis and would have been scared to death to set foot in his Pit.

Maxey admired the kind of generosity Willis typified and tried to emulate it himself. Legal assistant Marsha Dornquast said that every black minister in Spokane would come to Carl at Christmastime and ask for money, and he usually said, "You bet." And if he had clients who couldn't pay, he gave his services away for free. He once told the *Chronicle* that "lawyers do things for free far more than the public is aware." By "lawyers" he actually meant himself and his new firm, the Maxey Law Offices.

Following the retirement of partners Leo Fredrickson and Robert Bell, Maxey, his two sons, and Pat Stiley decided to strike off on their own. They bought a plain brick building near the Spokane County Courthouse and opened the Maxey Law Offices, PS, in 1981. The firm had six lawyers (including the three Maxeys), four paralegals, six secretaries, and a full-time investigator. It would later grow even larger. Maxey was immensely proud that his sons were following in his footsteps. "He never pushed me to be a lawyer," said Bevan, who had been an English major at Washington State University. "He was not opposed to it in any way [either]. He never discouraged it and probably liked the idea . . . A lot of people say they couldn't work with their family or wouldn't want to, because they wouldn't want things to get antagonistic. But I always enjoyed it."

For Stiley, however, the partnership was getting tense by 1981. He and Maxey had argued vehemently about how to handle the Kevin Coe sentencing. Stiley believed that Maxey was stepping into a trap. "Carl believed Judge Shields and I didn't," said Stiley. "And Carl had raised *me* to be the cynic." When Stiley was proven right, he might have said "I told you so" a few too many times, and antagonism began to grow between mentor and protégé. "In my opinion at the time, Carl was changing a lot," said Stiley. "He was no longer as dynamic in the courtroom. We were settling cases I wanted to try." They also had serious differences of opinion about the day-to-day running of the firm and its priorities. The result was a complete blowup one day, in which every member of the firm tendered their resignations to Stiley, who was president of the corporation that year (they traded off the presidency each year).

"Carl was unhappy and he expressed that in fairly strong terms," said Stiley. "So I went home and wrote him a letter and said I really enjoyed my time with him, but I couldn't be dependent on him for the rest of my career and I really had to spread my wings." Maxey did not take it well. In fact, he was monumentally angry. Before the next day was out, he removed Stiley's name from the firm's bank account and canceled Stiley's one major perk, his free parking spot. Stiley, who had intended to stay on for at least another year while finishing out his pending cases, was shaken by how hard Carl took it. "Carl thought I was disloyal, to him and to his kids," said Stiley. "He had never had a partner change directions like that. He saw it as, 'Patrick, how could you possibly do this?' I had no idea it would be that emphatic." After a short, extremely uncomfortable limbo, Stiley left the firm and started his own. It took a couple of years before Maxey would even talk to him, and even after that their relationship never regained its previous intimacy.

Maxey instead relied on his sons, which came in handy when Maxey first began to develop health problems. It was no coincidence that these problems flared during the Roldan Q. Atacador first-degree murder trial in 1984. If ever a case was custom-made to cause high blood pressure, this was it. Atacador, of Polynesian descent, was a student at Spokane's North Central High School in 1981 when someone broke into the home of Jane E. Ward, age thirty-one, robbed her, and then bludgeoned her to death. No arrest was made until two years later, when one of Atacador's schoolmates informed police that Atacador was the murderer. This schoolmate said that Atacador had told him he entered the victim's home under the guise of needing to use the telephone. Then he beat and kicked the woman and threw her down the basement steps. When she tried to crawl back up, he beat her to death with a hammer. Atacador was arrested in Hawaii and brought back to Spokane for the trial in January of 1984.

The case was filled with infuriating developments, even during the pretrial phase. Maxey was angered to find that the prosecutors had withheld a number of key documents, as well as hair, blood, and finger-prints samples, during the discovery process. Among those documents was a letter by the informant in which he contradicted his later statements about Atacador. Maxey was especially incensed that the prosecutor's office (still headed by Don Brockett) would delay discovery in this particular case. "This murder is three years old!" he told Judge William G. Luscher.

Far more damaging was the revelation that a police detective had elicited an incriminating statement from Atacador using dubious, to say the least, methods. He had showed Atacador a picture of a bloody palm print taken from the victim's staircase and said words to the effect of, "If this is your print, how did it end up at the victim's house?" The problem was, it was not Atacador's palm print, or at least nobody ever proved it to be. "That's the oldest con game in the world, judge," an exasperated Maxey told Luscher. The judge agreed and ruled that Atacador's statements were obtained through "trickery" and would not be admissible. This ruling was later upheld by a state appeals court and the state supreme court.

Still, when the nonjury trial finally started, the schoolmate's testimony was devastating. Among other things, the friend said that Atacador had "mocked the victim and then laughed about it." Maxey attempted to show that the schoolmate and his brother actually had far more motive to commit the crime than Atacador. They had lived with the victim before and had engaged in fights with her. But before Maxey could present his defense, a Perry Mason–like development threw the trial into turmoil. A woman, through her attorney, called Maxey's office four days into the trial and said she had information that strongly implicated a different acquaintance of the victim in the murder. Furthermore, she had given this information to a police detective, but the prosecution had never told the defense team. Carl and Bevan Maxey immediately moved for a mistrial based on "prosecutorial misconduct"—the deliberate withholding of exculpatory evidence. The next day, Judge Luscher ruled that there was "no excuse" for withholding the evidence, comparing it to "trial by ambush." He granted the mistrial and ordered a retrial.

The *Spokesman-Review* ran an editorial chiding Brockett and his office for its missteps in both the Atacador case and the Coe case and suggested that "he [Brockett] and the police department spend some time in the woodshed." That retrial took place in September of 1984, and Atacador walked free. Judge Luscher acquitted him, saying that no physical evidence had ever tied Atacador to the scene. The judge also said he was "distressed" by the numerous inconsistencies in the statements of the witnesses who implicated him. Atacador said, "I'm just glad to get out."

Maxey was not present for the acquittal, however, having handed the case over to Bevan and another attorney two months prior, tersely citing his health. He would say only that he was following advice from his doctor and did not want to discuss his health problems. The problems turned out to be a serious case of high blood pressure, a disease for which Maxey carried two risk factors: he was a black man and a type A personality. He may well have had a genetic predisposition as well, but that was anybody's guess. This diagnosis marked a turning point in Maxey's career and his life. "From that point on, he discernibly tried to slow down," said Bevan. "He kind of *had* to."

He finally opened up about the problem in 1986 to a *Spokesman-Review* reporter, saying that the stress during the Atacador case had been especially potent and at some point "something was telling me that something was wrong." His doctor told him his blood pressure was "soaring." Maxey said he "had to accept the fact that one lawyer wasn't going to change the world around . . . [I had to] make some adjustments in my habits to reduce stress." Maxey had cut his caseload and virtually stopped taking the most stressful cases, criminal cases, referring those to Bill and Bevan instead. He was pedaling away on an exercise bike, trying to walk more often, and was spending less time in the office. "I put in my hours," he said. "It's just that I'm not going to come in at 7 or 8 and work until 8 or 9 anymore. I come in when I feel like it."

Maxey had by no means abandoned his civil rights work, but for the previous five or ten years it had mainly involved fighting rearguard actions against proposals such as mandatory sentencing guidelines and a national movement to reinstate the death penalty. He believed that both of these issues had an inordinate impact on minorities. "They're going to be executing the same people," he said. "And the same folly [exists] that occasioned the moratorium in the first place—the total numbers of black[s] and minorities [being executed]." When Washington instituted new uniform criminal sentencing guidelines in 1983, Maxey told reporters, with considerable hyperbole, that it was "the worst thing that's happened since they approved slavery . . . These guidelines are a way to keep rich white people out [of prison] and to put poor black people in." The guidelines would simply compound the current appalling situation, he said, in which "two percent of the state's population is black, but 22 percent of the state's prison population is black."

"The reason that our number is disproportionately high in the penal system is . . . that minorities (blacks in particular) are more likely to be arrested and prosecuted, less likely to have an attorney immediately, more likely to have appointed counsel, less likely to make bail, more likely to be convicted (by judge or jury) and likely to get longer sentences," Maxey wrote in a 1983 guest editorial for the *Spokesman-Review*. He argued loudly and publicly against the new guidelines, often pitting himself against Brockett, who was a vocal proponent of mandatory sentencing and who served on a committee that helped draft the guidelines. Brockett claimed that mandatory sentencing would prevent many absurd abuses of the system. Just to take one example, a sixty-one-year-old woman convicted of trying to kill a judge and a prosecutor would not get one lousy year of work release. She would get a minimum of five years in prison.

By the 1980s, one of the most insidious racist groups in the United States, the neo-Nazi Aryan Nations, moved in practically next door. The group's leader, the Reverend Richard Butler, built his compound just across the state border, in Hayden Lake, Idaho, about thirty-five miles from Maxey's law office. An assortment of Aryan Nations losers, drifters, and skinheads proceeded to burn crosses and stage "white power" parades in Spokane and Coeur d'Alene. They also plastered the Maxey Law Offices one night with handbills that featured a drawing of a "running nigger" with a target superimposed. Maxey spoke out loudly and publicly against the Aryan Nations and he wrote the U.S. attorney general in 1981, urging a probe of the group's Klan links. Nothing, he said, was done about it until much later. "There were a bunch of people up there in North Idaho who were dangerous and nobody perceived it," Maxey told the *Spokesman-Review* in 1985. He continued to speak out against the Aryan Nations whenever he could.

Maxey also continued to complain about racial conditions in his hometown, but with an ever-increasing tone of frustration bordering on despair. In 1978, he noted incredulously that Spokane still had no black doctors or dentists. And, after all of those legal fights with the social clubs, there was exactly one black member of the Elks and "no others I know of in fraternities and social clubs." He said this indicated the general "social unacceptability" of blacks in Spokane. In fact, he claimed that the black people at the time faced a "larger personal affront from the white community than during the days of Jim Crow," saying that "the white citizenry has made up its mind that we've come so far, so fast, that we are now equal with them. That's a bunch of damn nonsense." He added that there was no reason to suspect that Spokane would ever attract more black professionals. Even if it did, he said, "I don't think they'd be accepted." Clearly, Maxey was taking this lack of progress personally.

Despite his own growing doubts, the greater world seemed to be coming to the conclusion that Maxey *had* made a difference. The first evidence arrived with a letter in 1982 informing him that he had won the William O. Douglas Bill of Rights Award, the highest award given by the American Civil Liberties Union (ACLU) of Washington. The award was named after the revered U.S. Supreme Court justice from Yakima, and the announcement noted that Maxey had "never backed away from defending constitutional rights, no matter how unpopular the cause." Maxey "overcame obstacles that would have crippled a lesser person, but lit a fire of determination in him that sent him to the forefront of every battle he could join against injustice and discrimination," said the ACLU.

At the awards banquet in Seattle in December of 1982, Maxey did not deliver the usual polite thank-you speech. "I saw bums in your alleys and people begging for your food," he told the crowd, describing what he had just seen on Seattle's streets. "Don't give me no goddamned award. Give those people some food." He then implored the crowd to seize this "one last chance" to help America fulfill its promise of equality. And he reminded the mostly white civil libertarians that blacks suffer disproportionately in the land of the free. He noted that black people were far more likely to be unemployed, and not coincidentally, far more likely to be in jail. "What is it you do when you're unemployed?" he asked. "When I was 10, 12 or 13 and unemployed, I stole."

He received plenty of letters congratulating him on his award, but none probably meant as much to him as the one from DeSmet, Idaho, written in the spidery handwriting of Father Byrne, age eighty-nine. The revered old priest, still living at the Sacred Heart Mission, told Maxey that the news of the award had "filled me with pride." A year later, Maxey was named to a list of Best Lawyers in America, and Father Byrne wrote again, saying, "How greatly honored—honored—we at DeSmet are to have contributed to some extent during your stay with us." Then in 1987, Maxey received notification of another award, the Legal Foundation of Washington's Goldmark Award for Distinguished Service. This was given to the individual or group who "best reflects commitment to the principle of equal access to justice for all." The board of the Spokane Bar Association had nominated him because of his unflagging commitment to pro bono work.

A growing consensus was emerging that Maxey had made a difference for the better. Even those who were not his natural philosophical allies were coming around. "Whether you love him or despise him, you have to admire Maxey, who has gone from birth at society's bottom rung to its heights—but never so far up that he has lost sight or touch with those still struggling behind him," said the *Spokesman-Review* editorial board, with whom he continued to spar in letters to the editor.

Other awards followed. In 1993, Mayor Sheri Barnard proclaimed Carl Maxey Celebration Day. That same year the Gonzaga University School of Law chose him for its highest honor, the Gonzaga Law Medal, which was presented to Maxey at the school's commencement ceremonies. "Carl Maxey's impact must be measured not only by the many cases he has taken, but also by the sheer deterrent effect his presence has had on actions that otherwise would have denied civil rights," said Gonzaga's president, the Reverend Bernard J. Coughlin. "He has been a vigilant watchman—a pre-emptive presence who caused many a retreat before the battle was even engaged." Not bad for a student who had barely squeaked by and whose law professor had predicted he would flunk the bar exam.

These awards meant a great deal to Maxey, but perhaps no more than two other nonlegal honors: his admission into both the Gonzaga Sports Hall of Fame and the Inland Empire Sports Hall of Fame. His old boxing coach, Joey August, gave the induction speech at the Inland Empire shindig in 1983, using the same general theme he used at the Gonzaga Sports Hall of Fame induction speech. "I know there's some people out there who don't like him—attorneys who have lost cases to him," said August. "And there are some husbands out there who are still paying [alimony]. But I'm very proud of this fellow."

The highest honor yet to come—one of the highest that any lawyer can contemplate—was about to be dangled before him: an appointment to the state supreme court. The possibility arose in the most unlikely manner, when Washington State Supreme Court justice William Goodloe announced his retirement in 1988 and then suggested Maxey as his successor. "It's long overdue for a minority to go on the Supreme Court," Goodloe told reporters. "Carl Maxey is the obvious choice. I have checked with members and officials of the bar association and received nothing but outstanding reports as to his ability and competence as a lawyer." This recommendation came as a shock for two reasons. First, Goodloe was an outspoken conservative Republican, nearly the last justice anyone would have suspected of being a Maxey fan. Second, according to the state's constitution, a retiring justice is not entitled to choose his own successor. That role is strictly reserved for the governor. Never had a justice had the audacity to even *suggest* a successor. Maxey was initially flattered. "I have to say that with this gracious invitation of Judge Goodloe's, it would be almost inappropriate to decline," he said. "After you get over the shock of what's occurred, you have to settle down and make some determinations. I will contact the governor's office."

As soon as jaws recovered from dropping, they started flapping. A spokesman for the state's prosecuting attorney association said that Goodloe had breached the bounds of proper judicial behavior by proposing his own successor. Some suggested that Goodloe's recommendation was more like a kiss of death. Governor Booth Gardner, a Democrat, said that Goodloe's recommendation probably "embarrassed" Maxey but didn't actually "hamper" Maxey's chances. When asked why he thought Goodloe made his unconventional announcement, Gardner only smiled and said, "He's a unique individual." Within a few weeks, others had come to the conclusion that Maxey's chances were indeed hampered; if the governor chose Maxey it would appear that he was ceding his own executive right to choose a justice. Maxey eventually reached that conclusion himself. "Goodloe didn't do me any favors by putting me in this situation," said Maxey three weeks after the announcement. "None of this was done with my approval or consent." Some went so far as to suggest that Goodloe had cunningly torpedoed a Maxey appointment. However, Goodloe appeared sincere in his belief that the court needed a strong minority voice and that Maxey possessed that voice.

The longtime Maxey love-him-or-hate-him debate was finally pushed into the public arena. Reporters found it easy to find passionate admirers, including superior court judge James M. Murphy, who told reporters, "He knows how people live—not only in the ivory tower, but on the streets. I think he has a good working knowledge of everyman." Another judge—a rather surprising one—was privately lobbying for Maxey. "I was pleased to read of Judge Goodloe's recommendation," wrote Judge Robert Bibb to Maxey from his courtroom in Everett. "As a matter of fact, I took it upon myself to recommend you to the Governor through State Senator Larry Vognild. I did this because of the excellent impression you made upon me in your handling of the Ruth Coe case."

It was just as easy to find those who had serious misgivings about the prospect of Justice Carl Maxey. Several told *Spokesman-Review* reporter Kim Crompton that they would not give their names so as not to create "professional ill will." Still, they brought up the issue of

Maxey's temper, noting that he had recently called up KXLY-AM radio host Martha Lou Wheatley and told her that if she weren't a woman, he would "come to your station and kick your ass." Maxey responded that he was justified in being angry with her. He was infuriated that Wheatley had said something on the air that would affect the defendant's right to an untainted jury pool in a case he was working. "Everybody's got some kind of temper," he said.

Other detractors suggested he was not a serious "student of the law." "If you conceive of a Supreme Court justice as one who is really a scholarly type," said one anonymous attorney, "Carl doesn't fit that mold." Still others pointed to his inexperience as a judge—he had only served pro tem—even though the state bar association rated him "most qualified." The *Spokesman-Review*'s editorial board, while calling Maxey's career "distinguished," did not exactly give him a ringing endorsement either. They warned against making a choice on the basis of "mere tokenism" and urged Governor Gardner to scrutinize Maxey's qualifications "from every angle." Then, of course, there was the charge that Maxey always played the race card. "The only thing that bothers me," said one anonymous lawyer, "is that if anyone disagrees with Carl, he has that one escape hatch, that 'You're a racist.'"

One critic who felt no need to remain anonymous was prosecutor Brockett. He told Crompton that Maxey was flat-out unqualified for the position for a litany of reasons. "I just don't think he has the proper judgment to be a Supreme Court judge," said Brockett. "It's much too important a position. One of his major weaknesses is that he turns every issue into a racial issue, which I think is unfortunate. I think that's a lack of judgment. I think Carl could be much more effective in destroying racial barriers by not doing that." Brockett said that Maxey once resorted to calling one of his deputy prosecutors a racist. Maxey didn't deny that, but said the guy deserved it. The prosecutor had suggested, during a trial about a killing at Chinese restaurant, that black people don't eat Chinese food. As for calling the deputy prosecutor a racist, Maxey said he had been called worse even by judges. "Sometimes, courtrooms are not the most pleasant arenas," Maxey said. "When I started practicing, I had judges refer to me as a nigger and it never upset me to the point where I couldn't discharge my duty. I think lawyers have to be forgiven for heat-of-the-moment comments."

Brockett also said that Maxey's overall philosophy was simply out of step with the public on law-and-order issues. He said that Maxey would use "too much of a fine-tooth comb" in questioning police activities. Obviously, Brockett was speaking from long experience on this issue. "He [Brockett] doesn't think defense attorneys have the same concern about law enforcement that he does," said Maxey in rebuttal. "That's an improper attitude. We have as high a regard for the judges—for the process—as [prosecutors] do."

When Governor Gardner finally made his selection on July 13, 1988, the appointment went to the only other black candidate on the six-person short list: Charles Z. Smith, a University of Washington law professor emeritus in private practice in Seattle. Maxey was unfailingly gracious in his public comments. He said he was gratified that the state supreme court would finally have a black justice. For Maxey, it was "half a victory—but the most important half." Yet those who knew him best said that he was disappointed not to be chosen. Lou Maxey said he saw it as evidence of a pattern in his life—no matter how much he achieved, he could never achieve ultimate acceptance. "A reasonable man could never argue against him in terms of qualifications," said Lou. "He had the judicial temperament, he really did. But Booth Gardner was scared to death of him. He, literally, truly was. That's pretty much an ongoing theme in Carl's life. He used to tell me, 'There's nothing more dangerous than a jealous white man.' And it's true. They are everywhere and they are deadly. His life was fraught with those kinds of obstacles that should never be put in front of anybody. He struggled with it every day. It killed him."

16

"LIVING THROUGH ALL THIS B.S."

Through the latter half of the 1980s and into the 1990s, Carl and Lou took more time to travel, visiting Hong Kong, London, and, when there was a championship boxing match, Las Vegas. Yet Maxey found cutting back from his law practice painful and, in many ways, impossible. He still took on divorce cases, the occasional criminal case and the occasional civil rights cause. His prime, however, was clearly behind him. Spokane attorneys who faced him during that era said he remained a skilled negotiator, but was no longer a formidable courtroom opponent. Even so, he was still probably the most in-demand defense lawyer in the region, strictly because of his reputation. When people in Spokane got in trouble, they still said, "Let's get Carl Maxey."

His blood pressure remained a problem and he knew he couldn't keep up his killer schedule. But retirement loomed before him like a sentence, and a mandatory one at that. All professionals eventually have to ease out of their jobs and most of them learn to come to terms with it. Retiring judge George Shields wrote Maxey a handwritten note on that very subject in 1993. "It seems strange to walk back in my old chambers stripped of the personal touches that made them mine," wrote the man who sentenced Kevin Coe. "Soon we will know the name of the new occupant, and I will be learning another lesson in how to 'let go.' That is not an easy lesson but in the long run it is good for one's health." Maybe Shields wrote this because he was concerned about Maxey. Or maybe he was merely being philosophical. In any case, Maxey continued to both resist and fret about retirement. "He was not a guy who golfed," said Bevan Maxey. "His hobby was to watch sports on TV. He liked to read and he liked to travel. But how he was going to keep himself occupied, I'm not really sure."

One way was by firing off guest columns, letters to the editor, and other outraged epistles. He dispatched an indignant letter to Los Angeles mayor Tom Bradley about the Rodney King beating in 1991. He sent an equally indignant letter a month later to National Basketball Association (NBA) commissioner David Stern about the league's lousy officiating. Other Maxey missives were on weightier topics of law and civil rights, including one heartfelt plea for local citizens to protest U.S. support for the apartheid regime in South Africa. "If Abraham Lincoln, 'The Great Emancipator,' had adopted a policy similar to that of Ronald Reagan, slavery would still exist in the United States," Maxey wrote with his ever-more-evident bombast in a December 23, 1984, guest column for the *Spokesman-Review*. Another angry letter went to the *Spokane Daily Chronicle* in response to its "derogatory" editorial about the first black winner of the Miss America contest. "Why didn't you suggest that the runner-up is black so they'd have a backup in case the winner got lynched?" wrote Maxey. "I'd ask you what does a black lady have to do to be perceived as a success by white people— maybe it's joining the Junior League, the City Club, the Moose, the Tri Delts or be an editorial writer? But then, that is all quite impossible, isn't it, because none of you will let us in."

With fewer fights in the courtroom, he seemed to be deliberately going out of his way to pick fights. In 1995, he wrote an outraged letter to U.S. attorney Smithmoore P. Myers, a colleague and friend from way back, who had delivered a talk at a Spokane Bar Association seminar. "During your presentation you made the statement that we do not want to emulate the 'rich, self-indulgent, narcissistic' professional basketball players, 'excluding, of course, John Stockton,'" wrote Maxey in his letter. "John Stockton was held out to be the good little white boy from Gonzaga as the ideal. Unfortunately, you made no exception for the 70 percent of basketball players who are black, thereby leaving the only inference that can be drawn: that they are the crybabies of which you spoke." Then Maxey said that "we are compelled to attend seminars to obtain [continuing education] hours, but we are not compelled to be insulted."

Myers was taken aback. "When I opened your letter, it was with the amiable thought, 'I wonder what Carl has in mind,' and I was astonished to learn what it was," said Myers, in a handwritten letter back to Carl. Myers defended his remarks on the obvious grounds: that he never said one word about race, that he didn't say and didn't believe that all black players were "narcissistic," and that he only mentioned John Stockton as a local crowd-pleaser. Stockton, raised in Spokane and schooled at Gonzaga, was Spokane's most popular sports export at the time. Myers said the entire reference to the NBA and Stockton "could have been left out with no real loss." He ended by saying that he would try to be more careful in the future to eliminate the possibility of offense, because "I know your complaint is sincere and I don't want it to happen again."

Maxey promptly wrote back that "all is forgiven and forgotten" and that "I know you would never intentionally do anything to harm anybody." Maxey didn't end there, going on to confess his increasing cynicism and despair about the world and his place in it. "Smitty, times have changed since you and I were young. As I look back over my 44 years of practice, I cannot really feel, with all of the modest successes I have had, that I have left the world a better place than where it was before I started. The newfound sensitivity that you are surprised at is occasioned by the present hostility that exists between people of all complexions, races, interests and classes. There is really not a concerted reason given by our political leadership as to why we exist at all."

This was simply the latest in a long litany of cynical and bitter remarks that Maxey had been making publicly since the 1970s. These remarks covered a range of political and civil rights issues, but usually came down to the same themes: All of his struggles and hard work had not mattered. The world is every bit as unjust as before, and maybe worse. "The thing that saddens me most is that it never really made that much difference to the people on the top and the people in power," he said in a 1975 *Spokesman-Review* profile. "You wonder why I am the way I am now? The sum total is that the whole damn country is a bunch of Archie Bunkers." He said he was disappointed that he never gained "respect, really, for keeping things non-violent and yet insisting on progress." In looking back on all of the fights and struggles, he bluntly told a reporter, "I don't think I would have done it again."

In a 1979 *Spokesman-Review* interview, he seemed more charitable, both toward the world and himself. "Let me make one thing perfectly clear—I am black and this is a white community," he said. "Of that there is no doubt. But I do feel this community has treated me well and I also think I have treated it well as an attorney. You have to give in order to get, and work hard. I'm satisfied with my personal progress."

Maxey's moods on this subject swung back and forth, often in the same interview. In 1981, he opened up to Rita Hibbard of the *Spokesman-Review*. "I look on life as a war and not a game," he told her. "I have basically a competitive nature against the establishment. It's a challenge to me, but on the other hand, these were important issues that I think we should make moral commitments to help solve. I have the lofty idealism, but I have the common sense to know that it extracts such a heavy toll—it's the difference between battling for what you want and battling for what you believe . . . I kind of think I've proved I can win the battle standing for something and also be successful." Then he confessed to a growing cynicism about the outcome of this "battle." "That's the disappointment—that you haven't made enough people play this game with blood in their eye and fire in their heart. It makes me sad. And it makes me mad. I doubt that many people are willing to pay the price. I don't know that I would, if I had to do it over again. Because the redemptive value is bullshit."

Bullshit. This discouraged and odiferous word cropped up one more time in 1981 when an interviewer asked him to name his single most worthwhile accomplishment. "Living through all this bullshit," he replied. When *The Washington Journal*, a law journal, asked him in 1993 whether or not he had accomplished what he had set out to do, his weariness overcame a token attempt at optimism. "Yes and no," he said, "in that there are always battles to be won. I am really discouraged because I have never seen so many devastated people." He had exactly the same doubts in private. "I had thousands of hours of conversation with him," said Pat Stiley. "There were stages where the theme would always be: he had not done enough, he was capable of doing more." Lou Maxey agreed. "At night—not every night, but a lot of nights—he'd talk about, 'You know, I just haven't done enough,'" she said. "And I would go, 'OK, Carl, let me run this down to you.' And I would say, 'Sunday closing, social clubs, et cetera, et cetera' and he'd go, 'Goddamn it, you're right. I really have kicked some ass, haven't I? You're goddamn right.'"

But did he really believe it? He appeared to need constant reassurance. As he turned seventy-three in June of 1997, this issue was more often on his mind because he knew that his most effective days were behind him. In July of 1997, he had come to a difficult decision. He had decided to announce that he would no longer handle any cases involving court appearances. His career as a courtroom fighter was over. The ex-boxer expressed relief on at least one occasion that he could finally retreat to his corner for good.

Apparently, however, Carl's emotions were far more complex. On the morning of July 17, 1997, Lou was downstairs in their house on F Street. She heard two gunshots. She raced upstairs. Carl Maxey was lying in bed, his handgun next to him on the sheets. He had fired one shot into the ceiling, possibly a test round, and then he had placed the barrel in his mouth and fired again. His journey from black scratch was over.

17

TYPE-A GANDHI

W hat if Carl Maxey had never existed at all? Or, what if that little orphan boy had taken the most likely path and lived down to the world's expectations? The entire region would have been able to continue in its comfortable, old-fashioned, socially restrictive ways for years longer, or even decades. Nobody else, at least in the 1950s, showed much interest in rocking the boat. And even if someone had set that boat to swaying, would they have had the power, the legal clout, to budge the entrenched system? Eventually, someone else would have come along—a white lawyer, a black lawyer, or a black community leader—to hold the school board's feet to the fire. Someone else would have put pressure on the social clubs and restaurants. Someone else would have eventually taken on the barbers who did not "cut colored hair." As laws and attitudes changed, Spokane would have gradually fallen in line with the changing times. Yet without a homegrown black attorney, one who was already a local hero, every increment of that change would have come slower, harder, and more grudgingly. In those first years of his career, there *was* nobody else who could talk "morality" to the Spokane school superintendent—and back it up with a legal threat.

And what if, in this vacuum, another kind of local African American leader had come along? One who had abandoned, or never believed in, Martin Luther King Jr.'s, gospel of nonviolence? Maxey, as belligerent as he could be personally, never once wavered from his commitment to social change through nonviolence. He rightly resented that the local establishment took his, and the black community's, peacefulness for granted. Yet Maxey's particular strength lay in his outsized personality, his eagerness to wade into any legal fight, which meant his peacefulness was never, ever confused with submissiveness. With Maxey in town, docility was forever off the table. The establishment didn't have to worry that Maxey would incite a race riot, but it had to constantly look nervously over its shoulder to make sure that he wasn't filing a lawsuit, holding an angry press conference, or firing off a ferocious letter to the editor.

Many in white Spokane had long considered Maxey a bull in a china shop, tossing his horns wildly and sometimes breaking too much of the dinnerware. Sometimes, white Spokane was right. Maxey was, by personality and training, reflexively opposed to almost any establishment initiative, even one like Expo '74, which proved to be a source of vast pride for the community. But as the decades went by and the city adjusted to a new, more just world, even the establishment came to understand that Washington was a much fairer place because of the existence of Carl Maxey—and certainly a much more colorful place. Meanwhile, the underdogs—the minorities, draft resisters, hippies, convicts, and divorcees—had known it all along. They had been filling Maxey's waiting room for years.

Which is why, on his death, Spokane mourned for Maxey as it had mourned for no other figure that decade. The *Spokesman-Review* bannered the news across its front page—"Spokane Loses a Champion"— and ran eleven stories about Maxey during the following week. The *Seattle Times* published a tribute headlined, "Maxey Was an Inspiration." The *New York Times* printed a quarter-page obituary on July 20 and followed it with a piece in the annual "The Lives They Lived" issue of the *New York Times Magazine* titled, "Carl Maxey: Type-A Gandhi," a phrase coined by Maxey's longtime paralegal Debbieann Erickson the day after his death. It was her way of saying "he could have been a real angry person and he chose not to be," explained Erickson, who, inspired by Maxey, went on to become an attorney herself.

The county's superior court judges voted, in a rare tribute, to act as the honor guard at his memorial service, held at the Ridpath Hotel on July 21. More than twelve hundred people packed the ballroom, a crowd that former mayor Sheri Barnard called "the largest gathering at this hotel I can remember." And the room wasn't big enough. A second memorial service was held, for mourners unable to get into the first service, at one of the city's black churches several days later.

The Ridpath service was jammed with notables, including Seattle mayor Norm Rice, former University of Southern California basketball coach George Raveling, and rows of judges. Rice called Maxey "one of Washington's greatest treasures." Raveling called him "my hero." John Schultheis, then a state court of appeals judge, took to the podium and recalled the time he and Carl were at an event, listening to a group of fine Irish tenors. "I said, 'I'd give up my judicial career if I could sing like that,'" said Schultheis. "The next day, I got a call from Carl: 'I'll pay for your voice lessons.'" Plenty of Maxey's clients, including a few accused drug dealers and Hell's Angels members, were tucked in next to the judges. Barnard looked around that room, at the men wearing suits and the men wearing leathers, and said, "Carl Maxey is bringing our community together one last time." Eli Thomas, his old boxing sparring partner, was there. So was Don Brockett, his old legal sparring partner. And there were the faces from Carl's past: Milton Burns, Ninon Schults, Bill Williams, Bob Gibson, and Frances Scott. They remembered a long-ago Carl, an orphan hoping to find a way to become something—anything—in a cruel world.

It was up to Raveling to touch upon the anguish everyone felt about the manner of his death. "Why didn't I tell him I loved him when he was still alive?" asked Raveling, who had met Carl while coaching at Washington State University. "Why didn't I tell him the world wouldn't be the same without him?" The ultimate question remained unanswered: Why did he do it? Even those closest to him had no easy answer. He left no suicide note and had never spoken of suicide. Lou Maxey said she was taken utterly by surprise. She knew that his decision to quit courtroom work had been difficult for him, sometimes to the point of agony. Yet half the time he seemed relieved to be finally leaving the arena. "Sometimes he was happy about it, because he said, 'I don't have to do anything I don't want to anymore,' and I'd go, 'Good,'" said Lou.

Less than a week before Maxey's death, his oldest friend, Milton Burns, drove to Spokane from Olympia and had lunch with him at the Ridpath. Burns had a legal matter he wanted to discuss. Maxey said the matter was outside his area of expertise and apologized almost too profusely. He tried to call some other lawyers who he thought would help, but no one was in. Maxey was obviously upset at not being able to help the friend he had protected all through the Spokane Children's Home and the DeSmet mission school. "He almost acted like he let me down," recalled Burns, who died of a stroke four years later. "He said, 'I've been at this for forty years and I'm just wore out. I've got to get out of this business.' I never picked up anything despondent or anything, but he said that a couple of times."

The night before his death, Carl and Lou called paralegal Marsha Dornquast and invited her over for a predinner drink. Sitting on his deck on F Street, he told Dornquast of his decision. "He was struggling with it a little bit, but he wasn't distraught," she said. After she left, he told Lou, "Let's go to dinner at Ankeny's [the Ridpath's restaurant]." They had dinner, came home, and he said, "Do we have any champagne?" They shared two splits of champagne and toasted his decision. Lou asked him, "You're not going to give up your ticket [to practice law], are you?" "Hell, no," he replied.

His anxiety over the decision seemed out of proportion, and it may have had a physical cause as well. Bill and Bevan Maxey both said they had noticed a significant change in their father's state of mind about a week or two before his death. "He had a couple of episodes where he was very anxious and was misconstruing certain conversations that people had with him," said Bill. "We'll never know for sure what it was," said Bevan. "But there was a drastic change in him. Something happened to him. It's been hypothesized that he had a stroke, or at least something that really affected him, because he wasn't himself. He was more hostile, but at the same time, not as strong . . . I'm having a difficult time putting it into words. It was kind of like being more aggressive toward myself and my brother, for no apparent reason. Something was wrong with him, but I didn't know what it was."

Bevan said that he and his brother were naturally worried about this sudden personality change, but didn't know what to do about it. "I couldn't call his doctor and ask him to go see him," said Bevan. "You kept thinking, maybe he'll get over it." Yet it worried Bevan so much that when he got the call from the police on July 17, he didn't even need to hear the words. "I just kind of knew what it was," said Bevan. "I didn't know it was *that*. I just had a sinking feeling he wasn't with us anymore." Bill later said that his father had seen some of his best friends and law partners go through extended disabilities. Maxey was shaken by it and may have feared it in himself. "My sense was that sometime earlier he had resolved that if he sensed some decline healthwise that he was not going to go gentle into that good night," said Bill. Bevan summed up, "Whatever happened medically, I don't know what to call it . . . But it happened."

Maxey had never been diagnosed with anything more severe than high blood pressure. Spokane police interviewed his physician, Dr. Fred Viren, an internist, who told detectives that Maxey had been in "excellent health." However, Dr. Viren did tell police that he had counseled Carl and Lou on July 9, just a week prior to his death, because Maxey had been struggling with his retirement decision. Dr. Viren described Maxey's condition as "extremely agitated and anxious," but not, in his opinion "depressed or despondent." Maxey had also been having trouble sleeping. Dr. Viren had prescribed an antidepressant, but only in a low dose as a sleep aid. The doctor could "give no medical explanation" as to why Maxey had committed suicide, except to say that he had been "extremely indecisive" about his law practice. He also added that Carl and Lou had "an extremely good relationship."

In retrospect, Maxey's anxiety about retirement may have been a surface symptom of a far deeper worry. Here was a man who started at nothing and had made himself into something through two remarkable attributes: his athletic prowess, which had filled "vacuums of unhappiness and loneliness," and his charisma in the courtroom. All of this was now in the past. Maybe he feared he was returning to where he had started: zero. And maybe, as a motherless child, his emotions were fated to always be more raw, less resilient, than those who had known childhood security. Even his substitute father figures, Father Byrne and Joey

August, were dead. A psychiatrist could have explored those issues, but Maxey never went to one. Pat Stiley laughed at the very notion. "You couldn't tell Carl what to do," said Stiley. "At no point in my life could I have convinced him to go see a shrink or take an antidepressant." Some of those closest to Maxey still believe that he didn't commit suicide at all—that it was an accident. "He wasn't the most careful guy with guns," said Dornquast. "I know one time he came in and he said, 'Oh, God, Marsh, you wouldn't believe what I just did. I shot the window out of my bedroom.' No one will ever make me believe that he killed himself."

The police reports, however, tell a straightforward tale. Lou called police at 6:34 A.M., and when the first officers arrived she was standing in the driveway saying that her husband had shot himself. She mentioned his retirement worries. They went upstairs to find Maxey sprawled in bed, a handgun near his cheek. Two spent cartridge casings were found and a hole in the ceiling. Blood was coming out his nose and mouth. On one nightstand was the holster of the .380 automatic he had used; on the other nightstand was a Beretta 9 millimeter. Containers of ammunition were found in several places in the bedroom. There was no indication of a struggle. Blood spatter on his wrist and right forearm were consistent with the theory that he had held the gun in his right hand, turned it upside down, placed the barrel in his mouth, and fired. The bullet had entered his head through his mouth and not exited. The coroner arrived on the scene, inspected Maxey's body, and filled out the certificate of death, which specified "pulpification due to a self-inflicted gunshot wound" as the cause of death, with "depression" as a contributing factor. The coroner said that no autopsy would be necessary. Police did not recommend an autopsy either, because, said the report, "there has been nothing discovered during the investigation which would indicate anything other than a self-inflicted gunshot wound to the head." The body was released to Hennessy's Funeral Home and was cremated.

For the deepest insight into his death, maybe we need to go back to Maxey's oldest friend, Milton Burns, the only man who could truly comprehend Maxey's long and arduous path. "I'll tell you what I really feel," said Burns. "He was in the eye of the storm all of his life. I think he was just wore out. I think he had done so many things for so many people, that it finally got to him." After standing up for Milton in the orphanage, after scrapping for equality in his city, after raging against injustice wherever he saw it, after defending every underdog in every lost cause, maybe Carl Maxey was simply exhausted.

His name and his legacy endure in a number of ways. Bill and Bevan Maxey still take on pro bono cases and controversial causes at the Maxey Law Offices. Gonzaga University's Carl Maxey Memorial Scholarship Fund assists aspiring minority students who might otherwise not be able to attend college. The Spokane YWCA presents its annual Carl Maxey Racial Justice Award to the person who most exemplifies Maxey's ideals. The Washington State Senate passed a resolution in 1998 paying tribute to Maxey as a man of "great character, compassion and intelligence" and a "giant in civil rights." Every day, harried students in the Gonzaga University School of Law's library walk past a bronze bust in the lobby. The pedestal reads, "Carl Maxey: He made a difference."

How much of a difference? Jerrelene Williamson, an old friend from Spokane's civil rights struggles, remembers a moment that didn't make it into the news or onto an award plaque. It occurred in 1961, when the Spokane School Board was threatening to shut down Lincoln Elementary School. This school happened to be the only school in the district that was predominantly African American and Japanese. The parents sat in discouragement at one meeting as the board lectured them about why this school, and not some more affluent school, absolutely had to close. These parents felt powerless, resigned to their fate. "Then the door opened, and in walked Carl Maxey," said Williamson. "Everyone began to whisper, 'Carl's here. Carl's here.' Carl was a big man anyway, but when he came through that door, to us parents, he looked like a giant."

He must have looked that way to the school board as well. He plopped his briefcase on the floor and sat down. After a brief, urgent semihuddle, the board made an announcement: the school would remain open.

Carl Maxey had not uttered a single word.

NOTES ON SOURCES

In most cases, information and quotations are attributed within the chapter text. Interviews were a rich source of detail, and transcripts—in some cases, recordings—of the following interviews are in possession of the author.

Bonino, Rick, June 2006, Spokane, Washington
Burnette, Henry, 1998, by phone
Burns, Milton, August 15, 1998, Olympia, Washington
Dellwo, Robert, 1999, by phone
Dornquast, Marsha, March 1, 2006, Spokane, Washington
Elliott, Mildred, 1998, by phone
Erickson, Debbieann, June 2006, by phone
Freeman, Clarence, 1998, by phone
Gibson, Robert D., no date, by phone
Hagin, Wally, 1998, by phone
Kelly, Joe, May 2006, by phone
Lerner, Michael, June 2006, by phone
Lippman, Roger, May 2006, by phone
MacDonald, Kenneth, June 2006, by phone
Marashi, Mohammad, December 2006, by phone
Marchioro, Karen, December 2006, by e-mail
Maxey, Bevan, May 21, 2006, Spokane, Washington
Maxey, Bill, February 13, 1999, Spokane, Washington
Maxey, Carl, April 14, 1997, Spokane, Washington
Maxey, Lou (Merrie Lou Douglas), June 27, 1998,
    and March 1, 2006, Spokane, Washington

Nichols, Ruth, 1998, by phone

Salina, Martin, May 2006, Spokane, Washington

Scarpelli, Nick, 1998, by phone

Schults, Ninon, 1998 and 2006, by phone

Scott, Frances, 1998, by phone

Steinborn, Jeff, June 2006, by phone

Stiley, Patrick, June 8, 2006, Spokane, Washington

Thomas, Eli, 1999, by phone

Williams, William H., 1998, by phone

Williamson, Jerrelene, 1999, by phone

I made extensive use of the clipping archives of the *Spokane Spokesman-Review* and the *Spokane Daily Chronicle*, both referred to in the chapter sources that follow as S-R reference library or S-R electronic archive. The clippings number in the hundreds and are contained within files titled "Carl Maxey." Virtually every chapter contains some information from these clippings. Major articles and profiles I found most useful include John Blanchette, "Carl Maxey Found Equality Inside the Ring," *Spokesman-Review*, October 14, 1983; Alden Cross, "Spokane's Two Black Lawyers," *Spokesman-Review*, March 2, 1975; Rita Hibbard, "Life of Throwing Stones at Goliath Officialdom," *Spokesman-Review*, March 29, 1981; "Q&A: Attorney Carl Maxey Discusses Issues and Goals," *Spokesman-Review*, June 24, 1979; John Webster, "Carl Maxey: From Black Scratch," *Spokane Daily Chronicle*, March 17, 1981. I also used a number of other clipping files in the S-R reference library, many of which are specified in the chapter sources that follow.

I relied heavily on Carl Maxey's papers and other documents housed at the MAC Archive in the Joel E. Ferris Research Library and Archives at the Northwest Museum of Arts and Culture/Eastern Washington State Historical Society in Spokane, Washington, referred to in the chapter sources that follow as MAC Archive.

Several scholarly works about Northwest black history and the overall civil rights era were invaluable in providing context, including Joseph Franklin, *All through the Night: The History of Spokane Black Americans* (Fairfield, WA: Ye Galleon Press, 1989); Dwayne Anthony Mack, "Triumphing through Adversity: African-Americans in Spokane, Washington, 1945–1965, a Social History" (PhD dissertation, Washington State University, 2002); Quintard Taylor, *The Forging of a Black Community: Seattle's Central District from 1870 through the Civil Rights Era* (Seattle: University of Washington Press, 1994); Taylor Branch, *Parting the Waters: America in the King Years, 1954–63* (New York: Touchstone, 1988); and Taylor Branch, *Pillar of Fire: America in the King Years, 1963–65* (New York: Simon and Schuster, 1998).

Sources of particular relevance to certain chapters follow.

CHAPTER 1

Discrimination-Racial file and Spokane Children's Home file, S-R reference library; Spokane Children's Home records, MAC Archive; Certificate of Live Birth, Carl Maxey, Washington State Department of Health; Order of Adoption, Superior Court, Spokane, No. 20877, July 15, 1927; Certificate of Death, Carolyn Maxey, Washington State Department of Health; Timothy Egan, "The Lives They Lived: Carl Maxey, Type-A Gandhi," *New York Times Sunday Magazine*, January 4, 1998; Jim Kershner, "Segregation in Spokane," *Columbia: The Magazine of Northwest History* 14, no. 4 (Winter 2000–2001).

CHAPTERS 2 AND 3

Cornelius Byrne file, S-R reference library; Timothy Egan, *Breaking Blue* (New York: Knopf, 1993).

CHAPTER 4

Joey August file, S-R reference library; Doris Kearns Goodwin, *No Ordinary Time* (New York: Simon and Schuster, 1994).

CHAPTER 5

Joey August file and Gonzaga Boxing file, S-R reference library; E. C. Wallenfeldt, *The Six-Minute Fraternity* (Westport, CT: Praeger, 1994).

CHAPTER 6

Eugene Breckenridge file, and Discrimination-Racial file, S-R reference library; *Olsen v. Delmore*, 48 Wn. 2d 545 (1956); "Hot Nights, Cool Club: The Harlem Club Was Spokane's Original Hip Hangout," *Spokesman-Review*, November 2, 1997; Sammy Davis Jr. and Jane and Burt Boyar, *Yes I Can: The Story of Sammy Davis, Jr.* (New York: Farrar Straus Giroux, 1965).

CHAPTER 7

Spokane NAACP files, S-R reference library.

CHAPTER 8

Charles Will Cauthen file, Jangaba Johnson file, and John Wheeler file, S-R reference library.

CHAPTER 9

"An Oral History with Henry Brooks Coker, Jr.," Mississippi Veterans' Oral History Project, vol. 782, pt. 1 (Center for Oral History and Cultural Heritage, University of Southern Mississippi, 2004), reprinted with permission of the publisher; anonymous hate letter, Carl Maxey collection, MAC Archive; Stokely Carmichael with Ekwueme Michael Thelwel, *Ready for Revolution: The Life and Struggles of Stokely Carmichael (Kwame Ture)* (New York: Scribner, 2003); *Reporting Civil Rights: Part Two, American Journalism 1963–1973* (New York: Library of America, 2003).

CHAPTER 10

Spiro Agnew file, Discrimination-Housing file, Robert Greiff file, William Greiff file, Peter J. McDonough file, and Sunday Closure files, S-R reference library; speech manuscript and letters from and to McDonough, Carl Maxey collection, MAC Archive; Samuel J. Smith, "Samuel J. Smith: An Oral History," www.secstate.wa.gov/oralHistory/smith/smithsmall.pdf; *City of Spokane v. Peter J. McDonough*, 79 Wn. 2d 351, 485 P. 2d 449 (1971); *County of Spokane v. Valu-Mart Inc.* 69 Wn. 2d 712 (1966); *Maxey et al. v. Washington State Democratic Committee*, 319 F. Supp. 673 (W.D. Wash. 1970); Clayborne Carson, *In Struggle: SNCC and the Black Awakening of the 1960s* (Cambridge, MA: Harvard University Press, 1981); Dominic Sandbrook, *Eugene McCarthy: The Rise and Fall of Postwar American Liberalism* (New York: Knopf, 2004); Jules Witcover, *Party of the People: A History of the Democrats* (New York: Random House, 2003).

CHAPTER 11

Elections 1968 file, S-R reference library; manuscript of Washington State Democratic Convention speech, Carl Maxey collection, MAC Archive; Robert G. Kaufman, *Henry M. Jackson: A Life in Politics* (Seattle: University of Washington Press, 2000); Peter J. Ognibene, *Scoop: The Life and Politics of Henry M. Jackson* (New York: Stein and Day, 1975); William W. Prochnau and Richard W.

Larsen, *A Certain Democrat: Senator Henry M. Jackson, A Political Biography* (Englewood Cliffs, NJ: Prentice-Hall, 1972).

CHAPTER 12

Seattle Seven file, S-R reference library; Seattle Seven case, Case No. 51942, U.S. District Court, Western District of Washington, National Archives and Records Administration, Pacific-Alaska Region (Seattle); Walt Crowley, *Rites of Passage: A Memoir of the Sixties in Seattle* (Seattle: University of Washington Press, 1997); Roger Lippman, "Looking Back on the Seattle Conspiracy Trial," 1990, http://terrasol.home.igc.org//trial.htm; Susan Stern, *With the Weathermen: The Personal Journal of a Revolutionary Woman* (New York: Doubleday, 1975).

CHAPTER 13

Craig S. Jordan file, Long Lake Lawsuit file, and Mohammad Marashi file, S-R reference library; letter from Martin Salina, Carl Maxey collection, MAC Archive; Ted Cilwick, "The Saga of Joe Schock, War Protester," *Moscow Idahonian-Pullman Daily News*, March 10 and 11, 1990; J. Williams T. Youngs, *The Fair and the Falls: Spokane Expo '74; Transforming an American Environment* (Cheney: Eastern Washington University Press, 1996).

CHAPTER 14

Frederick (Kevin) Coe files, Gordon Coe files (which include Ruth Coe), and transcripts of Ruth Coe undercover tape, S-R reference library; letter from Judge Robert Bibb, Carl Maxey collection, MAC Archive; audiotapes of Carl Maxey's testimony in second Kevin Coe trial (1984), in possession of the *Spokesman-Review* reporter who covered the trial; Connie Bruck, "Will a Prosecutor's Missteps Free the South Hill Rapist?" *The American Lawyer*, December 1982; Jack Olsen, *Son: A Psychopath and His Victims* (New York: Atheneum, 1984).

CHAPTER 15

Roldan Q. Atacador file, S-R reference library; Goldmark Award letters, Gonzaga Law Medal and related letters, William O. Douglas Bill of Rights Award letter, letter from Judge Robert Bibb, letter from Father Byrne, Carl Maxey collection, MAC Archive; Kim Crompton, "Maxey 'the Obvious Choice?' "

Spokesman-Review, July 10, 1988; Carl Maxey, guest editorial, *Spokesman-Review*, June 5, 1983.

CHAPTER 16

Letter from Judge George Shields, letters to Tom Bradley and David Stern, and letters to and from Smithmoore P. Myers, Carl Maxey collection, MAC Archive; Alison Kartevold, "A Spokane Legend," *Washington Journal*, July 5, 1993; Carl Maxey, letter to the editor, *Spokane Daily Chronicle*, September 29, 1983; Carl Maxey, guest column, *Spokesman-Review*, December 23, 1984.

CHAPTER 17

Various articles on Carl Maxey's death, memorial service, tributes, etc., in the *Spokesman-Review*, July 18–27, 1997, S-R electronic archive; videotape of Carl Maxey memorial service, July 21, 1997, Carl Maxey collection, MAC Archive; Spokane Police reports, detective's statements, logs, and interviews about Carl Maxey death, Case No. 97–190966, July 17, 1997; Certificate of Death, Carl Maxey, State of Washington Department of Health; Timothy Egan, "The Lives They Lived: Carl Maxey, Type-A Gandhi," *New York Times Sunday Magazine*, January 4, 1998; Robert McG. Thomas Jr., "Carl Maxey, 73, Spokane Civil Rights Lawyer," obituary, *New York Times*, July 20, 1997.

INDEX

One World Club, 52
Opendack, Henry, 95
Oregon Shakespeare Festival, 55–56
Orndorff, C.A., Jr., 94
Orris, Peter, 125–26

Parchman, Mississippi (Mississippi State Penitentiary), 124, 126
Parker, Horace (Red), 170–72
Parks, Rosa, 101–3, 128
Pasco, Washington, 79
Payette Lake, Idaho, 26
Peck, Chris, 210
Perkins, Melvin, 114
Phi Beta Kappa, 53, 55
Pike County, Georgia, 112, 116, 119
Pitkin, Stan, 165, 168, 170, 172
Pittsburgh Courier, 48
politics, Maxey's involvement in: justice of the peace candidacy, 94–97; McCarthy delegate, 143–45; Senate race against Scoop Jackson, 151–61; speeches about Nixon, 196–97; state House candidacy, 92–94; vice-presidential candidacy, 197–98
Portell, Dewitt, 61
Portland, Oregon, 100
Powell, Adam Clayton, Jr., 79
Powell, Charles L., 117–18, 131
pro bono work, 106, 108, 148, 226, 232
Prochnau, William W., 156–59
Purdy, Washington, 28

Quincy, Washington, 113

Rakow, Ross R., 149
Rankin, Gene, 70
Raveling, George, 244
Reagan, Ronald, 205, 238
Rebel Without a Cause, 105
Reed, Emmett, 90
Reilly, Edward J., 94
Reilly, Jim, 63, 67, 69
restaurants, discrimination in, 5, 27, 49, 79, 89–91
Reynolds, Bobby, 53
Ribicoff, Abraham, 144

Rice, Norm, 244
Rickey, Branch, 66
Ridpath Hotel, 34, 59, 201, 204, 207, 243–45
Riggins, J. A., 119
Ringsiders (boxing booster club), 68, 71, 73
riots, 50, 142, 163
Robeson, Paul, 52
Robinson, Jackie, 51, 66, 89
Robinson, Mack, 51
Rodgers, David H., 191
Roe, Rebecca, 220
Rogers, Willie, 124
Romeo and Juliet, 218
Rookery Building, 200–201
Rosellini, Albert D., 103–5, 113–18
Rosellini, Hugh J., 149
Ross, Fred, 62
Royal Air Force, 44
Ruth, Babe, 18

Sacramento, California, 62, 67, 92
Sacramento Bee, 67
Sacred Heart Mission and School, 20–30, 232
Salina, Martin L., 181–82
Sam's Pit, 189–90, 225
San Francisco, California, 61–62, 96
Sanders, Carl E., 119
Scarpelli, Nick, 37–42
Schaeffer, Don, 61, 67, 69
Schmeling, Max, 36
Schock, Joe, 195–96
schools, segregation, 5, 87–89
Schueler, Fred, 10, 14–16
Schultheis, John, 183–84, 202–3, 244
Schults, Ninon: background of, 52–53; on boxing, feelings about, 73–74; on boxing tournament, 68; caseworker, 78; courtship with Maxey, 52–56; on dancing incident at Spokane Club, 33–34; divorce from Maxey, 186–87; on early law career struggles, 85–87; on Father Byrnes' influence, 28–29; at funeral, 244; on Gonzaga High School recruiting Maxey, 31; on her initial

CPSIA information can be obtained at www.ICGtesting.com
Printed in the USA
LVOW08*0818080616

491654LV00001BA/1/P

9 780295 997346